Bungkulan

agaraga

raja

Menyali

Sembiran

Tejakula

BANGLI

△ Mount Batur

Desa Pinggan

Trunyan

Penulisan

Kintamani

Lake Batur

Penelokan

△ Gunung Agung

KARANGASEM

Besakih

Karangasem

Bangli

Sebatu

Asak Tenganan

Tegallalang

Pujungan Kalar

Bugbug

Ubud

Pejeng

Mandangan

Klungkung

Peliatan

Gianyar

Kamasan

GIANYAR

Mas

Serongga

Gelgel

Tunjuk

Bongkasa

Bona

Jempai

Blahbatuh

Lebih

Tabanan

Kediri

Saba

Matolah

tan

Sibang

Batuan

Celuk

Sukawati

ngan Jawa

Singapadu

Cemengawon

Benoh

Kesiman

Guang

Tegah Tamu
Pagutan
Den Jalan
Batubulan

OUNG

Ketewel

Denpasar

Kelandis

Kedaton

Sanur

Pedungan

NUSA PENIDA

Benoa

Balinese Dance in Transition

Siwa Nataraja, the Creator God of Balinese dances. Choreographed by Ni Luh Swasthi Wijaya; Wredhi Budaya Arts Centre. (I Madé Bandem)

BALINESE DANCE IN TRANSITION

Kaja and *Kelod*

Second Edition

I Madé Bandem
Fredrik Eugene deBoer

Kuala Lumpur
OXFORD UNIVERSITY PRESS
Oxford Singapore New York
1995

Oxford University Press

Oxford New York
Athens Auckland Bangkok Bombay
Calcutta Cape Town Dar es Salaam Delhi
Florence Hong Kong Istanbul Karachi
Madras Madrid Melbourne Mexico City
Nairobi Paris Shah Alam Singapore
Taipei Tokyo Toronto

and associated companies in
Berlin Ibadan

Oxford is a trade mark of Oxford University Press

Published in the United States
by Oxford University Press, New York

© Oxford University Press 1981, 1995
First published as Kaja and Kelod: Balinese Dance in Transition, 1981
Second edition 1995

British Library Cataloguing in Publication Data
Data available

Library of Congress Cataloging-in-Publication Data
Bandem, I Made.
Balinese dance in transition: kaja and kelod/I Madé Bandem.
Fredrik Eugene deBoer.—2nd ed.
p.   cm.
Rev. ed. of: Kaja and kelod. 1981.
Includes bibliographical references (p.   ) and index.
ISBN 967 65 3071 9:
1. Dance—Indonesia—Bali (Province) I. DeBoer, Fredrik Eugene.
II. Bandem, I Made. Kaja and kelod. III. Title.
GV1703. I532B34322   1995
793.3' 19598'6—dc20
94-41032
CIP

Typeset by Typeset Gallery Sdn. Bhd., Malaysia
Printed by Kyodo Printing Co. (S) Pte. Ltd., Singapore
Published by the South-East Asian Publishing Unit,
a division of Penerbit Fajar Bakti Sdn. Bhd.,
under licence from Oxford University Press,
4 Jalan U1/15, Seksyen U1, 40000 Shah Alam,
Selangor Darul Ehsan, Malaysia

This book is dedicated to our first teachers:
I Madé Kredek, dancer, 1907–1979,
and I Nyoman Rajeg, dalang, 1915–

Preface to the First Edition

THIS volume is intended to present an overview of the Balinese dance today, with background information and some conceptual apparatus helpful to understanding the subject. In our discussion, we seek to bring together traditional Balinese and contemporary Western ways of approaching the arts of performance. We address a general audience interested in learning about the fascinating and beautiful dances of Bali, rather than the specialist, but we hope the reader will already have had the opportunity to become acquainted with the basic aspects of the traditional Balinese culture. In the past, writers on Balinese dance had to assume that their readers might never see the dances under discussion, and they therefore devoted a substantial proportion of their accounts to pages of description and evocation so that the reader might get a feeling for the subject as well as an understanding of it. In recent years, however, many troupes of Balinese dancers have toured the world, and a growing number of films and videotapes have been produced in which the dances themselves can be seen; we hope the reader will have access to such opportunities for seeing Balinese dance, or, best of all, will be able to visit Bali and see the dance there in its appropriate context.

Our plan of arrangement is to move from the dances which are correctly performed in or emanate from the most sacred spaces of the island, through genres of lesser sanctity performed in semi-sacred spaces, to dances of a secular nature performed in essentially secular spaces. We then discuss some 'demonic' performances given in ritually dangerous spaces, and finally some tourist performances, perhaps most dangerous of all for the Balinese dance in the long term, are discussed in the epilogue.

Fundamental to understanding the spatial premise on which the arrangement of our book depends is an old Balinese system of directional orientation, the *kaja* to *kelod* axis (Figure 1). *Kaja* in Balinese means 'toward the mountain', while *kelod* means 'toward the ocean'. In Balinese tradition, the gods have permanent dwelling-places on the heights of the mountains, especially on the great central volcano, Gunung Agung. Bali's most sacred shrine, Pura Besakih, is located high on the flank of this enormous peak. The area beneath the mountain, the middle world, is considered to be the appropriate place for human beings, while the lowest level, the

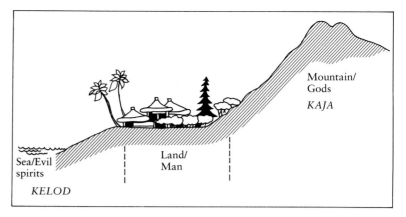

FIGURE 1 *Kaja* to *kelod.*

sea, is habitation for demons and devils. In the ancient Balinese system, the direction *kaja* leads toward the sacred, the divine, the good. *Kelod* leads toward the demonic, the chthonic, the evil. The middle world alone is secular space, uncharged with special spiritual forces.

To move from *kaja* to *kelod* at the scale of the macrocosmos is to go from Siwaloka, the highest heaven, by way of the world, to Yamaloka, or hell. At the all-Bali level, to go from *kaja* to *kelod* is to go from the top of Gunung Agung to the southern sea, by way of the inhabited land between them. At the village level, it is to go from the most sacred shrine in the inner temple courtyard to the crossroad, the haunted place, and graveyard. In the household compound, it is to go from the family shrine enclosure toward the refuse pit. The progression is from the sacred to the demonic by way of the secular. All important spaces and buildings on the island are (or should be) laid out in proper alignment on the *kaja*–secular–*kelod* axis.

We wish to express our sincere thanks to all those who have made this work possible, especially to our many Balinese informants, who are too numerous to mention individually. We must, however, invoke the names of a special few of them, great masters of the subject: I Ketut Rindha, Blahbatuh village, Gianyar Province; the late I Madé Kredek, Singapadu, Gianyar; the late I Gusti Bagus Sugriwa, Bungkulan, Buleleng; I Madé Sidja, Bona, Gianyar; and I Nyoman Rembang, Sesetan, Badung. We wish to thank also the JDR III Fund and its director, Mr Richard Lanier, for helping to make this collaboration possible. Our sincere thanks are also due to John Emigh, Richard Schechner, and Hildred Geertz, who kindly read our manuscript and commented on it; we are grateful for their penetrating observations and helpful suggestions, although we have not always followed their advice. We also wish to gratefully acknowledge technical consultation on musical matters from Andrew Toth, and we wish to thank Danielle Toth for making available several valuable photographs. Responsibility for errors, however, is entirely our own. Unless otherwise attributed, our work is based on interviews with Balinese authorities and on field research by the authors.

Middletown,   I Madé Bandem
Connecticut   Fredrik Eugene deBoer
June 1979

Preface to the Second Edition

IN the fifteen years that have elapsed since we began work on the first edition of this book, a great deal has changed on Bali. Development has been occurring at a very rapid pace, standards of living have improved, urbanization has brought many changes, and the island has become aware of the world beyond Bali through more modern education, communications, and television. New forms of performing art have come into being: some of these have lasted for only a brief moment, while others have become very well-established and seem destined to be a more or less permanent part of the continuing scene. Our intention in presenting this second edition of our book is to bring the original up to date, as well as to make a few minor corrections in the original text. To accomplish this, some rearrangement of the material has been necessary in those chapters which cover the post-Second World War period. We have also acquired a new and much improved set of photographs to illustrate the forms discussed.

Denpasar, Bali   I MADÉ BANDEM
Middletown, Connecticut   FREDRIK EUGENE DEBOER
June 1994

Contents

Preface to the First Edition   *vii*
Preface to the Second Edition   *xi*
Colour Plates   *xv*
Plates   *xvii*
Figures   *xviii*

1   Dances of the Inner Temple   *1*
        Berutuk   *3*
        Sang Hyang Dedari   *10*
        Rejang   *15*
        Baris Gedé   *18*
        Procession   *21*
        Gabor, Mendet, and Baris Pendet   *22*

2   Classical Dance of the Second Courtyard   *26*
        Gambuh   *27*

3   Masked Dances of the Bebali Group   *44*
        Topeng Pajegan   *46*
        Interlude: Barong Kedingkling   *56*
        Wayang Wong   *58*

4   Secular Dances in the Outer Temple   *70*
        Legong   *71*
        Kebyar   *74*
        Parwa   *78*
        Arja   *79*
        Modern Baris   *82*
        Topeng Panca   *83*
        Prembon   *84*

5   Secular Dances in Secular Spaces   *86*
        Joged Forms   *86*
        Abuang Kalah   *93*
        Gebyog   *94*
        Cakapung   *96*
        Godogan   *97*
        Janger   *97*

6 'Magic' Dances of the Street and Graveyard   102
   Barong Ket   102
   Jauk and Telek   106
   The Masks of Rangda   107
   Onying   108
   Wong Sakti   109
   Pengrebongan Ceremony   109
   Rangda in Performance   110
   Dance of the Sisya   112
   Calonarang   113
   Barong Landung   125
   New Year Processions   126

7 Balinese Dance in Transition   127
   Cak   128
   Barong and Rangda   131
   Prembon   132
   Modern 'Classical' Forms   133
   Sendratari-based Dances   138
   New Creations   141

Glossary   143
Select Bibliography   154
Index   159

Colour Plates

Between pages 30 and 31

1 Berutuk; Trunyan.
2 Sang Hyang Jaran; Bona.
3 Rejang, girl's ritual dance from Asak, Karangasem.
4 Baris Poleng, male ritual warrior dance from Sanur.
5 A pair of priests with offerings dancing the Mendet; Bangli.
6 The Demang and Tumenggung, a pair of portly ministers, in Gambuh; Batuan.
7 Panji with Semar and an attendant in Gambuh; Batuan.
8 Mask of Sidha Karya.
9 Mask of Danawa, a demonic god, in Topeng Pajegan, made by I Wayan Tangguh.
10 The Dalem, or refined king, in Topeng Pajegan; Singapadu.
11 Mask of Luh Géro, a *bondres* or comic character, in Topeng Pajegan; Singapadu.
12 Mask of Sugriwa, King of the Monkeys, in Wayang Wong; Wredhi Budaya Arts Centre.
13 Sugriwa with Twalen and Wredah in Wayang Wong; Tunjuk.
14 The *condong*, or maidservant, in Legong; Ubud.
15 Princess Rangke Sari in Legong; Peliatan.
16 Kebyar Duduk; Ubud.

Between pages 94 and 95

17 A female performer in Oleg Tumulilingan.
18 Ni Nyoman Candri as Mantri Manis in Arja; Singapadu.
19 Modern solo Baris.
20 Mask of Tua, one of many characters in Topeng Panca.
21 The *gamelan gong kebyar* which accompanies Prembon.
22 Janger; Kedaton.
23 Barong Ket mask; Singapadu.
24 Onying; Batubulan.
25 Wong Sakti I Gusti Gedé Raka and his Rangda mask.
26 Entranced dancers in Calonarang; Kerambitan.
27 Jero Gedé and Jero Luh in Barong Landung; Tegalalang.
28 A *pemangku*, or priest, with a Barong Landung performer, one of Jero Gedé and Jero Luh's children.
29 Sekar Jagat welcoming dance; Wredhi Budaya Arts Centre.

30   Rawana in Sendratari Ramayana; Wredhi Budaya Arts Centre.
31   Kijang Kencana; Wredhi Budaya Arts Centre.
32   Belibis; Wredhi Budaya Arts Centre.

Plates

1   Sang Hyang Dedari; Bona. The dancers in a trance.   *11*
2   Sang Hyang Bojog, in which the performer is
    possessed by the spirit of a monkey; Bangli.   *15*
3   Procession with *pratima*.   *16*
4   Young girls waiting to perform Rejang; Tenganan.   *17*
5   Baris Tumbak; Kintamani.   *19*
6   The gamelan orchestra playing for Gambuh;
    Batuan.   *31*
7   The *condong* and *kakan-kakan* dance in
    preparation for the entry of the Putri in Gambuh;
    Batuan.   *34*
8   Panji, the refined hero in Gambuh; Batuan.   *35*
9   The Prabu, or foreign king, in Gambuh; Batuan.   *39*
10 Mask-maker I Wayan Tangguh at work,
    Singapadu.   *46*
11 Dancer Ida Bagus Puja blesses the offering in
    Topeng Pajegan.   *48*
12 The Patih, or prime minister, in Topeng Pajegan;
    Peliatan.   *50*
13 The Tua, or old courtier, in Topeng Pajegan, from
    the Klungkung Palace.   *51*
14 Kebyar Bebancihan; Legong Peliatan Group,
    Ubud.   *77*
15 Parwa; Mas.   *84*
16 Kunti Seraya scene from the Barong dance;
    Den Jalan.   *99*
17 One of the Janger dancers from Singapadu.   *103*
18 Barong Ket; Batubulan.   *103*
19 Barong Bangkal; Wredhi Budaya Arts Centre.   *119*
21 Entranced dancers in Calonarang; Kerambitan.   *121–3*
22 Cak; Teges, Peliatan.   *129*
23 Cak; Wredhi Budaya Arts Centre.   *130*
24 Barong play for tourists; Den Jalan.   *132*
25 Composer and choreographer I Wayan Beratha.   *136*

Figures

1 *Kaja* to *kelod*. *viii*
2 Plan of a Balinese temple. *2*
3 Plan of Trunyan. *4*
4 Typical instruments used in most forms of Balinese dance and drama. *28*
5 The *kalangan*, the basic Balinese dance stage. *30*
6 Typical costumes worn by males and females in Wayang Wong. *62–3*
7 Typical head-dresses worn by the human characters in Wayang Wong and other genres. *64–5*
8 The places of a Calonarang performance. *115*

1 Dances of the Inner Temple

THE genres considered in this chapter belong to the most sacred (*wali*) category of Balinese performing arts.[1] They all appear to be of indigenous origin, although later Hindu-Javanese elements can be seen in them, as well as the characteristic poses, gestures, and locomotive movements which make up the fundamental vocabulary of movement of Balinese dance. All of these forms belong to what might be called the communal, village-centred aspect of Balinese culture, and involve a strong element of audience participation. Typically, the degree of training and basic talent required of the performers is not demanding by Balinese standards. Aesthetic factors, however, are important in some of them. In Gabor, for example, the skill of the dancers is as important as the beauty of the offerings presented.[2] Trance is often present in these genres and, with it, the presumption of possession by divine or, occasionally, demonic spirits. *Wali* dances are performed in connection with religious rituals, and are often given in the context of the elaborate schedule of festivals of the Balinese religious calendar. Some of them are specifically associated with the traditional Bali Aga villages, where many very old Balinese traditions and practices have been maintained, while others are found in villages throughout the island.

The *wali* dances are customarily performed in, or originate from, the *jeroan*, or inner temple courtyard (Figure 2). This is the most sacred temple space, the inner sanctum. The essential form of the modern Balinese temple is thought by many authorities to be of indigenous origin, dating back to the neolithic culture of ancestor-worshipping Malayo-Polynesian people, who migrated to Bali from the South-East Asian mainland between 2500 and 1000 BC. These progenitors of the modern Balinese are thought to have already believed that the spirits of departing ancestors went to dwell on the top of the mountain peaks to the north of Bali's fertile southern heartland. From these peaks, and especially from the tallest, Gunung Agung, come the waters necessary to cultivate rice, and from their dwelling-places on the peaks, the gods also come periodically to visit the realm of human beings below. The visiting gods were received in terraced temples at special times of the year. According to the Dutch archaeologist, Stutterheim, the temples were ringed by a wall to set apart the consecrated area, and were

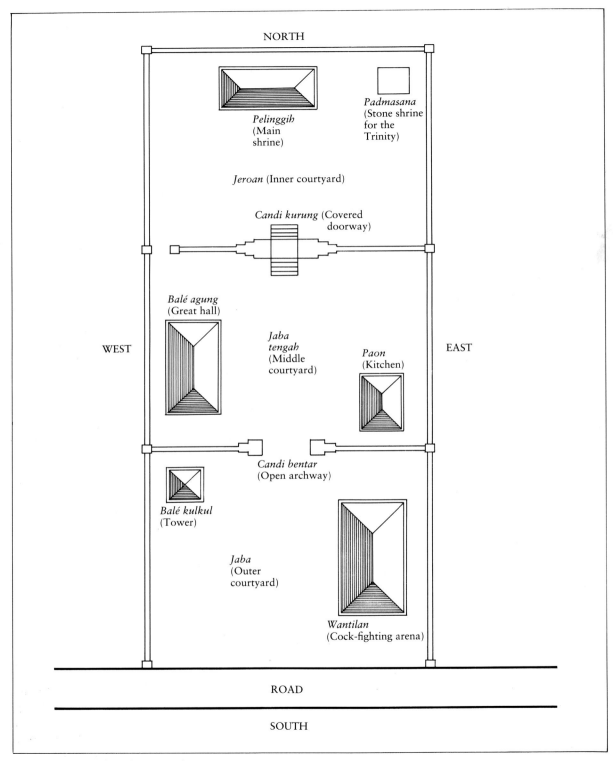

FIGURE 2   Plan of a Balinese temple.

paved with stones to mark a sacred dancing place before the shrine of the gods. The modern Balinese temple serves similar functions.[3]

Berutuk

In the lower mountain region of Bali, on the shore of Lake Batur in the province of Bangli, stands the ancient village of Trunyan, a Bali Aga village in which many traces of Bali's ancient past are preserved (Figure 3). Near the lake stands the old temple, Pura Pancering Jagat (Navel of the World), a shrine of modest proportions situated in the shade of an enormous sacred banyan tree. The temple covers an excavated pit, several metres deep. In the pit stands a large statue of a naked man, about 3.6 metres tall. His face is rudely carved and fierce of aspect; his arms hang loose at his sides; his genitals are large and prominent, although flaccid. This is His Lordship, Déwa Ratu Gedé. Only males may enter his presence, and out of respect for him, must be entirely naked when they approach. None may look boldly at him, and all who come near make appropriate gestures of respect.[4]

Every few years, the annual Odalan, or regular calendrical festival, in honour of this god, becomes the occasion for as strange and interesting a ritual dance-drama as is known in Bali—the dance of the Berutuk. Performances are seldom given, and occur at unpredictable intervals, for any uncleanness (sebel) in the village, such as an epidemic, a crop failure, or even a death, will be reason for the ceremony to be cancelled. The most recent performances were given in 1969, 1976, and 1992. It has not been determined when the next one will be held.

Performers of the rite are drawn from the Seka Taruna, an association of the taruna, or young bachelors, of the village. The number of participants varies, depending on how many are eligible in the chosen year, but it is always an odd number. As only twenty-one masks are available, that is the maximum possible number who can take part. Only strong, healthy, and unblemished youths are thought worthy to serve Ratu Pancering Jagat, and to receive him into their bodies.

For forty-two days prior to the ceremony, the young men leave their family households and go to live in the temple. From there, they must go in a group to Desa Pinggan, a village on the other side of the lake, high in the mountains, where they gather special banana leaves for their costumes. For the entire six weeks, they may not make any contact with any of the female members of the village group. They sleep each night in the temple at the feet of the statue, where an old pemangku, or priest, teaches them ancient chanted Balinese prayers.

In the morning of the day of the performance, the taruna are awakened early. Wearing only small loincloths, they are led before the pelinggih, or shrine, of the Sun God, Batara Surya. There, they

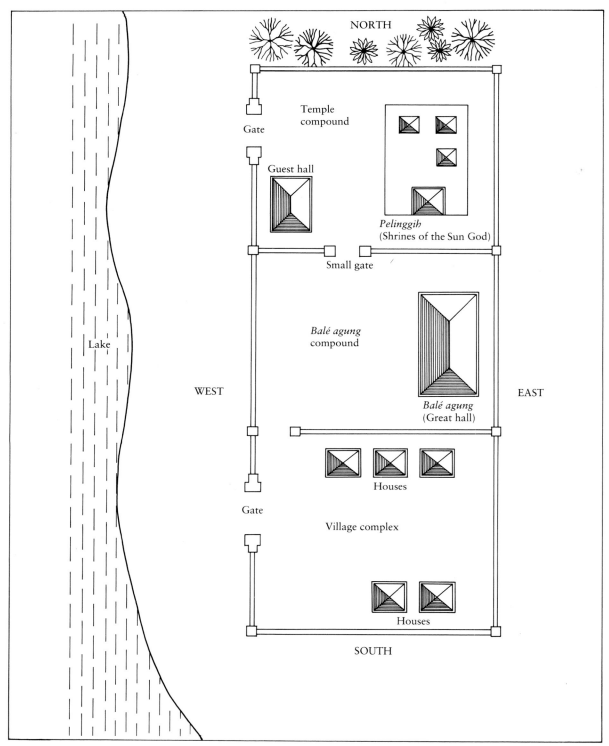

FIGURE 3   Plan of Trunyan.

are sprinkled with holy water and shrouded with sweet and pungent smoke, while prayers are intoned. When the *taruna* have been purified in this fashion, they go into the underground shrine of the great statue once more, and there they put on the costumes for the coming event.

The costumes consist of large aprons made from dried banana leaves gathered in the forest. These have been stacked to dry beside the temple, and subsequently sewn into the skirt-like aprons. Each dancer wears two of them; one hangs around his neck, while the other is tied around his waist. The lower skirt is given additional support from a pair of criss-crossed braces made from dried fibres of the same banana plant. Once the skirts have been tied on, the dancers murmur short prayers and put on their masks—which have been stored in the shrine—and head-dresses. Half of the masks are white or yellow in colour and are said to be female, while the other half, painted brown or red, represent males. When the performers are ready, they go out, one by one, through the doorway of the underground shrine. Each takes up a nasty-looking fibre whip, approximately 3 metres long, as he goes through the door. The *taruna* have thus been transformed into Berutuk! They look like animated haystacks on legs, with their masks frozen into a permanent expression of astonishment (Colour Plate 1).

Flourishing their whips, they circle the shrine three times. Then, having finished the established 'choreography', each of the monsters wanders about at will in the courtyard, 'guarding' the shrine with fierce determination. Their whips whistle menacingly and the spectators are warned not to come near. Finally, the four most sacred masks come out of the underground shrine. They form a kind of royal family—the Patih (Prime Minister), the Queen's brother, the Queen, and the King—entered by the god, Ratu Pancering Jagat.

These characters have special head-dresses decorated with flowers, and distinctive masks. Each also has an individualistic manner of walking. When the King and Queen appear, a priest comes forth with special offerings for them. The King and Queen also circle the shrine three times, and then they too rush about whipping furiously as excitement mounts among the performers and in the audience.

The spectators cheer and shout, teasing the Berutuk and testing the boundaries of their territory. The more daring members of the audience, men and women, come forward and try to snatch pieces of the sacred banana leaves away from the costumes of the Berutuk. The monsters, in turn, attempt to prevent it, and a slashing cut of the whip is the punishment for a spectator who is caught. As further punishment, anyone who has been whipped must later pay a fine to the village treasury. But the bits of banana leaf are highly charged with spiritual power—they offer protection against disease and encourage fertility in the rice-fields—and thus many men and women risk the strokes of the Berutuk's whip, hoping to bring home a lucky leaf to keep in the rafters of their houses.

About noon, this phase of the ritual concludes, and the dancers rest in anticipation of the violent exertions yet to come. Their masks are raised, like the visors of knights' helmets, and they lie inert under the shade of the temple roof while older members of the village fan their bodies. This pause is only a brief intermission as soon the second section of the rite will begin. Once more, the Berutuk stake out a territory to defend, but now it is the nearby *balé agung* that they must protect, a secular space, also ringed by a wall, that is the centre of the village's social and governmental existence. Excitement soon rises to a peak as dancers and spectators play what might be considered to be an ancient ceremonial game, a game akin to a number of children's games played in the West. Many spectators attempt to snatch away pieces of the Berutuk's costumes, and in turn the performers are entitled to whip anyone entering the arena, except for the festively dressed women who come at regular intervals with offerings to Ratu Pancering Jagat.

Later in the afternoon, some of the women present a special group of offerings to the Berutuk themselves, celebrating the fact that they have been entered by the god. These gifts consist of fruit, flowers, and sweet cakes, and are taken by the shaggy dancers but not eaten. Members of the audience, edging cautiously near, offer to exchange cigarettes for bits of the offerings, and the Berutuk, apparently tame for a brief while, allow themselves to be approached. They exchange fruit and cakes for cigarettes. Some of the more enterprising members of the audience use this opportunity to snatch a piece of the lucky banana leaf as well, and run out of the temple with their prize. The bits of offerings are eaten on the spot by members of the audience lucky enough to get them.

Towards evening, the final phase of the ritual performance takes place. Led by the priest, the women bring in new offerings for the King and Queen Berutuk. As with the earlier phases, no music accompanies their actions. When the offerings have been presented, the King and Queen dance together, while the other Berutuk and the audience watch. The Patih and the Queen's brother continue to rush wildly about, trying to beat back the spectators and prevent them from seeing the courtship dance of the King and Queen.

The couple, like two great haystacks, now dance an ancient step, which imitates the behaviour of the woodfowl, a beautiful bird, common in the forests in the vicinity of Trunyan, which resembles a pheasant. The King dances as the *keker*, or cock, the Queen as the *kiuh*, or hen. They bob and dip and peck and strut, scratching the ground and making sudden rushes past each other while flapping their 'wings', in a rough *pas de deux* that has as much of the cock-fight about it as of the mating display. As it continues, excitement mounts among the noisy crowd of spectators.

6

By now, the dancers have moved down very close to the lake, and the day is drawing to a close. The 'male' Berutuk, in their red masks, take up their position in a row behind the King; the white-masked 'females' line up opposite them, behind the Queen. A line is drawn on the ground between two ceremonial banners to mark the separate territory of the King and the Queen, with the King occupying the space between the Queen and the waters of Lake Batur.

The courtship dance of the King and Queen continues for half an hour while the male and female Berutuk stand in their lines. Except for the courting pair, only the Patih and the Queen's brother are active. They flourish their whips at the crowd, but are hardly able to maintain order. The spectators surge about, struggling to see the dancers while avoiding the whips. The mood is one of excitement and gaiety.

The dancing then takes on more of the quality of a contest than a performance as it progresses to a new phase. Now, the Queen will try to evade the King, choosing a good moment to run from the safety of her own territory to the safety of the waters of the lake. The King does his utmost to capture her, encouraged by the shouts of his followers. The two contestants eye each other across the boundary, and the Queen begins evasive action, with eye and body faking, feinted rushes, and other preliminary manoeuvres. The Queen tries to find a good opportunity to dodge past the King, seeking the safe 'goal' of the water.

At last, the less agile youngster playing the Queen takes the plunge and makes a dash across the line marked by the banners. The Berutuk all shout as the King takes off after the Queen, and (usually) catches her by clasping his arms around her in a flying tackle. At that moment, the young men shout simultaneously and rush down to the water, hurling themselves in. There, they strip off the remains of their banana leaf costumes, and swim and frolick in the water after their exertions of the afternoon. The costumes are left floating on the water, while the sacred masks are retrieved by the older villagers who come down to the lake's edge to assist. The young men are delighted to be rid of the very heavy costumes; they are hot and tired from their day of frenzied service to the god.

The old men lay out the masks on pieces of sacred cloth spread on the sand, and when all have been assembled, they are taken to the temple for a final offering and prayers. The masks are then set aside until the next time the ceremony is performed. Six months before the next Berutuk festival, they will be brought out again for cleaning and ceremonial repainting with powdered rice, betel-nut, and ground turmeric. But now, at sunset on the day of the festival, they will be put away. Performers and audience go their separate ways for the evening meal after the activities have ended.

How are we to interpret this strange and beautiful event which combines aspects of a game, a ceremony, and a ritual drama, all performed simultaneously? Let us trace, very briefly, some of the sources of the elements we see.

There is a legend in Trunyan concerning the founding of the village. Once, long ago, a group of sixteen bachelors migrated west from the traditional Bali Aga territory in East Bali, in what is now the province of Karangasem. These *taruna* were farming people in search of new lands to work. After a dangerous trek through hostile country, they stopped at the high mountain slope above Lake Batur. Here, they formed a settlement and established plantations. Living so deep in the wilderness, they were confronted with many dangers. Often there were crop failures, and on occasion wild animals from the jungle carried off their livestock and even some of the villagers themselves. They also found relations with their neighbours to be difficult, for their neighbours had quite different beliefs and customs. To get wives, the young men had to kidnap women from other communities. The newcomers were able to establish themselves in Trunyan only after a long struggle.

This legend may correspond to historical fact, for it is clear that the villagers have many customs in common with the Bali Aga groups in East Bali, and many such migrations are known to have been made over the years. It is also obvious that the citizens of Trunyan, although living beside a large lake rich in fish, have little expertise on the water and make their living almost entirely from farming, just as people to the east do.

The legend finds expression in the Berutuk ceremony in a number of ways. The *taruna* become temporary vessels for the god, Ratu Pancering Jagat, who appears in a demonic aspect. In the first stage of the performance, the masked figures and the audience carry out the game of whipping and theft, thus re-enacting the struggle of the village founders to wrench blessings and fertility from a hostile and demon-filled environment. Here, as in other *wali* dance forms, the audience participates directly in the performance. In this case, the audience symbolizes one of the contestants in a ritual battle, namely, the protagonist. For the event to be as successful as possible, it is important that the Berutuk be not too effective in protecting their mana-laden costumes.

The afternoon activities are also based on the origin legend. The ritual kidnapping of the Queen represents the theft of brides by the sixteen original *taruna* of the village. It is in the interest of the village that the King should achieve his goal and capture the bride, and the 'casting' of the event is arranged accordingly. The successful capture of the Queen ensures fertility for the village.

For the youths and for the village community as a whole, another process is in motion during the performance, for it is clear that the Berutuk event is also an initiation ceremony, a rite of passage. In Trunyan, it is the custom for young men to marry late. They are also expected to choose partners from the village. The matches made are of intense interest to the elders of the village, for they affect important considerations of inheritance, as well as traditional social and ceremonial responsibilities. The planning of the Berutuk ceremony thus gives elders an important say in when the young men of the group are considered ready for marriage. The very complex calculations involved in setting the proper day for the ceremony, and the elaborate list of reasons for postponement become, in practice, a means by which the elders can exert control over when youths can marry and when they may, subsequently, be admitted to full membership in the village. Many of the men who danced in 1976 had, in fact, been living as husbands with women for some time prior to the ceremony, but only after the ceremony were they eligible to formally marry and take their seats in the village council.

As a rite of passage, the Berutuk event has much in common with similar ceremonies from other cultures. The period of retreat, the quest for mana in the wilderness (getting the special banana leaves), tutelage in tribal traditions, and the chanting of prayers are among these. As in similar ceremonies, the Berutuk rite involves an ordeal; in this case, it is the assumption, for a day, of the demonic aspect of Ratu Pancering Jagat. To take the role of the Berutuk, is to take part in two ceremonies/dramas at the same time: one is the enactment of the origin legend; the other is the ordeal of the initiate who, following his impersonation, receives a kind of baptism in the purifying waters of the lake.

Still other layers of significance may be found in the ceremony, particularly in the odd identification of the King and Queen with the male and female wild woodfowl, the *keker* and *kiuh*. In another dance ceremony enacted in Trunyan, called Mabuang, the tribal elders form two lines, each led by the eldest member of the sub-group. The leaders carry gold representations of *keker* and *kiuh* birds, and dance with them in a kind of stately imitation of the cock-fight. Here, the *keker* and *kiuh* have an additional significance: apart from the sexual symbolism of the male and female, a social division of the tribe into rival subgroups is expressed in the dance of these totemistic animals.[5] In the Berutuk event, this element also appears, although in a truncated form, in the fighting dance of the King and Queen.

We have used the terms 'rite', 'event', 'ceremony', and 'performance' to describe the festival of the Berutuk and the activities connected with it in Trunyan. In truth, it is all of these, and more. The Odalan of Ratu Pancering Jagat is at once a festival, a religious service, an occasion for presentation of offerings and prayers, a sequence of games, and a dramatic performance. Everyone in the village has a role to fill in the proceedings, from the smallest child who braves the monsters' whips to bring home a piece of good luck for the household, to the oldest men who take care of the masks. Each participates in a way appropriate to his or her age and situation.

Recently, the event has acquired yet another dimension, as many dignitaries from the government, people from the tourism industry, and scholars attend, contribute money, and observe the festivities from VIP seating set up at a convenient location near by.

Sang Hyang Dedari

Another dance genre with ancient roots is the set of dances known as Sang Hyang. There are nearly two dozen varieties of Sang Hyang, most of them found only in remote northern and eastern mountain villages.[6] All involve putting one or more dancers into trance by means of incense, chanting, and prayers, in order to receive possessing divinities. Inhabited by either divine or demonic spirits, the performers then interact with the audience, and occasionally with each other, dancing, mimicking animal movements, and in some localities, speaking as oracles. The performance invariably involves improvisation by the visiting spirits, which takes place along pre-established lines. These possessions differ greatly in kind and content according to locality and the particular type of Sang Hyang. They range from the celestial nymphs of Sang Hyang Dedari to the horse spirits of Sang Hyang Jaran, the pig spirits of Sang Hyang Celéng, and the monkey spirits of Sang Hyang Bojog. In all varieties of Sang Hyang, there is an element of ritual purification, even of exorcism.

Sang Hyang Dedari is the best known of these dances of ritual possession, and is the most accessible to the visitor to Bali (Plate 1). The title means, roughly, 'Honoured Goddess Nymphs', and refers to the likeness of the young female dancers to the *widyadari*, or demigoddesses, in Hindu mythology. Other elements of Hindu culture are difficult to trace in the genre, which is pre-eminently a form of the village community, rather than of the sophisticated culture of the palaces.

Like the Berutuk performers, the dancers in Sang Hyang Dedari are selected from a special subgroup in the village—in this case, preadolescent girls, between nine and twelve or thirteen years of age. Four or five of them are usually in service at any one time, although no more than two dance in a single performance. The girls have special responsibilities in the temple, and are often family members of a *pemangku*, or priest. In some localities, it is traditional for the young dancers to choose their own successors from among those eligible, shortly before puberty enforces retirement. These youngsters are not trained dancers, although—like almost all Balinese villagers—they are quite familiar with the various kinds of dance-drama.

Sang Hyang Dedari dancers are considered to be a kind of temple servant, and are subject to restrictions on their conduct. They are expected to refrain from using bad language and from quarrelling, and they are subject to special taboos, for example, they must not walk under a clothes-line. They are required to sweep the temple

1 Sang Hyang Dedari. The dancers in a trance; Bona. (Danielle Toth)

and help with cleaning the shrines. They also assist with preparing offerings, and otherwise help the *pemangku*. They learn the holy scriptural songs called *kidung*.

Unlike most traditional Balinese dance performances, the Sang Hyang Dedari has no place in the great calendar of recurring festivals and ceremonies. It is performed at irregular intervals when needed to ward off or mitigate an epidemic or other disaster. If an outbreak of smallpox were to occur, the dancers might perform nightly until the danger had been averted, and then might not perform again for years. The climate and topography of Bali have long made the island susceptible to epidemic diseases; it is thus a prominent theme of great antiquity in Balinese literature.

11

The performance is usually given at night, and begins in the inner, most holy courtyard (*jeroan*) of the village's principal temple (*pura puseh*). The entire village is in attendance. At the beginning of the ceremony, the audience sits quietly on the ground in the *jeroan*. Near the *pelinggih*, or main shrine, the priest and his assistants, a chorus of women singers, and the group of dancers are placed, including both the pair who will perform that evening and the other members of the Sang Hyang group.

The first part of the performance is called the *penudusan*, or purification by smoke. During this, the goddesses are invited to descend, while the girls who will dance inhale quantities of pungent incense. They kneel side by side before the priest, who arranges the many offerings presented to the goddesses and controls the brazier in which the incense is burned on glowing charcoal. The female choral group sings *kidung* to establish an appropriate mood and to encourage the goddesses to appear. In a variant of this dance, called Sang Hyang Deling, performed in Kintamani, Bangli district, small wooden dolls are suspended before the girls and caused to dance and vibrate during the *penudusan*.

After an hour or so, if it pleases the goddesses to descend, the Sang Hyang dancers fall back in a state of possession that the Balinese call *kerawuhan*. With their eyes closed, they begin to sway sideways and backwards, supported by older women assisting in the ceremony. The priest wipes the girls' faces with a piece of cloth, for they perspire profusely. Once he is satisfied that the deities have arrived and entered the bodies of the young girls, he asks them to speak. In high, tense voices with a patterned, nervous sing-song drawl, utterly unlike normal speech, the 'goddesses' address the villagers: 'Don't be afraid, my followers, we are arriving now! The cure for your sickness is at hand. Listen! Listen!' They then prescribe medicine—usually a mixture of herbs, rice, bark, grasses, and other natural products of the island—and the ritual steps necessary to stem the epidemic. The girls distribute special bracelets made of thread on which a Chinese coin has been strung, for the villagers to wear. Holy water is prepared by the priest.

Once the girls have gone into a trance, the women's chorus, which has been singing *kidung*, falls silent and often, at the request of the visiting goddesses, is replaced by a *Cak* chorus, a group of men drawn from the temple congregation, who chant and sing and make distinctive vocal percussive patterns. Meanwhile, fires have been prepared in front of the girls. At this time, to test the depth of their trance, the girls jump on to the red-hot embers and walk on them with their bare feet. If they are sufficiently possessed, their feet will not be burned and they will feel no pain. Stepping off the coals, they call out, 'Come, come, my followers. Why don't you join me to chase the bad spirits now? Hummmm?' The girls seem almost to plead as they begin, at last, to dance. The *gamelan legong*, a classical Balinese percussion orchestra, begins to play in the outer courtyard of the temple, where the girls will soon be carried.

The dance itself is an improvisation, 'performed' by the visiting goddesses through the bodies of the youthful mediums who contain them. The girls, in their white skirts and head-dresses, are lifted to the shoulders of waiting men and carried about while still in a possessed state. Standing on the shoulders of their fast-moving carriers, they sway and undulate above the crowd which forms into a kind of rough procession behind them. To be a bearer of one of the goddesses is considered a great honour by the village *taruna*.

The movements made by the girls on their high and unsteady perches are inspired by natural phenomena. For example, the movement known as *soyor* imitates trees swaying in the wind; *ngelayak* is the movement of a tree bowing under the weight of many flowers; *capung mandus* is based on the flight of a dragon-fly; and *kidang rebut muring* represents a deer pestered by biting flies. This vocabulary of movement is very old in Bali and has been adapted in the more recent genres of the dance. Conversely, the villagers, whose movements formed the basis for the more sophist-icated forms, have been influenced by the later types. Thus, the movements of the entranced Sang Hyang dancers show definite influence of the classical court styles they have seen.

Led by the *pemangku*, the carriers leave the *jeroan*, and the procession winds out into the street. The girls are carried to all corners of the village and to the central crossroad, where they make repelling gestures toward the demons who have caused the epidemic, while the *pemangku* sprinkles holy water about, thus purifying the village by means of the ritual. After an hour or two, the small dancers are taken back to the temple, where the orchestra has continued to play.

At this point in the ceremony in Cemengawon village, Gianyar Province, the girls are lowered to the ground. There, they dance together in close co-ordination with the gamelan; this was not possible during their travels to the four corners of the village. Imitation of the Legong court dance style is clearly seen. Else-where, the girls are taken back into the temple at once.

In the temple, the girls are brought out of their trance with the aid of holy water, prayers, and the presentation of offerings to the departing goddesses. These are prayed over by the *pemangku*, accompanied by the chorus of female singers, who render an appropriate *kidung*. The girls slowly return to consciousness, tired from their exertions but otherwise unharmed by their experience as receptacles for the powerful energies of the goddesses who temporarily inhabited them. For many, their experience as per-formers is so enjoyable, they are inspired to study classical dance after retiring from service to the temple.

The subject of trance and ritual possession is of great interest to many visitors to Bali, although little of a precise or scientific nature is known about the physiological aspects of the phenomenon. Indeed, it is somewhat difficult to increase our understanding of *kerawuhun*, for the condition involves both an individual and a context, and one can hardly perform scientific measurements in the normal situation where possession occurs without disrupting the context. Many observers have commented on the similarity of the *kerawuhan* state to advanced levels of hypnosis. For the Sang Hyang dancer, the crucial test is the walking on fire, which proves to the *pemangku* and the spectators that possession has, in fact, taken place. The condition manifested by the little girls is much more refined and controlled than the frenzied self-stabbing of the kris dancers found in various other performance situations in Bali.

It must be emphasized that all Balinese dance is not performed in a state of 'trance'. Quite another term and conception apply to the trained performer's inspiration, which is usually called *taksu*. The dances of possession are of a different kind from the more secular performances, and make different demands on the performer. For the former, the essential prerequisite is that the performer be able to *nadi*, or become possessed; the ability to dance is of secondary importance. For the professional, these factors are reversed. These two conditions can, however, become confusingly mixed in some Balinese performing situations, for example, where possession rituals have become embedded in the performances for tourists. Here, the 'trance' behaviour seen by the spectator may quite simply be an example of highly realistic acting, while on other occasions, actual possession may occur.

What trance provides to the Sang Hyang dancers is, above all, a specific characterization with a distinctive vocal pattern and a conventionalized set of movement elements that the dancers combine improvisationally. In all the Sang Hyang dances, the gods are, in a sense, the servants of the village, called to perform an unvarying action, which is to drive off the dangerous *buta* (demons) responsible for the epidemic. It is a simple but very powerful rudimentary dance-drama, with no literary content of any importance. As in other dances of this group, complex plots and pre-established dialogue are absent.

In the other varieties of Sang Hyang, most often a lower, usually animal-like, spirit is drawn into the body of the dancer. In Sang Hyang Jaran, for example, which is still performed in some wards of the capital city of Denpasar, horse spirits imbue the adult male dancers, who, in the *kerawuhan* state, run neighing bare-footed through the embers of bonfires astride straw hobby-horses (Colour Plate 2). Sang Hyang Bojog presents monkey spirits who climb into the nearby trees (Plate 2). In such cases, the exorcism of the demons is accomplished when the possessed dancers frighten them away. In another variant, Sang Hyang Celéng, the dancer is entered by a pig spirit who impels the performer to eat (for the

2 Sang Hyang Bojog, in which the performer is possessed by the spirit of a monkey; Bangli. (Stuart Rome)

most part only symbolically) the accumulated filth and impurities responsible for the epidemic, volcanic eruption, or other disaster.[7]

Rejang

In the Berutuk ceremony and in the Sang Hyang dances, we have seen some of the many varieties of Balinese dance in which deities or spirits enter the dancer(s), inhabit them, and control their behaviour. In another important category of Balinese religious dance, the performance is given for the gods rather than by them.

15

At every Balinese temple festival, visiting gods descend into doll-like sacred wooden effigies called *pratima*, which are gaily dressed, decorated with flowers, and placed in special portable shrines for the festive occasion.[8] The gods who dwell for a time in these *pratima* are carried in procession and bathed (Plate 3). They are presented with offerings of food, flowers, and other tangibles, and also—very often—with offerings in the form of performances. The dancers perform to delight and amuse their celestial guests, and to pay them appropriate respect.

Rejang is one of the most ancient and most formal of these entertainments. It can still be seen in many villages throughout Bali, and most villages have a group devoted to it. Although it is one of the simplest Balinese dances, it possesses a dignity and elegance that are distinctive and very beautiful. In its mood, it is far removed from the struggling tumult of the lashing Berutuk or the frenzied crowd that surges around the Sang Hyang Dedari and their bearers.

Rejang is a processional group dance performed by the female members of the temple congregation. It is never performed professionally. Women of all ages take part in the performance in most villages, but in the more traditional Bali Aga villages of Tenganan and Asak, the performers are drawn only from among the children and young women of the village (Plate 4). In a typical

3   Procession with *pratima*. (Koes)

4   Young girls waiting to perform Rejang; Tenganan. (Stuart Rome)

performance, some forty to sixty women take part. All are dressed in formal Balinese costume, with an *anteng*, or long sash, tied around the waist, and an elaborate semicircular head-dress consisting of a gold frame to which fresh flowers are attached (Colour Plate 3).

Rejang is performed in the daytime, usually in the early afternoon. Through a single gateway, long lines of dancers in pairs enter the *jeroan* from the less sacred precincts outside. Upon entering, they execute a simple choreography which divides them into four lines facing the *pelinggih*, where the *pratima* have been placed. The front dancers from each line dance toward the gods. They progress slowly, waving their fans, and holding out their *anteng* at waist height. They undulate as they advance, their faces drawn into serious, rather preoccupied smiles. When they reach the *pelinggih*, the line divides, with two dancers going off to each side. The next row, in turn, approaches the *pelinggih*, and the dance continues as each row comes forward, to the accompaniment of appropriate music. The *gamelan gong gedé* is traditionally played in Batur, Bangli Province, while the sacred *selonding* ensemble accompanies the dancers in Tenganan. When each row of dancers has been presented to the *pelinggih*, the performance is over, and the dancers and audience move on to the next event in the day's schedule of activities.

In Batuan village, Gianyar Province, Rejang is better known by the name Sutri. The movements in this variant form are especially slow and highly refined, befitting the village, famous for its many *brahmana*, or priestly caste, families, and its long tradition of excellence and conservatism in the dance and drama. Sutri is also unique among the varieties of Rejang for its exorcistic qualities. The annual performance at the Usaba Nini festival at the *pura désa*, Batuan, is thought to help protect against the danger of epidemic diseases. If any sickness does break out in the village during the year, special performances of Sutri are given in the *jeroan* of that temple every five days until the danger is past.

Baris Gedé

Complementary to the Rejang is the Baris Gedé, a group dance performed by the adult males of the village on the occasion of an Odalan. Baris dancers have been known in Indonesia at least since the sixteenth century. *Kidung Sunda*, an old poetic, historical romance, which is dated about 1550, mentions that seven kinds of *bebarisan* were performed on the occasion of the funeral of an important personage.[9] The word *baris* means 'line' or 'row', and refers to the military formations assumed by the dancers. *Gedé* simply means 'great', and designates Baris dances performed by groups of men. Baris Gedé is often given in the afternoon, just before or after a performance of Rejang, although the two forms are not invariably associated. Just as special semicircular floral head-dresses are distinctive of Rejang, the Baris Gedé is characterized by the triangular-shaped helmets worn by the dancers. These may consist of many pointed fragments of mother-of-pearl thrusting upwards in a pyramid. The fragments are attached to springs which cause them to quiver as the dancers move.

The dancers in Baris Gedé can be considered the bodyguard of the visiting deities temporarily residing in the *pratima*. The men carry sacred heirloom weapons, such as spears, lances, shields, daggers, or even, in some villages, rifles. Each dancer-soldier carries the same kind of weapon, and thus each type of Baris is distinguished by the type of weapon employed. The size of the group can vary from four men to several dozen, depending on the custom of the village and the number and kinds of weapons available in the village repository of inherited treasures. The largest and grandest of the varieties is Baris Tumbak, which is performed at Batur, Bangli province (Plate 5). Here, the group is often made up of more than sixty dancers.

In the performance at Batur, the dancers enter from the south through a large and ornate single gateway opening into the *jeroan*. Each dancer wears the characteristic helmet and carries a 3-metre *tumbak*, or lance. The rest of his costume consists of tight-fitting white trousers, a white shirt, and a decorative uniform apron hanging down from the shoulders in front and behind. The costume is completed by the dancer's kris, or dagger.

The dancers come in, marching and shouting in unison, accompanied by the great old *gamelan gong gedé* that is the pride of Batur village. The first dancers march in place until everyone has

5   Baris Tumbak; Kintamani. (Danielle Toth)

19

entered and the formation is complete. Then, at a signal in the music, all shout together and kneel to pray. The music stops. Facing the *pelinggih*, with weapons held straight, the dancers remain kneeling silently for five minutes or more, offering themselves and their weapons to the service of the gods in the *pratima*. The *gamelan gong gedé* then resumes playing, providing spirited martial accompaniment for the next section of the dance.

At this signal, the men rise and execute a rather complex choreographic manoeuvre, which divides the group into two subgroups facing each other. Shouting again, the two 'armies' execute a stylized mock combat drill. The soldiers of each side move in unison, in turn attacking and defending against the attack of the opposing side. The emphasis is on co-ordinated group action rather than individual combat; there is no leeway for individual variation in the contest of one soldier against another. The dancers pause on signal, and march to a new alignment before they commence another round of stylized fighting. When this has concluded, all face the *pelinggih* again and bow. The dancers stop where they are as the piece concludes.

In the mountain villages of northern Bali, the performance of Baris Gedé usually involves a series of similar dances following each other in close succession. In each phase, a new group of weapons is presented and manipulated. In Batur, for example, a smaller group of dancers from the Baris Tumbak group leaves at the conclusion of that dance to equip themselves with boat-shaped shields of the Baris Dadap, which follows quite soon after. The choreography is very similar to that of Baris Tumbak, although the number of dancers is much smaller.

Baris Dadap is of particular interest for, in addition to its place in the Odalan, it is often seen at cremation ceremonies. The special wedge-like painted shields carried by the dancers are made from the wood of the *dadap* tree, which is valued for its medicinal and magical qualities. The shields are less weapons than abstract representations of boats, and are vestigial survivals from ancient Balinese funerary practices. Similarly shaped votive objects are employed in burial rites elsewhere in Indonesia.[10] The movement and structure of Baris Tamiang, which concludes the series of Baris Gedé dances at Batur, is similar to the others; this form takes its name from the round shields that the dancers present and brandish. Another variant, Baris Poleng, is named for the chequered cloth from which the costumes are made (Colour Plate 4).

The *dadap* tree itself has special meaning and importance in Balinese ceremonial and performing arts. The ritual shadow puppet play, Wayang Lemah, held in the daytime, is performed against a thick string stretched between the trunks of two small *dadap* trees. *Dadap* leaves are an ingredient in many folk medicinal remedies. The head-dresses of the classical Gambuh dance are also traditionally decorated with fresh *dadap* leaves. The significance of the plant, apart from its inherent pharmacological properties, lies in its association with the high end of the *kaja–kelod* axis. The *dadap* grows in the mountains, and especially on the slopes of Gunung Agung where the gods dwell. It is so important in Balinese religious usage that many households in southern Bali grow it in their gardens.

There are other non-ceremonial forms of Baris dancing: Baris Melampahan, or dramatic Baris, in which a story is told employing a company of dancers clad in Baris costumes; and solo Baris, a dance by a single male performer, adult or child, dressed in Baris costume, who presents a plotless character study of a young warrior.

Procession

Following the performance of Rejang and/or Baris Gedé at a typical Balinese Odalan, the *pratima* are taken to the sacred bathing-place a kilometre or so away from the temple to receive their ritual cleansing. The entire temple congregation joins in the procession. Members of the celebrating group, male and female, remain dressed in their best ceremonial attire; the dancers still wear their Baris and Rejang costumes. Individual pots and kettles, small gongs, drums, and cymbals are taken up from the gamelan and beaten by the musicians in a lilting pattern (*bebonangan* or *bala ganjur*) as the procession winds down the highway and then along a narrow pathway to the bathing-place. As they are carried along, accompanied by colourful offerings, the gods in their gaily decorated shrines are shaded by parasols and guarded by the weapons consecrated in the Baris Gedé performance. As seen so often in Bali, the movement of the group, as it winds down from the *pelinggih* in the *jeroan* to the chthonic watering-place, is along the axis from *kaja* to *kelod*. The route is chosen to ensure a maximum display of the visiting deities and their magnificently turned-out followers.

After the *pratima* have received their ritual bathing, and the offerings brought for the purpose have been presented, the procession forms again and the congregation returns to the temple. The gods are returned to their place in the *pelinggih*. Now, the main offerings, specially prepared for presentation on behalf of the entire village, are dedicated by the attendant priests. This process requires several hours, and during it, the dancers in the Rejang and Baris Gedé groups often go home for refreshments and a change of clothing.

The dedicatory prayers offered by the priests are accompanied by elegant hand gestures of great antiquity and delicate formality, especially when the officiant is a *pedanda*, or high-caste priest. His prayers are in Sanskrit and his *mudra*, or ritual gestures, descend from those of the Indian Hindu and Buddhist sages of a millennium or more ago.[11] The *pedanda* sits on a high platform, praying and ringing his bell, and making his *mudra*. Beneath him, on the ground, at his right, are set up the *dadap* poles and thread of the

Wayang Lemah, while on the left a *gamelan gong* is positioned to accompany the ritual Topeng Pajegan, a form described in Chapter 3.

Prayer, performance, and offering are interwoven in Balinese Hinduism, and in the Balinese art, as in Balinese religion, there is a linking of three elements in every considered expressive assertion. These are *bayu*, *sabda*, and *idep*: action, word, and thought. Thus, when the *brahmana* priest prays, there is—simultaneously—a thought in his mind, a word on his lips, and an action with his hands. Similarly, when an offering is presented, the idea symbolized in the object employed must be completed by the act of presentation and the word of the appropriate prayers. The *bayu-sabda-idep* trinity also expresses itself in the dance, both in specific technicalities of linking a phrase of movement or sequence of gestures to the spoken or sung dialogue, and in the larger dimension that leads the Balinese to prefer dance-drama to more abstract forms of the art.

Gabor, Mendet, and Baris Pendet

The simple three-part Balinese prayer finds elaboration in a group of temple dances that are usually performed in the evening of an Odalan. These dances develop the action (*bayu*) involved in the presentation of prayers and offerings. In these dances, the performers carry the offerings to be consecrated, and dance with them before the deities in their shrines. The verbal dimension (*sabda*) is provided by a chorus of women, who sing the sacred *kidung*, 'Wargasari', describing the arrival of the goddess and her entertainment. The female chorus consists of a dozen or so singers who have rehearsed regularly for the occasion. In keeping with the multi-media nature of the Balinese performance, a gamelan plays instrumental music for the accompaniment of the dancers, while the a cappella choir of *kidung* singers carries on relentlessly in their own corner, without co-ordination with the other elements of the performance.

In Gabor, the elaborate presentation of offerings is done by female dancers, who are usually members of the Rejang group. In Singapadu village, Gianyar district, the Gabor performance begins late in the evening. When the priest has presented the large group of offerings on behalf of the village as a whole, the members of the Rejang society gather near the *pelinggih*. They are no longer wearing their Rejang costumes, but have changed into normal temple dress. The women are called together by a lower-caste female priest, who encourages them to begin the Gabor. Only the best dancers will actually take part. The girls are shy at first, and must be urged to begin, but after a time the first pair is ready to dance.

The *gamelan gong* strikes up the Gabor melody, and the dancers begin, in pairs. Each carries a bowl of flowers or another offering in her right hand. They dance side by side, advancing toward the *pelinggih*, always facing the gods in their *pratima*. The vocabulary of movement employed is far more complicated than any we have discussed so far and is drawn from the full range of classical Balinese dancing. Gabor requires talent and training in Balinese dance technique. The basic walk is stylized elaboration of the walking step of Rejang, but the dancers execute a variety of complex patterns of movement, in close co-ordination with the drummer and accompanying gamelan. Each pair performs for five minutes or so in front of the *pelinggih* before the offerings are deposited at its foot. Four to eight pairs dance on a particular occasion, and a performance can last up to an hour.

Complementary to Gabor is Mendet, which is performed by adult men from the temple congregation or, occasionally, by the *pemangku* (Colour Plate 5). The dancers wear their regular temple costumes, but without shirts. They dance a rather simple step based on the Baris Gedé group of movements; the music is also from the Baris repertoire. In some villages, a dance called Baris Pendet is given, much like a Baris Gedé but performed by eight men. Ritual vessels filled with flowers are used instead of weapons. Baris Pendet, which can be seen at temple festivals in Sebatu village, Gianyar Province, or in Tejakula village, Buleleng Province, is usually performed in the daytime, rather than late at night. These dances, like Gabor, are performed by pairs of dancers with offerings, who dance their way to the *pelinggih*, where the offerings are left. In some locations, such as in Badung or Buleleng Provinces, these dances are often performed in a trance state, associated with the playing of a particular piece of music, 'Klincang Klincung'.

The dances in which offerings are presented may be seen as an extension and development of the idea inherent in the use of *mudra* to accompany prayer. They elaborate the act of presentation; the performance process itself takes on the character of offering.

When Gabor and Mendet dancers have finished presenting the offerings, the *pemangku* and his assistants approach the altar while the congregation prepares to offer individual and family prayers. Men sit and women kneel on the ground in the *jeroan*, facing the *pelinggih*. The priests distribute liquor—arak, or rice wine—which is poured on to the ground to pacify the demons. Then, each individual, alone or with the family group, lights a stick of incense and puts it in the ground near by. The priests distribute consecrated flower petals which the worshippers hold fervently to their foreheads. At each phase of the nine-part prayer, petals are thrown toward the *pelinggih* in a gesture of humility and respect, as each villager unites *bayu–sabda–idep* in the process of praying. With these prayers, the formal activities of a typical Odalan come to an end.

In this chapter, a number of sacred ritual dances of the inner temple courtyard, grouped by Balinese authorities in the *wali* category, have been discussed. As such, their performance is considered to be essentially an act of worship. They are not to be performed for financial gain, but as a sign of devotion and service to the temple. While non-members of the temple congregation are usually welcome to watch the temple dances at an Odalan, or other religious ceremony, it is important that due respect be paid to local customs and rules.

In all of the dances of the *wali* group, the actual participation of the deities is essential. Even in Rejang, where the gods remain passive in the *pelinggih*, they must, in some sense, accept the offerings extended by the young women. In *wali* dances, the attention of the gods is kept under control by the participating priests, and their time is tightly scheduled and programmed.

For Balinese audiences, *wali* dances are not of particular aesthetic interest, for they are directed at the divinity rather than at the crowd of human spectators. This has been clearly shown when such groups have been brought to perform at the Bali Arts Festival, held in Denpasar each summer. Local people have not demonstrated any great enthusiasm to see temple dances from the outlying areas of Bali, even for old forms of great dignity that seem very beautiful to outsiders. The same people, on the other hand, regard the sacred performances of their own village as something quite indispensable.[12]

1. The classification of Balinese dances into *wali* (sacred), *bebali* (ceremonial), and *bali-balihan* (secular) genres was first proposed by the late I Gusti Bagus Sugriwa at a seminar held in Denpasar in 1971. See 'Proyek Pemeliharan dan Pengambungan Kebudayaan Daerah Bali' (1971: 3).

2. Soekmono (1973) provides a convenient summary of Indonesian cultural history. See also Hanna (1976) and Vickers (1989) for Bali. Covarrubias (1937) is still the best introduction to Balinese culture in the colonial period. H. Geertz (1973) describes the Indonesian context. Ramseyer (1977) is an excellent compendium on Bali. De Zoete and Spies (1938) has been the standard reference on Balinese dance and theatre, except for the shadow play, since it appeared more than fifty years ago; now out of date, the book is still a trove of information and vivid description. Other general considerations of Balinese dance include Holt and Bateson (1944), McPhee (1948), and Sanger (1985).

3. Stutterheim (1935: 1–5).

4. Archeologist Bernet Kempers (1978: 167–8) describes the temple and statue. Danandjaja (1985) considers the Berutuk ceremony in some detail from an anthropological viewpoint.

5. Scholars may wish to consider these dances in the light of the fascinating, if erratic, essay by Rassers (1959: 10–62). Ras (1973) attempts, with considerable success, to sort out Rassers' arguments.

6. Belo (1960) investigated Balinese trance performances of many types in the years before the Second World War. Most of the performances she studied were given especially for visitors, outside the usual ritual context. Since then, Suryani and Jensen (1993) have considered Balinese trance phenomena from a psychiatric viewpoint. O'Neill (1978) provides a complete description of the Sang Hyang Dedari of Cemengawon village, Gianyar Province.

7. These 'lower' varieties of Sang Hyang and others, such as the Sang Hyang Bojog (monkey), Sang Hyang Bumbung (bamboo), etc. are described in Belo (1960). It is evident that, apart from their exorcistic content, they also provide the occasion for fun and frolic. The crowd teases the dancer and has a good laugh, while the dancer seizes the opportunity to run wild and, in the case of Sang Hyang Bojog, 'go ape', without danger of social disapproval.

8. Belo (1953) describes a rather typical Odalan, from preparations to clean-up, in considerable detail.

9. Relevant passages are quoted in Holt (1967: 288).

10. Especially among the Toraja people of Sulawesi (Celebes).

11. De Kleen (1924) provides excellent drawings.

12. See Sanger (1985).

2 Classical Dance of the Second Courtyard

ANOTHER important category of Balinese dance is the group of ceremonial performances called *bebali*. These genres are also performed in connection with Odalan and other important religious occasions, but are of a different, somewhat lower, level of sanctity from the *wali*, or sacred, group discussed above. The *bebali* dances are all dramatic dances with a narrative element, and may be understood as optional entertainment for the gods who are attending a festival. Unlike the *wali* dances, those of the *bebali* type do not compel the gods' attention, nor are they a necessary part of the ritual embedded in the performance. They are, none the less, explicitly religious in intention, for they are meant to entertain the divinities present, as well as the human spectators. The celestial guests are treated as visiting dignitaries who must be kept amused during the long hours of the festival day.

In Chapter 1, *wali* dances were characterized as belonging to a native Balinese tradition centred in the village community. The *bebali* genres, on the other hand, are associated with another, almost antithetical, strand in the composition of Balinese culture, which might be called Hindu-Javanese. This is a tradition of foreign, rather than native, origin coming directly from Java and possessing indirect roots in India. With it are associated the caste system, a centralized state government under a single powerful noble ruler, and a Javanized form of the Hindu religion.[1]

Hindu-Javanese culture came to Bali in successive waves of Javanese power and influence between the ninth and sixteenth centuries AD. At times during this 700-year period, connections between the two islands were quite close; at others, Bali was free of strong outside influences. After the expedition of the Javanese War Minister, Gajah Mada, in the mid-fourteenth century, in which he successfully put down a local Balinese despot, Bali became a part of the Majapahit Empire which was to hold sway over Java and Bali for the next 150 years. During this time, the cultural life of the palaces of both islands was united. Then, about 1520, Majapahit fell before the advance of Islam in Java.[2] The last courtiers moved to Bali, where the Hindu-Balinese culture was left to develop for several hundred years in virtual isolation.[3] The *bebali* dances in existence today, are forms which have descended

26

from the dance-dramas of the courts of the Majapahit period and of the Hindu-Balinese courts which were formed, in their likeness, over the next two centuries.

Historical and literary records from the Majapahit period tell us something of the great sophistication, elegance, and refinement of the dance performances given in the palaces and great houses of the era. The performing arts were clearly highly developed, being heirs to a tradition extending back five centuries or more in Indonesia and beyond that to India. We thus read in old tales, set in the palaces of the medieval East Javanese kingdoms, of dance-dramas given by masked and unmasked dancers. Incomplete descriptions of such performances are also included in historical documents like the *Kidung Sunda*, and the *Nagara Kretagama*, while Balinese documents include accounts of similar court performances, though of a somewhat later period.[4]

The old accounts also reveal that the Hindu princes and their wives were enthusiastic patrons of the arts. Some of them were amateur performers as well, and took part in public performances. The princes subsidized and employed a professional corps of highly skilled artists and teachers who were attached to the palaces. Courtly audiences of the day were revealed as being especially appreciative of comic talent, wit, skill in improvisation, grace, refinement, and subtlety. However, ritual aspects of the performance were taken for granted by the old authors and are not emphasized in the accounts, although provisions for offerings given in connection with the performance are described.

Gambuh

One of the types of courtly dance-drama mentioned in the old records survives in Bali today, preserved by a continuous performing tradition that goes back 400 years. This is Gambuh, a *bebali*, or semi-secular, dance of the temple's second courtyard, which is performed without masks.[5] In Gambuh, aspects of the manners and ideals of the sophisticated courtiers of the Majapahit era are preserved, as well as the musical repertoire, choreographic ideas, and highly refined literature of the period. Archaic, formal, and stately, Gambuh is accompanied by its peculiar form of music, dominated by wailing flutes (*suling*), and is presented by grave dancer-actors who chant and intone lengthy speeches.

Gambuh is also of great importance in Balinese dance because of its influence on later forms; it is the source and prototype for the more modern forms of dance-drama like Topeng, Wayang Wong, Arja, Legong, and Baris Melampahan. Balinese choreographers have relied heavily on Gambuh for notions of structure, characterization, means of dramatization, compositional elements, costume, musical repertoire, and other features. In addition, Gambuh is the point of origin for much of modern Balinese music, especially the drumming patterns which are the essential point of contact and communication between the dancer and the accompanying gamelan in every type of dance that developed later (Figure 4).

The traditional locus for the Gambuh performance is the *jaba tengah*, or second courtyard, of the temple. This space serves as the ante-room to the *jeroan* and, like it, is enclosed by a wall about 2 metres high. It contains buildings and pavilions in which kitchen equipment, ceremonial paraphernalia, musical instruments, and costume items are stored between festivals. Tall ceremonial gateways (*candi bentar*) give access to the outer courtyard and to the *jeroan*. As the middle space in the traditional Balinese temple, the *jaba tengah* is, in effect, a transitional zone between the sacred and secular space.

For most of the year, the *jaba tengah* is not used for performances. Only when serious preparations for an upcoming festival are underway, does it come to life. By the time of the Odalan, it is bustling with activity as people hurry about performing various duties. Groups also gather here before proceeding into the *jeroan* to present their offerings. Food is chopped and cooked in the area, to be eaten there later.

The *jaba tengah* also serves as an important performing space during a festival and in the days leading up to it. Many centres of interest will form in the crowded courtyard, and often several

FIGURE 4   Typical instruments used in most forms of Balinese dance and drama. (I Nyoman Mandra)

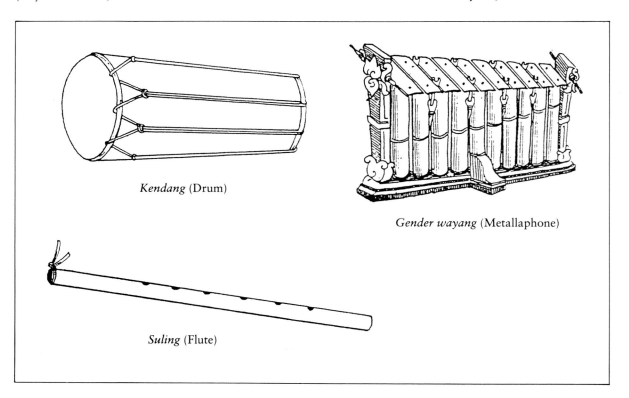

Kendang (Drum)

Gender wayang (Metallaphone)

Suling (Flute)

gamelan groups will play at the same time in connection with subsidiary rituals. One focal point is the special space where dramatic dance performances are given. This area, called the *kalangan*, is the basic Balinese dance stage (Figure 5).

As noted above, the *jaba tengah* where the *kalangan* is set up for a Gambuh performance is not a ritually consecrated space. Therefore, here, in the *jaba tengah*, as well as in any place outside the temple where a stage might be set up, the performance space must be set apart and consecrated before the performance can begin. A *pemangku* is required for the ritual consecration, which involves presenting offerings to the earth spirits, along with pouring libations, burning incense, and chanting appropriate prayers. The demons must be invoked and placated, for the performance will take place on the ground, which is their territory. The dancers do not wish to step on them or otherwise cause offence.

Another set of offerings must be presented before the actual Gambuh performance can begin. These are given to the high god, Wisnumurti, Patron of Dance, to mark the bringing out of the *gelung*, or sacred head-dresses, just before the performance. These head-dresses, drawn from fifteenth-century Javanese prototypes, symbolically represent the entire dance costume, and are specially consecrated when first put into service. They are handed down from generation to generation as venerated objects. The offerings to the *gelung* consist of fruit, flowers, a coconut, Chinese coins, rice cakes, an egg, and a length of thread which symbolically ties the whole together.

Another small ceremony is required after the *gelung* have been blessed. Now it is the turn for the dancers themselves to receive a purifying sprinkle of holy water, as additional offerings are presented at the *sanggah taksu*, a shrine dedicated to what we might call 'the divine force of inspiration'. The dancers pray for assistance from the gods in performing their roles, and ask that the audience might enjoy their work. Thus, even for a semi-secular *bebali* performance, a full complement of ritual preparations is required.

The *kalangan* itself consists of a rectangular performance area roughly 9.0 metres deep by 5.5 metres wide, marked off from the surrounding space by a 0.3-metre-high bamboo fence. A decorative ceiling made of greenery is often erected overhead. Decorative lances are placed at the sides of the stage, as are bright umbrellas, emblems of power and status. These lances and umbrellas also serve as points of orientation for the dancers during the performance. The gamelan orchestra is seated at one end of the *kalangan*, to the side (Plate 6). Near it is a row of mats, where performers who are waiting between appearances may rest and take refreshments. The entrance is located at the top of the flight of stairs leading up to the archway going into the *jeroan*.

The *kalangan* is a temporary stage, prepared anew for each performance. Like the temple in which it is housed, it is aligned carefully on the axis of the ritually significant directions, *kaja* and

29

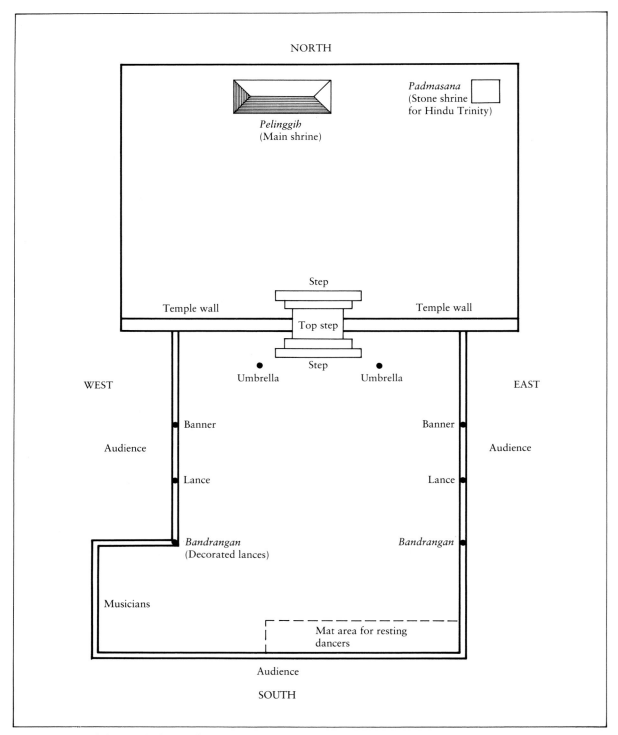

FIGURE 5   The *kalangan*, the basic Balinese dance stage.

1   The Patih, or Prime Minister, Berutuk rite; Trunyan. (Ida Bagus Alit Yudhana)

2   Sang Hyang Jaran, the hobby horse trance dance from Bona village. (Stuart Rome)

3   Rejang, girl's ritual dance from Asak, Karangasem. (Koes)

4　Baris Poleng, male ritual warrior dance from Sanur. (Koes)

5   A pair of priests with offerings dancing the Mendet; Bangli. (STSI documentation; courtesy Nik Wheeler)

6   The Demang and Tumenggung, a pair of portly ministers, in Gambuh; Batuan. (Danielle Toth)

7   Panji with Semar and an attendant in Gambuh; Batuan. (Danielle Toth)

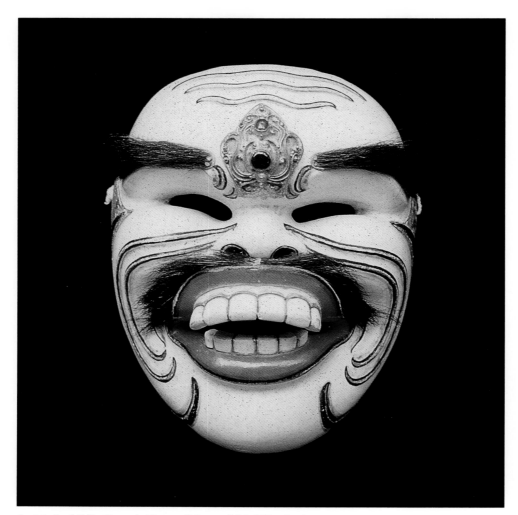

8   Mask of Sidha Karya in Topeng Pajegan. (I Madé Bandem)

9   Mask of Danawa, a demonic god, in Topeng Pajegan, made by I Wayan Tangguh.

10   The Dalem, or refined king, in Topeng Pajegan; Singapadu. (Pino Confessa)

11   Mask of Luh Géro, a *bondres* or comic character, in Topeng Pajegan; Singapadu (Pino Confessa)

12 Mask of Sugriwa, King of the Monkeys, in Wayang Wong; Wredhi Budaya Arts Centre. (Swasthi Wijaya)

13 Sugriwa with his servants, Twalen and Wredah, in Wayang Wong; Tunjuk. (Swasthi Wijaya)

14 The *condong*, or maidservant, in Legong; Ubud (Stuart Rome)

15 Princess Rangke Sari in Legong; Peliatan. (Stuart Rome)

16   Kebyar Duduk, or Kebyar Trompong. A squatting male dancer plays the *trompong* while dancing; Ubud. (Stuart Rome)

6   The gamelan orchestra playing for Gambuh; Batuan. (Danielle Toth)

kelod, and is adorned with flowers, greenery, and other temporary decorations. Lighting is provided by the sun, for Gambuh is traditionally performed during the day.

In its subject-matter, as well as its origins, Gambuh is associated with the life of the medieval Hindu-Indonesian courts. The stories are usually taken from a long romantic poem called *Malat*, which comprises a set of tales concerning the adventures of a handsome prince, Panji Inu Kertapati, and his destined bride, Princess Candra Kirana. The language spoken by the principal characters in the drama—as in most forms of Balinese theatre—is the language of

31

the old poem itself, called Kawi by the Balinese, who consider it to be their ancestral language. It is also the name of the Old Javanese language, which was employed in the courts of Bali and Java during the medieval period. Translations are provided by attendants and comic retainers as the performance goes along, for few in the audience can understand the ceremonial tongue. But, just as Latin was considered by many to be the appropriate language for the Mass long after most in the congregation had lost all comprehension of what was being said, Kawi is kept in the Balinese theatre out of respect for its long tradition and venerable (*wayah*) majesty.

The story is an important element in Gambuh, providing a structure for the succession of dances. The narrative is presented by means of a fairly standard progression of stock scenes and stereotypical characters. The characters are generally identified by their titles, which remain unchanged. In addition, each principal character may assume a particular character name peculiar to the story. Thus, the hero, Prince Panji, might be called Prince Panji Damar Wulan in one story, but Panji Mahisa Jayanti in another. A character such as the Old Patih (Prime Minister), would not, however, change his name from one tale to another. The stock scenes are hardly differentiated from play to play, except for minor variations in the dialogue. Only minor alterations are required to change a scene to fit a different story.

In a typical Gambuh performance, the Putri, or principal female character, is usually presented in the first scene under her specific character name, usually Putri Candra Kirana or Putri Kencana Wungu. She is a female character of the refined/sweet (*alus/manis*) type, with a high, drawling, falsetto voice, small (preferably almond-shaped) eyes, a delicate figure, and restrained movements. She wears a distinctive *gelung* decorated with fresh flowers. Before the Putri makes her entrance, her ladies-in-waiting must first appear to prepare the way for her. The first of these is the *condong*, or maidservant. Although the *condong* is a retainer, she is of noble family and ranks first among the court ladies. (In the past, it was the custom for all the female roles in the Gambuh to be danced and acted by men, but nowadays women very often take part, to the extent of playing the refined male characters.)

The performance begins with an instrumental overture by the accompanying *gamelan gambuh*. The ensemble and the genre it accompanies take their name from a quartet of *gambuh suling*, or long flutes, which are the core of the melodic section of the orchestra. These are blown with a difficult circular technique that produces a continuous sound. Another melody instrument, a bowed, fiddle-like, spiked lute, called the *rebab*, plays in unison with the *gambuh suling*. The musical ensemble is completed by a lead singer (*juru tandak*) and an extensive percussion section, including drums, cymbals, bells, and gongs of various sizes and shapes.

At the conclusion of the overture, the *condong* appears at the head of the entrance steps, facing the direction *kelod*. The *condong* sings and dances to her own identifying melody as she descends into the *kalangan*, where she dances in a complicated, energetic pattern that covers a great deal of the stage area. Her movements, in the realm of pure dance, without pantomimic or other narrative features, are drawn from the old indigenous vocabulary of movement seen in simpler form in the old *wali* and Joged dances (see Chapter 5). The choreographic sophistication and the complex patterns of accent, in which the dancer works in tight co-ordination with the orchestra, are from the later tradition of the Hindu courts.

The *condong* dances for about fifteen minutes before she summons the second group of preliminary dancers, the four *kakan-kakan*, or ladies-in-waiting. They enter in a group and dance together, in a style somewhat more refined than that of the *condong*. Their movements, reminiscent of Rejang, display marks of trained choreographers working with movements taken from the oldest, more primitive, dance forms of the island.

As the four *kakan-kakan* execute their slowly unfolding sequence of symmetrical patterns, moving languidly and fluidly, they call to one another in high, refined voices: 'Quickly, quickly, sister, don't be late!' The *condong* takes a position to one side, where she delivers comments on the progress of her sisters: 'How beautifully you dance, sisters! How lovely are your costumes!' Then the music speeds up, marking the beginning of a more energetic phase of the dance. The *condong* joins in and the five women dance together in preparation for the entrance of the Putri (Plate 7). At last, perhaps 45 minutes into the performance, the *condong* brings the gamelan to a halt with a sharp clap of her hands.

The *kakan-kakan* then move to the row of fibre mats laid on the ground at the far end of the *kalangan*. Here, they may drop out of character and eat, drink, and chew betel-nut while awaiting their next appearance in the performance. The *condong*, meanwhile, approaches the foot of the steps, calling her mistress to come out. The flutes strike up a new melody for the heroine, who appears at the top of the steps. The *condong* kneels respectfully. Slowly the Putri dances down the stairs, while singing a verse from the *Malat*. Between phrases she calls to the *condong*: 'Be prepared to follow me!' When the Putri reaches the ground, the *condong* rises and the two dancers execute a duet over the entire stage area, in which each counters the other's movement. The idiom is pure dance.

The Putri wears a long train which sweeps the ground between her feet, and her dancing emphasizes the characteristic Balinese jerking and winding head movements. The *condong*, in contrast, dances with the proper subservience and respect. Her arms are crossed and she favours a low position in relation to her partner. Her jumps in a squatting position are developed from the old Balinese movement called *gelatik nguwut papah*, an imitation of the paddy or rice bird jumping sideways on the branch of a tree. At the end of the duet, approximately an hour after the performance

7 The *condong* and *kakan-kakan* dance in preparation for the entry of the Putri in Gambuh; Batuan. (Stuart Rome)

has begun, there is a short pause. The preliminaries are complete. The Putri is left standing alone in the centre of the *kalangan*, as the musicians play an intermezzo. She waits, expectantly, her demeanour modest but self-assured.

The next section of the performance is devoted to dialogue. The *condong* calls the *kakan-kakan*, who rise from the mats and approach the Putri, kneeling before her. The dialogue begins with the Putri addressing the ladies, who always reply in unison. The talk, in Kawi, is highly stereotyped and is translated, for the benefit of the audience, by the *condong*.

After elaborate courtesies have been extended, the subject turns to the storyline, although this is not developed at length in this scene. The heroine usually expresses sadness, in very general terms, at being separated from her beloved Panji. Very often she is in captivity in the palace of a foreign king. At the end of the conversation, the *kakan-kakan* report that they are ready to dress the Putri, which gives the cue to the orchestra to begin the departure music. The Putri retires up the stairs and through the archway with her followers. This concludes the first of the stock scenes. It is interesting to note that in the most traditional Gambuh companies, such as the one in Pedungan village, Badung Province, the women would never return to the stage after this scene.

34

Inevitably, the second scene in the Gambuh performance introduces Panji, the male hero, the typical refined/sweet leading man (Plate 8). (Nowadays, the role is often performed by a female dancer, as in Batuan village, Gianyar Province.) Panji wears a distinctive head-dress decorated with fresh flowers, burning sticks of incense, *dadap* leaves, and *pandanus* blossoms. His voice is a high, monotonous falsetto, and he walks with a glide, crossing one leg over the other as he moves.

Before Panji appears, his attendants must be presented. First come a pair of portly ministers, the Demang and the Temenggung, whose bulging eyes indicate they are coarse characters, although they are on the side of the 'good' party in the drama (Colour Plate 6). They perform a comic routine punctuated by loud, deep, stylized laughter. They call to each other as they dance: 'Hey, brother, don't stay too far away, come closer!' The comedy of their dancing is established in a fixed choreography which takes them to the four corners of the *kalangan* to do comic and animal movements in unison, in a burlesque idiom.

Once the comic ministers have finished their routine and are seated on the waiting mats, it is the turn of the *arya-arya*. This group of four dancers represents the army of the good party in the story, and is analogous to the *kakan-kakan* in the Putri scene. (Later,

8   Panji, the refined hero in Gambuh; Batuan. (Danielle Toth)

35

we shall see that the antagonist in the story has an equivalent group.) The *arya-arya* enter one by one, each performing a simple routine composed of steps quite similar to those of the Baris Gedé dances. As the *arya-arya* dance, they call to one another: 'Hey, brother, come on! Get ready to meet King Panji!' They then sit together on the mat with the two ministers.

Next, the Old Prime Minister, or Patih Tua, appears. Being a refined nobleman, his movements are similar to those of Panji, but are distinguished by a slight stiffness or awkwardness, to indicate old age. The Old Minister's voice is high, his bearing dignified, and his manner grave. He dances down the entrance stairway, and when he has introduced himself, circles back to the foot of the stairs where he calls for Panji to enter. The Prince joins him in the *kalangan*, and they dance together for a time, parallelling the earlier duet of the *condong* and the Putri.

When this 5-minute duet is over, Panji returns to the top of the stairs, pausing for a few moments in the archway. He then dances what is considered to be the most difficult solo in Gambuh. Although the *condong* must render a wider range of movements, the Panji has the more difficult task of smooth linkage between isolated movements. He must also sing throughout, co-ordinating the phrasing of his chant perfectly with the phrasing of his gestures.

After a time, Panji is joined by his servant, Semar, who will later serve as his interpreter (Colour Plate 7). Semar is a coarse, comic type, of the servant class. He wears a simple Balinese cloth head-dress, often made of propitious chequered cloth, instead of a Javanese-style *gelung*, and dances a simple step. Holding his costume in one hand, he extends the other forward, thumb up, in a gesture of humility. His task, as Panji nears the end of his introductory solo, is to extend the correct ceremonial greeting to a Balinese monarch. Semar compares Panji to the gods in beauty and wisdom and grace. He follows the Prince as he dances, begging his pardon, and beseeching his royal blessing. As they move about, the men seated on the mats join in the chorus to the accompaniment of the gamelan.

This section is equivalent to the interaction of the *condong* and the Putri in the previous scene, and it is also echoed in the following scene in which the major antagonist is introduced. What is represented—the entrance of a noble character—is elaborated and ceremonialized. Dramatic time stands still while courtesies are extended and rituals of courtly etiquette observed. Through Gambuh and other forms of dance-drama, the Balinese have been able to preserve, in detail, a long tradition of formal courtly behaviour, a code now only personally remembered by the oldest living Balinese.

Once Panji has completed his lengthy entrance and has been properly received, the music and dance come to a halt. The courtiers are called from the resting mats by Semar, and they take their places in front of the Prince. A section of dialogue now follows, called the *pegunem*, or meeting. The content of this scene varies according to the plot of the particular story presented, but inevitably, the scene progresses in a fixed pattern.

First, lengthy courtesies are exchanged: 'How are you? Why do you summon us today?' etc. After a while, Panji raises the central issue of the play. The assembled courtiers reply to their leader in unison, speaking in voices pitched high, middle, and low. Panji replies in a high falsetto drawl, while Semar translates and interprets for the two groups, thus enabling the audience to understand the plot. During this part of the performance, Semar's character is perfectly correct in deportment and speech; clowning is reserved for later.

The dialogue from a typical scene goes much like this:

Panji (in Kawi): 'Uduh! My uncles are you all, my lords. I would now meet with you all together.'

Semar (in High Balinese): 'Aduh! My lords! My lord Panji is delighted to meet with you now. He has something important to discuss with you. Yes, with you, Uncle Demang, and with you, Uncle Temenggung; oh yes, and with you also, sir, with you, the Venerable Adviser, and yes, he is pleased to meet with all of you, family members and soldiers all!'

All Ministers (in Kawi): 'Yes, my lord, we are all ready and happy to greet you. Please accept our respects and do not strike us with your dreadful curse.'

Semar (in High Balinese): 'My lord Panji, your Ministers greet you and offer their humble respects. They crave to know what task you have in mind for them today.'

Panji (in Kawi): 'Now it comes to mind that my fiancée, Candra Kirana, has been lost in the forest of Gegelang and captured by the king of that country. News has come that he wants to marry her. Therefore, I would have you accompany me to that country to bring her back again. Perhaps we will have to fight.'

Semar (in High Balinese): 'Ministers of King Panji, hearken to what the King has said! Now His Highness remembers that the love of his life, Princess Candra Kirana, has been kidnapped in the woods of Gegelang by its king. She is heartsick for love of Prince Panji and, therefore, we must go to help him get her back. I'm afraid you'll have to fight, for the King of Gegelang is a dangerous fighter. Now you must gather food and weapons. Get the equipment, prepare to march for days!' etc.

The scene continues with a discussion of the particular method to be employed for the quest. Invariably, it will be decided that Panji will go to the court of the foreign antagonist in disguise. Always there is an assumed identity or similar stratagem: in one

Gambuh play, Panji goes as a *dukun*, or folk doctor; in another, he is a dancer; in another, a shadow puppeteer. The meeting scene concludes with the agreement by all the ministers to Panji's proposed plan.

The dancer portraying Panji now gives a signal to the gamelan, and the orchestra strikes up the music for the next subsection of the performance, the *pangkat*, or formal departure. No matter what the particular incident of the story is, there will usually be a formal departure at the end of the Panji scene. The characters form a line behind Panji and circle the *kalangan* a few times to represent travelling toward the foreign kingdom. The music may change as they walk along, to set the mood of the scene to come.

This section also creates the opportunity for more modern Gambuh groups to introduce comic interludes. In Batuan, for example, a group of comic villagers and peasants, called *bondres* characters, appear during the *pangkat*. The travellers dispatch Semar to ask the idiotic rustics for directions. Predictably, the locals argue among themselves, and cannot agree on the right direction to follow. When all seems hopeless, a friendly monkey appears and points out the way. Finally, Panji and his followers leave by the steps, making their exit through the stone archway.

In the third scene of a typical Gambuh performance, the antagonist, the foreign king, called the Prabu, is introduced (Plate 9). (His name varies according to the particular story.) This scene is similar in structure to those which have preceded it. Before the Prabu can make his entrance, his retinue of followers must be introduced, and, in turn, must receive him with appropriate ceremony.

The first minister to appear is Prabangsa, a 'rough' character. He is handsome, with a large moustache, protruding eyes, and a loud, low voice. Like all the principal characters, he wears a *gelung* decorated with flowers and burning sticks of incense that leave a fragrant trail of smoke wherever he moves on the stage. Prabangsa comes down into the *kalangan* and dances and sings alone for a time. He then calls to his men, the *potet*, a comic group of soldiers, who appear together at the top of the stairs.

The *potet* come down into the *kalangan* to dance with their chief. Prabangsa switches from Kawi to ordinary Balinese as he dispatches them in all directions, marching and counter-marching, until they are in hopeless confusion. This scene is a great favourite with the children in the audience, who look forward to it impatiently through the long first scenes of the play.

The comic military routine lasts for about ten minutes before Prabangsa and his men sit down on the mats to rest. They are followed by the *kade-kadehan*, four heralds, who enter in pairs and perform a group dance with an elaborate choreography. They call to one another as they dance: 'Hey, brother!' 'Come closer!' 'Get ready!' 'Be prepared!' 'The King is coming!' At the conclusion of

9 The Prabu, or foreign king, in Gambuh; Batuan. (Danielle Toth)

their routine, the *kade-kadehan* and the *potet* are brought to order by the Prabangsa in readiness for the entrance of the Prabu.

In contrast to the extended introductory solos performed by the Putri and Panji in their scenes, the Prabu dances only briefly, before moving quickly into the dialogue section of the scene. The Prabu is a 'strong' character, like the Prabangsa, but has his own way of moving, with arms held high, to emphasize his pride. He laughs as he dances down into the midst of his waiting retinue, and sings a line or two from the *Malat*. He is followed by his *penasar*, or buffoon, named Togog, who is the equivalent to Panji's attendant servant, Semar. Like Semar, Togog received his name from Java; both names are still used for the comic servant characters in the shadow puppet theatre.

The meeting in the Prabu's court advances the dramatic narrative. Very often at this point in the play, a stratagem for the disguised Panji to gain admittance into the court is established. For example, the King may call upon his ministers for advice after experiencing impotence while trying to force a union with his captive, Candra Kirana. The suggestion will be given that a *dukun* be summoned to prescribe an appropriate medicine. Later, Panji will come into the Prabu's court in that disguise.

In this rather typical variation of the plot, Panji appears at the conclusion of the meeting scene between the Prabu and his ministers. 'What is the reason for that commotion in the outer courtyard?' asks the Prabu. Togog is sent to find out and is met by Semar. The two clowns then improvise a comic routine in rather vulgar Balinese. 'Who are you? What do you want?' asks Togog, after extended horseplay having little to do with the depicted situation. 'Let's see your identity card!' 'I didn't bring it with me,' Semar protests. 'Please don't add to my problems. I've got two dozen mouths to feed at home, and I don't know where to get rice to feed them all.' 'What's the matter? Don't you know about family planning?' is his reply, bringing laughs from the audience. The dialogue can grow quite earthy, to the general merriment of the crowd.

After a time, the subject is brought around to the plot once more, and Semar reveals that his master is a *dukun*, very skilled at curing people with romantic problems. 'Just the thing! You must come to treat my master and his wives, especially the new one.' Thus, Panji is admitted to the court, and the King explains his problems to the disguised Prince. 'I lose all desire when I approach my new wife, Candra Kirana. Help me, please.' Panji agrees to try, but says that first he must interview the melancholy bride. By this ruse, he gains admittance to her quarters.

In some villages, the Gambuh performance includes a *pengipuk*, or love scene, at this point, performed by Panji and Putri. The dance is in characteristic Gambuh style, but is probably a relatively recent addition, based on the love sequences in more modern dance. Panji and Putri circle each other flirtatiously, before—very slowly and gradually—coming close enough to touch. The Princess affects surprise that these advances are coming from a mere folk doctor and draws back, until Panji reveals his identity to her by dropping the white overskirt he has put on to indicate that he is impersonating a *dukun*. Their dance represents love-making in a highly conventionalized, restrained, and decorous sequence of movements. As the intensity of the wooing increases, Semar appears at the corner of the stage and burlesques the proceedings with obscene witticisms and gestures.

In this juxtaposition of the vulgar with the sublime, an essential ingredient of Balinese dance is clearly displayed: a pairing of the divine and the chthonic. This asserts itself time and again in all the Balinese performing arts, as well as in the shadow theatre and in literature.

Semar (in Low Balinese): 'Aduh! Look at that! Delicious, yummy, yummy!' (He pants and kisses one of the poles at the side of the *kalangan*, humping obscenely. Panji notices him and comes over to tap him on the shoulder, which brings him to his senses.) 'Sorry, boss, I just got carried away—I've been away from my wife too long!' (Panji and Putri resume their cool and stylized love-making.)

After one or two episodes in which the plot is developed, the play moves to its conclusion—a prolonged sequence of fighting scenes. Togog discovers the lovers at the conclusion of the *pengipuk*. 'Aduh, what's this? The *dukun* is making love to the Princess! Call the guard!' The stage is cleared and a series of highly energetic mock combats ensues, in which characters of equal rank are pitted against one another. The *kade-kadehan* of the Prabu square off against the *arya-arya* of Panji in a group combat inspired by Baris Gedé. The Prime Ministers of both sides contend in a duel, and, finally, Panji fights against the Prabu. Each of these episodes results in victory for the good side. Between serious fighting sequences, which are carefully choreographed and highly pantomimic, there is a comic battle between Semar and Togog which is more improvisational. The performance ends with the Prabu being defeated by Panji. The dancers now retire. The sacred *gelung* are returned to storage in the *jaba tengah* with minor rituals performed to lay them away. The musicians get up as well; the flautists have been blowing continuously for about five or six hours.

Although the above describes a typical Gambuh performance, in practice there is much variation among different villages and Gambuh clubs. In the most conservative villages, as well as in those with a shortage of female talent, the scenes involving the female characters are omitted. In others, the first scene, with the *condong* and Putri, is performed, but the *pengipuk* omitted, reflecting the days perhaps when the dancers were all male. What is certain in any Gambuh performance is that there will be the meeting scene with Panji and his retainers. There will also be a *pangkat*, an intrigue involving Panji's disguise, and at least one comic (*bondres*) scene. The play will conclude with the obligatory sequence of battles. An alternative to the love scene is a weeping scene, which is accompanied by set music. These scenes are the elements from which Gambuh is made. A typical village group might have five or six different stories in its repertoire, but only 40 minutes of the complete 6-hour performance will include variations.

As mentioned earlier, Gambuh arose in the courts of the Majapahit Empire, and in the courts of the princes of the Balinese kingdoms that succeeded Majapahit.[6] This connection of the genre with the court was maintained throughout the entire nineteenth century, as recorded by European travellers in Bali, on diplomatic business, who were entertained with performances of Gambuh while visiting Balinese nobles.[7] The Gambuh troupes described by these travellers had all-male casts, including preadolescent boys trained to play the female roles. At this time, performances of Gambuh do not seem to have been limited to special ritual occasions. The noblemen sponsored a Gambuh group either in the palace itself, or in a convenient nearby village. When distinguished guests arrived to visit, or when the Prince wished to divert himself and his family, the group was summoned. Performances were also given in connection with religious festivals, as a part of the nobleman's contribution to the event.

When Bali finally came under Dutch control in the early years of the twentieth century, the power of the nobility was largely checked, and many of the former ruling families were reduced in circumstances. Although patronage of the arts by the upper-caste families did not cease immediately after Dutch conquest, it gradually diminished. Large retinues of artists, musicians, and dancers were no longer supported by the former gentry.

It was thus necessary for the villages themselves to take on responsibility for the Gambuh groups, particularly as performances had come to be considered an indispensable element of a success-ful Odalan. Certain particularly wealthy villages, with strong Gambuh traditions, were able to do this. In some villages, such as Batuan, Gianyar Province, where most of the Gambuh dancers were traditionally drawn from certain families, keeping the form alive was a matter of clan as well as village responsibility. In many other places, however, Gambuh disappeared early in the twentieth century.

Despite the efforts of certain villages, Gambuh declined in importance during the 1920s and 1930s, and was all but abandoned in the enthusiasm for new dance forms generated by a renaissance in all the Balinese arts after the First World War. By the mid-1930s, the painter and Baliphile, Walter Spies, noted that Gambuh was on the verge of extinction, performed only rarely in a few very traditional villages.[8] He reported that the performance was given without any real interest or enthusiasm. It had declined to a mere formality, and was but a vestigial remnant of its former importance. It was preserved merely out of respect for its antiquity and its still potent associations with the palaces.

Since the end of the Second World War, however, and especially in the 1980s and 1990s, Gambuh has taken on new life. Several old groups have been revived, and new ones have been started. Scholars and artists associated with government schools and other institutions have been instrumental in drawing Balinese attention to this part of the island's heritage. The role of the palaces of former times is now being taken on, to some extent, by the government-sponsored STSI, or College of the Arts, in Denpasar. Gambuh style and technique have been added to its curriculum.

In the early 1990s, some ten or twelve groups were active in Bali, supported entirely by the villages or wards to which the members belonged. Like many Balinese performing arts groups, the Gambuh clubs are voluntary associations, formed for the prime purpose of contributing to ceremonies at the village temple. Most of the village performers are not professional dancers, and have other primary occupations. The training of the group is also conducted not by a professional dance teacher, as would have been the case in the palace a century ago, but by older dancers who remember how the performance was done. Staff and students from STSI have also gone into the villages to provide instruction and advice to the renascent groups.

Since 1978, the opening of the Wredhi Budaya Arts Centre in Denpasar has provided an opportunity for secular performances of Gambuh to take place once again. Condensed versions of the dance-drama have been created by groups from Batuan and Pedungan, as well as by dancers at STSI. In these shorter performances, designed to appeal to a general audience of Balinese and foreign visitors, dramatic values have been re-emphasized and the narrative element heightened. Repetitive sections of choreography have been cut or condensed, and the dancers more carefully trained, with a renewed emphasis on skill, refinement, and consistency. In the case of Gambuh, it would thus seem that modernization in the Balinese context has involved a return to the values of the sophisticated courtiers of the Majapahit Empire.[9]

1. Stutterheim (1935: 6–25).

2. Suleiman (1974: *passim*).

3. Boon (1977: 1–90) provides some accounts of early contacts between Bali and the West, as does Vickers (1989).

4. Holt (1967: 281–9); various Balinese *Babad* manuscripts, some with references to dance, are on deposit in the Listibya Library, Denpasar. Robson (1971: 85–91) describes court Gambuh through the eyes of a Majapahit era poet.

5. See Vickers (1986) for a comprehensive discussion of *Malat* as text, in its many manifestations, of which Gambuh is but one. See also Bandem and deBoer (1978).

6. See also Ras (1973), referring to Rassers (1959).

7. Jacobs (1883: 91–2) provides a good example of an account by a Dutch official traveller who was entertained by Balinese kings with Gambuh.

8. Spies (1936: 59).

9. These are described in Robson (1971).

3 Masked Dances of the Bebali Group

In this chapter, dramatic dances, which share with Gambuh an association with Hinduized court culture, are considered. Topeng Pajegan (which is also in the *wali*, or sacred, domain) and Wayang Wong are masked dance genres belonging to the *bebali*, or ceremonial, category of sacred dances. Both, however, are later developments than Gambuh and are products not of the Hindu-Javanese courts of the sixteenth-century Majapahit Empire but of the seventeenth- and eighteenth-century Hindu-Balinese courts which evolved in the capital city, first at Samprangan, then Gelgel, and then Klungkung (now Semarapura).

These dance genres were created by artists who deliberately set out to establish new forms at the request of the King or head of a noble family. Originating in the great central palace of the Balinese capital city, Topeng Pajegan and Wayang Wong were disseminated to the lesser courts in Badung, Bangli, Gianyar, and other places. The development, elaboration, and propagation of these forms were associated with particular families of sponsors and artists. The all-important masks and head-dresses employed in the performances have been handed down in particular families, acquiring with each generation greater *pasupati*, or magical quality. In addition to the sanctity bestowed by age, these treasures have often been additionally charged with the power of magical inscriptions.

Many categories of the sacred in Bali can become relevant to the arts: gestures, syllables, images, plays, melodies, clothing, weapons, etc. The sacral quality, called *tenget*, inheres in the specific object, locale, etc., and is particular, definite, and fixed. Unlike the doll-like *pratima*, which are only temporarily inhabited by the visiting deities at an Odalan, a sacred kris (dagger), for example, or a sacred mask, is permanently empowered, and that power is handed down from generation to generation within a particular clan. The heirlooms that are *tenget* both literally embody and symbolically represent the family's sustaining power, a power which is both displayed and replenished from time to time by appropriate reconstruction and public presentation of the objects. The use of at least one sacred mask and/or head-dress is an essential part of every *bebali* performance.

Masked dancing has been known on Bali for more than a millennium. The Berutuk masks referred to on page 3, as well as many native Balinese animal masks, are quite similar in style to masks found on other islands of the Indonesian archipelago, such as the Topeng Hudoq of East Kalimantan (Borneo), and those used in dances of various groups in Sulawesi (Celebes) and Irian Jaya (West New Guinea). None of the surviving Balinese dance forms employing masks of this type make use of a developed narrative or story, although rudimentary dramatic features are occasionally present in them.

The oldest record of masked dance on Bali dates to the copperplate charter, *Praçasti Bebetin* (AD 896), inscribed during the reign of King Ugrasena of Bedulu.[1] The charter lists masked dancers (*partapukan*) along with other court artistes, servants, and functionaries. The charter is inscribed in the Old Javanese language, showing that Hindu influence had already reached the island by this time. Unfortunately, we know nothing of the nature of the dances performed by these ancient civil servants. The earliest descriptive accounts we have are given in the considerably later Panji stories, such as the *Malat* and *Wangbang Wedeya*, and concern forms of dance quite similar to Gambuh.[2]

The masks made in modern Bali retain many traditional features, especially those intended for use in performance rather than for sale to tourists (Plate 10). The craft itself most often passes down from generation to generation in particular families. Thus, the mask-maker is a special kind of artisan, who must be consecrated to his calling in a special ceremony. He must know the necessary prayers and ceremonies connected with masks and an entire code of ritual lore, the *Dharma Sangging*, which applies to the maker.

Making a magically powerful mask commences with the selection of the wood from a potent tree growing in a sacred place. The *pohon kepuh*, or graveyard tree, or the tree in the village *pura dalem*, or death temple, is propitiated with prayers and offerings before a mask-sized slab is cut from the living wood of its trunk. The wood is soaked in water for a few days, and then set aside to dry for several seasons before it can be carved. The first cut made by the mask-maker is accompanied by an appropriate ritual, and another ceremony is undertaken when the mask has been finished. At that time, a magical letter is written on the interior face of the mask, and it is taken to a sacred place, along with a large offering. There, spirits are invited to enter the mask, while the future users and the mask-maker watch from a safe distance. It is said that often it is possible to see the power entering the mask, in the form of a glowing nimbus, like St Elmo's fire. The mask is then ready for use in the *bebali* dances. Not all masks will have received this special treatment, but there will always be at least one of them in a *bebali* performance. In Gambuh, in contrast, it is the *gelung*, or head-dresses, which are infused with magical power.

10   Mask-maker I Wayan Tangguh at
work, Singapadu. (Pino Confessa)

Topeng Pajegan[3]

On the narrow road leading from Denpasar to Gianyar, above the
Petanu River, is located the lovely old Balinese village of Blahbatuh.
This prosperous community, with its rich ricelands, has a large
population of families who were, until the late nineteenth century,
associated with the court of the paramount Balinese kingdom,
located first in Gelgel and later in Klungkung.

One of these families, a *ksatrya* (knight)-caste clan called the
Pemaksan Gusti Ngurah Jelantik, maintains its principal temple in
Blahbatuh, and in that temple, the Pura Penataran Topeng, is kept
an especially sacred collection of *lontar* (palm-leaf) manuscripts,
wayang (shadow play puppets), and *topeng* (masks). The word
topeng comes from the root *tup*, meaning 'cover', and refers to
something pressed against the face, that is, a mask. The term is used
specifically to denote the masks used in the genre of dance-drama
called Topeng. The *topeng* kept in Blahbatuh, belonging to the
Jelantik family, are said to be the oldest in Bali.

The masks themselves, which are now regarded as too sacred to
photograph, are of two types. The first, and probably the oldest, is

46

represented by six masks covering the full face, each with a mouth-piece on the inside for the wearer to clench between his teeth while dancing. This method of securing a mask is still seen today in Sunda (West Java) and in Central Java, but not at all on Bali. The remaining masks, fifteen in number, are more similar in style to modern Balinese masks; they are held to the dancer's face by means of an elastic band. This group was probably made by native craftsmen inspired by the six examples imported from Java.[4]

The collection of sacred *lontar* manuscripts, kept with the masks and puppets, includes a legendary historical account of the Jelantik clan, from its founding in the time of Dalem (King) Batu Renggong (AD 1460–1550) to the year 1779, when the clan moved from Klungkung to Blahbatuh.[5] This account, called the *Babad Blahbatuh*, recounts history from the point of view of the family, emphasizing its exploits, and tracing its lineage. While little attention is given to other matters, it does present a feasible account of how Topeng Pajegan came to Bali.

According to the manuscript, in the late sixteenth century, Dalem Batu Renggong sent an expedition to attack the East Javanese kingdom of Blambangan, under the leadership of his two war ministers, Patih Ularan and Patih Jelantik, the founder of the present Blahbatuh Jelantik line. The Balinese invasion succeeded in sacking the palace of the King of Blambangan, although Jelantik was killed in the battle. Patih Ularan brought home a basket of masks as booty, which he showed the King in Gelgel as proof that the expedition had been successful. The treasures were then stored in the palace treasury, where they lay unused for a century.

Descendants of the first Jelantik followed their illustrious ancestor into the service of the kings of Bali, and often served in the position of Patih, or Prime Minister. Sometime between 1665 and 1686, during the reign of Dalem Batu Renggong's grandson, Dalem Dimadé, Patih I Gusti Pering Jelantik composed a dance-drama. The captured masks were brought out and used for the first time in the première performance, called Topeng Pajegan. Following this, it became customary for the masks to be used in performance in the palace every six months, on the occasion of an Odalan, at first in Gelgel and later in Klungkung, after the court moved there about AD 1715. The manuscript ends with the report that, as a result of political intrigue and a *coup* in the court of Klungkung, the Jelantik family went into exile to lands they held in the Blahbatuh area, taking the masks with them. The family survived the transition to Dutch colonial rule, and later to life under the independent government of Indonesia, with little loss of power or prestige. Members of the family are still active patrons of the performing arts, and especially of Topeng.

Alone among the *bebali* dance forms, Topeng Pajegan contains ritual aspects similar to those of *wali* dances described in Chapter 1.

For this reason, it is sometimes known as Topeng Wali. At an Odalan, therefore, the performance is given in the *jeroan*, the most sacred part of the temple. But temple festivals are not the only events calling for a performance of Topeng Pajegan: weddings, cremations, tooth-filings, and other ceremonies associated with rites of passage are also highly appropriate occasions. The dancer serves in both sacred and secular capacities—as high priest and entertainer—and thus works in the most sacred area available. When performing in a private household compound, he dances in the *sanggah*, or family temple. In either location, he presents a small offering and pours a libation to consecrate the ground for his performance (Plate 11). The main ritual will take place later, after the conclusion of the story.

The distinguishing feature of Topeng Pajegan is that it is a monodrama. A single dancer tells a story by portraying a succession of masked characters. The word 'Pajegan' itself comes from an expression used in purchasing rice: when someone buys an entire crop of paddy, rather than by the kilo, he is said to *majeg* the crop, that is, he does the whole thing on his own. With the help of a few simple theatrical conventions, the soloist in Topeng Pajegan is able to tell a complicated and engrossing story single-handedly.

11 Dancer Ida Bagus Puja blesses the offering in Topeng Pajegan. (STSI documentation; courtesy Nik Wheeler)

Topeng Pajegan is by far the most dramatic of the *bebali* genres; in none of the others are the intricacies of the narrative of much interest to either dancer or audience.

The stories presented in Topeng are always taken from the chronicles of Balinese history and deal with the semi-legendary feats of the Hindu-Balinese kings, their ministers, and their high priests. The dancer composes his own plays from the manuscript sources by following traditional procedures. The story presented on a particular occasion is chosen by the dancer in accordance with the needs and desires of the sponsor. The story of the expedition, whereby the first Patih Jelantik attacked Blambangan under the orders of Dalem Batu Renggong, is itself a popular subject in the repertoire.

The ritual aspect is not integrated with the story-telling but is reserved for the end. In a sense, then, the performance is a prologue to the ritual. At the end, regardless of what story has been presented, a strange white-faced, buck-toothed, smiling character with long, wild hair comes to the stage. His name is Sidha Karya, which means 'The one who can do the task' (Colour Plate 8). When he is wearing this mask, and only then, the dancer serves a specifically priestly function.

The playing space for the performance is a small, oval area on the bare earth, some 2.5 by 3.5 metres in size. The dancer places his basket of masks in front of the *gamelan gong* which will accompany him. Usually there is no curtain. His performance is oriented toward the shrine where the gods are sitting, invisibly, to watch. During the performance, his masks are spread out on a small table. A straight-backed chair is at hand, if needed.

The performance invariably begins with the presentation of three introductory character studies (*pengelembar*), which gives the performer the opportunity to demonstrate his skill as a dancer; later, there will be few opportunities to interrupt the story with extended passages of pure dance. These characters, in fact, have no connection to the story and, when introduced, demonstrate a mood of wonder and astonishment, as if suddenly wrenched from the distant past into the world of the present, a process characterized by Emigh (1979) as 'ancestral visitation'.

The first introductory mask is always the Patih, a character of the strong and crude type (Plate 12). His red face indicates that he is brave and easily angered. His movements are broad and extended, conveying strong tension. He is followed by two additional masked characters, chosen by the dancer (Colour Plate 9). Often another Patih will be presented, with a brown face and big moustache. His movement is rather comic and very vigorous. The final introductory mask may depict a comic yet dignified old gentleman, known as the Tua (Plate 13). Each of these dances begins with a particular set of movements known as *mungkah lawang*, or 'opening the door', in which he indicates parting a curtain.[6]

12 The Patih, or prime minister, in
Topeng Pajegan; Peliatan. (Stuart Rome)

Story-telling in Topeng Pajegan follows a firmly established set
of conventions. The dancer generally alternates the full-face masks
of high-born and noble characters with the half-masks, allowing
speech, worn by the servants and comic peasant characters. The
kings and noblemen convey their meaning through gesture, while
the attendants may speak for their masters in Kawi or for themselves in Balinese. Occasional dissociation of voice and body is a
striking and exotic aspect of the story-telling mode: at times, the
dancer will bend his body in cringing subordination in keeping

50

13 The Tua or old courtier, in Topeng
Pajegan, from the Klungkung Palace. (I
Madé Bandem)

with his role as palace servant, while from his lips come the
imperious commands, in Kawi, of his invisible master.

The language employed in Topeng Pajegan is a rich and varied
medium of literary and theatrical expression. A series of levels,
ranging from the most sacred (at the *kaja* end of the linguistic
spectrum) to the demonic and obscene (at the *kelod* extreme) is
employed. The top level, used only for prayers, is Sanskrit. Below
it, quotations from the Kawi literary classics are sung in verse at
appropriate places in the action, lending majesty and dignity to
the moment. Somewhat lower on the scale is the prose Kawi,

51

spoken by the high-ranked characters of the drama. In practice, since these characters usually wear full-face masks, the Kawi is spoken for these characters by their servants. The *penasar*, or retainers, themselves use the 'high' Balinese when addressing their masters, but ordinary vernacular Balinese when addressing low-ranking people. *Bali kasar*, 'low' Balinese, is not a complete language but consists of vulgar terms and expressions considered quite shocking in everyday life. It is used in the performance only by the *bondres*, or comic, characters and servants who may taunt and insult the enemy as the drama moves toward its sometimes violent climax.

As in the Gambuh dance-drama, the dramatic action in Topeng Pajegan is built on a series of stock scenes occurring in a predictable order. After the *pengelembar* have been presented, the dancer begins to relate the particulars of the chosen tale. This is invariably begun by the *penasar*, who is a descendant of the character Semar from the older Gambuh form. In Topeng, the *penasar* can be of two different types, either the *penasar kelihan*, or 'older brother', or the *penasar cenikan*, or 'younger brother'. The former may also be known by his proper name, Punta, and the younger by Wijil. In Topeng Panca, the *penasar* always appear as a comic team, the older brother serving as a foil to the antics of the younger. In Topeng Pajegan, in contrast, the two servants alternate in making jokes and explaining the action of the play.

The elder *penasar* begins his scene with singing and comic dance. He then establishes the theme of the story to follow. Wearing a brown-coloured half-mask, adorned with a large black moustache and bulging eyes, he speaks in a low voice, in this way:

Punta (singing in Kawi):
'When the Five Pendawas rose up at dawn,
Departing from the city of Wirata,
Like the rising sun were they,
Gleaming over the whole world. . . .

(Spoken) 'Ho, ho, ha, ha, ha! Lordy me! I'm so happy to be the chief servant here in the palace of Gelgel, great capital city of ancient Bali! My master, Dalem Batu Renggong, is going to arrive soon, here in the beautiful audience chamber. What a mighty King is he, my master! His power is known everywhere in the whole world.

'His people are happy, his lands are at peace. Why, we have a wonderful standard of living, with low taxes, no inflation, and plenty of coconuts for export! And you know, I'm also happy for another reason. My boss, King Batu Renggong has a terrific Patih, a mighty Prime Minister, doughty in battle, named I Gusti Ngurah Jelantik. There's supposed to be an audience held today, and I can't imagine what is going to happen. . . .'

The *penasar* continues until the background to the story is clear. He may also embellish the exposition with jokes that are relevant to the story and its theme.

The second character to appear in a Topeng performance is often the Dalem, or King, provided the performer is capable of dancing the role (Colour Plate 10). This mask is omitted when he can not manage the role. In the story begun in the example given above, he would be Dalem Batu Renggong; in another tale, he would assume a different name. The mask of the King is of the refined type, and covers the full face, which means the dancer must perform in silence when portraying this character. It is always white or very light green. The face represented on the mask is an idealized portrait, representing kings as a class rather than any specific individual. Although slight variations in appearance distinguish the masks of different regional traditions, the fundamental iconography is immediately recognizable no matter where the performance is given.

The scene presenting the Dalem follows a fixed format, commencing with an extended dance routine that demonstrates the ideal qualities of Hindu-Balinese kingship: dignity, grace, and refinement. This solo is a set piece and is performed whenever the Dalem first appears, regardless of the story-line. When danced by a master, it is at the very pinnacle of Balinese Terpsichorean art.

Only after his lengthy dance solo, which is always the same, does the Dalem enter the specific circumstances of the tale currently being presented. The music accompanying his entrance is brought to a quick transition by a commanding clap of his hands. Now, he will begin the second part of the scene, in which pantomime rather than pure dance is the means of expression. This section is quite short and also follows an established scheme. The King appears alert, and then indicates that he is seeing someone approach. With a gesture, he beckons the visitor to come closer.

At this point, the dancer leaves the stage, although the King's 'presence' remains there, invisible. During the following scene, another character, often a messenger, will enter, to advance the story. This character will wear a half-mask, permitting speech. He will speak Kawi, to represent the speech of the King, alternating with 'high Balinese' spoken by the lower-ranking character. During this section of the performance, a mission to perform a great ceremony or to attack an enemy is usually ordered.

The second character leaves the stage at the conclusion of the audience scene. Now, when the dancer returns, as one or another of the *penasar* characters, he can improve the audience's understanding of the dramatic situation and perhaps do a little clowning as well. The stance of the *penasar* is basically comic throughout the play, but he is always respectful of his masters. At this point in the story, the *penasar* must prepare for the entrance of the next essential character, the strong, good Patih, whose function is always to carry out the will of the refined King.

In Topeng, the refined King is never represented doing anything as undignified as fighting or working: mysterious, almost insubstantial, he is half-way between the common man and the gods themselves. His Patih, however, is a man of action as well as breeding. He is the quintessential *ksatrya* warrior. His face is brown, his eyes large, and he sports a fierce moustache. In some of the Patih masks, his teeth are bared, while in others his lips are closed. His movements are energetic and forceful, yet always controlled and dignified. The characterization might seem familiar, and indeed it is, for the good Patih has received his vocabulary of movement and general appearance from the character Prabangsa in the Gambuh. There, this character is a minister for the antagonistic King; here, with no change in his appearance, he becomes the active protagonist.

The Patih performs his own introductory dance solo, demonstrating the qualities of his character. This over, he gestures to his (invisible) *penasar* to make ready for departure on the planned expedition, the nature of which depends on the particular tale presented.

In the next section of the play, a gallery of comic characters (*bondres*), perhaps half a dozen in all, are impersonated by the dancer, a real test of his virtuosity. The audience looks forward eagerly to this section, which exists in one form or another in most of the genres of Balinese drama. The characters belong to the lower caste and are very eccentric (Colour Plate 11). They often represent oppressed villagers who need the services of the Patih to rescue them from some trouble. Often they are portrayed as suffering from physical defects and handicaps; one medical scholar has used a group of *bondres* masks to discuss common genetic defects found on the island.[7] Some characters have buck teeth, others have cleft palates; still others have long noses or no noses at all; some are represented as being blind or deaf, or as stutterers. The Balinese audience enjoys slapstick humour, to which these characters lend themselves perfectly. The jokes occasionally have a rather cruel edge. Travesty is also common, with the male dancer playing one or more comic female roles.

Another common stock scene, especially when the play concerns the holding of an important ceremony, has the *bendesa*, or village chief, or another character, even perhaps one of the *penasar*, lecture the common people on their spiritual and ethical responsibilities. This is as close as Balinese religious practice normally comes to sermonizing and is an important aspect of the performance, especially at life-cycle rituals in the home.

When the story concerns a battle, another character often appears after the last of the *bondres*. This is the antagonist King, who usually possesses supernatural powers. His mask is yellow or red, with a moustache and large eyes. His appearance is often bestial; visible fangs may protrude from his mouth. The antagonist King wears a characteristic *gelung*, similar to the head-dress worn by the Prabu, who is his counterpart in Gambuh. Very often his mask has an open mouth, which permits limited speech. This King enters the stage quickly because he does not have an extended solo. As he appears, dramatic tension begins to rise, for the audience knows that when he comes into view, the end of the story is near. He comes out talking and gesturing excitedly. It is clear that his country is being attacked, and he orders his followers to make ready to fight.

Once more, the Patih appears to the insistent pounding of 'Gending Batel' played on the gamelan. The Patih mimics a great hand-to-hand struggle, in which he battles against his (invisible) opponent, the antagonist King. This section comes to a quick conclusion as the dancer works his way up to his table of masks and then holds the face of the villain aloft, to signify the victory of the Patih and the beheading of the antagonist. A moment later, one of the *penasar* appears and explains that the story is over, that the enemy has been defeated, and that it is now time for a celebration. (In some performances, the conclusion of the story is merely narrated by the *penasar*.) The narrative portion of the performance is ended, and it is time for the ritual to begin.

At this time, the dancer puts on the mask of Sidha Karya, along with a wig of long, wild hair (see Colour Plate 8). The priest has already said prayers over the offering before the dancer seizes it and dances with it over to the shrine, shouting and laughing and praying in Sanskrit over the bowl of fruit and flowers. He gestures with the sacred *mudra* used by the priests when they pray. Once he has presented the offering to the gods, he turns back and showers the audience with handfuls of specially blessed Chinese coins kept with the offering. The spectators scramble to pick up the lucky money. To bless the spectators further, he sprinkles holy water and flings rice in their direction.

Suddenly, Sidha Karya lunges into the audience and snatches up one of the small children who make up a large part of the crowd. All of the youngsters in the audience, who have been waiting for this moment, rush here and there, shrieking with fright as he approaches, but the dancer is always able to catch one. He carries the struggling child over to the shrine and holds him up to the gods before giving him a small present from among the offerings there. The child is then put down and disappears into the crowd with his trophy. The performance is over, for now the ritual is complete. The members of the audience can approach the shrine for individual prayers. The dancer puts away his masks in their basket after presenting a small offering to the god Wisnumurti, Patron of Dance. He is ready to return to his own village.

Unlike the performers of Gambuh and of the *wali* dances, the Topeng Pajegan dancer is not usually a member of the group celebrating the occasion, but a professional engaged for the event. Few villages could hope to boast a member possessing all the necessary qualifications for the demanding Topeng Pajegan role. Like the mask-maker, the Topeng dancer needs to know the special code of his craft—the *Bebali Sidha Karya*—which prescribes prayers and offerings and behavioural taboos. In addition, he must be able to read the *Babad*, or historical chronicles, from which his stories are made, and be able to dramatize his own material from the bare outlines given in these sources. Comic ability is also a special requirement, as is the ability to impersonate a number of characters. The dancer must also be able to sing and chant lengthy passages of Kawi poetry from memory. And by no means least, he must be a talented dancer.

Before a dancer may give his first performance of Topeng Pajegan, he must undergo a dedication ceremony in which he is confirmed in the profession. Thereafter, he may perform at temple festivals in his own village, or at events sponsored by his clan. If some measure of fame is achieved locally, he may then be called by other villages or kin groups to perform on their behalf. The payment for these professional engagements is quite modest. In the early 1990s, it consisted of a fee of about US$15 for the entire performance, plus the leftover offering. At the present time, no more than a dozen performers of Topeng Pajegan are still active in Bali.

In recent years, among the larger Balinese clans, there has been a resurgence of interest in their origins. Many groups without heirloom copperplate charters or historical *Babad* manuscripts have commissioned new ones to reinforce their perceptions of the group's historical prestige and influence. In the wake of this development has also come fresh opportunities for the performers of Topeng Pajegan, for hand in hand with the commissions for written historical documents has come the desire to see the story of the kin group's origin enacted, visualized for the clan by a Topeng Pajegan dancer. Some of the dancers, in fact, do double duty, composing the newly 'discovered' *lontar* manuscripts in the daytime and performing a Topeng play taken from it that night. This kind of effort is work for a truly well-educated scholar and multi-talented artist.

Interlude: Barong Kedingkling

It is told in the village of Madangan, Gianyar Province, that a terrible pestilence threatened the people about 250 years ago, when King Batu Renggong's great-grandson was on the throne in Klungkung. The new King's elder brother, I Dalem Agung Pemayun, was driven into exile after he had refused to assume the title of King of Bali for himself. After I Dalem Agung Pemayun had wandered for some time in the wilderness of the northern mountain district, and meditated there, he travelled to the south and entered Madangan while the epidemic was raging. The desperate villagers appealed to the great man for help, and he proposed a possible remedy for their distress. 'In the palace in Klungkung are some wonderfully powerful sacred masks,' he told them. 'They represent the sacred monkeys of the holy *Ramayana*, and they have the power to drive out the disease.' He told the people of ceremonies conducted in the palace to protect against disease by driving out the demons. At his suggestion, the villagers made nine masks, copies of those in the Klungkung palace, and inaugurated a *wali* dance called Barong Kedingkling to protect themselves against disease. The ceremony is still performed at one of the village temples, the Pura Dalem Madangan, every six months. There, too, the old masks are kept between festivals.

Barong Kedingkling is similar to rituals performed in several other Balinese villages, where the form may be called Barong Belas-belasan. *Barong* is a general Balinese term for a mask representing a mythological animal or supernatural being; *kedingkling* means 'hopping', while *belas-belasan* means 'going in separate directions'. In Barong Kedingkling, we see a manifestation of the connection between dancing and exorcism, with ritual power attached to the properties, in this case the masks, used in the performance.

The event begins at noon in the *jeroan* of the temple. The leader of the dancers, usually an ordained *pemangku*, or priest, is called Sugriwa, King of the Monkeys, a name taken from the old *Ramayana* epic. Wearing a very handsome mask in the style of Wayang Wong (see below) and a costume made of white palm fibres, he enters the inner courtyard of the temple, dancing to the accompaniment of the *gamelan batel*, an ensemble consisting of percussion instruments used in the *gamelan gambuh* plus the *gender wayang*, a quartet of metallophones which accompanies the shadow play. Sugriwa carries an ornately worked silver tray, on which are arranged pieces of roast pork (*babi guling*), a much-loved culinary specialty of Gianyar Province. His dance is very simple, without rigorous technical demands, and is based on mimicry of monkey movement. He dances about in the *jeroan*, singing a Balinese song, before calling on his two Prime Ministers, Amoman and Anggada. The two apes are masked and costumed like their King, but are dressed in different colours: Anoman wears white, Anggada red. Between them they carry a live pig hanging upside-down from a pole. This animal will be sacrificed at the conclusion of the ceremony.

Anoman and Anggada are followed into the *jeroan* by four other monkeys, each bearing a different kind of offering on a plate, and two characters belonging to the general category of *penasar*. This particular pair of retainers are Twalen and his son, Wredah, who are very popular in several genres of Balinese dance and in the shadow theatre. Found in all plays that derive from the *Ramayana* and *Mahabharata* epics, they serve the characters of the good party. Twalen and Wredah thus attend King Sugriwa in Barong Kedingkling. They translate his commands from Kawi into Balinese for the benefit of the audience, as well as explain the ritual and comment on the action. Twalen and Wredah carry incense and holy water and dance a simple choreographic pattern with the seven monkeys in the inner courtyard.

With a shouted signal, the Monkey King calls his band to form a circle in the middle of the courtyard. All sit as Sugriwa exercises a *pemangku*'s function in presenting the offerings to the *pelinggih*. The live pig and the other meat offerings are kept to one side, for they will be presented later, to the demons rather than to the gods.

Sugriwa's troupe sits quietly for half an hour or so as the offerings are presented. They then rise, and with loud shouts and monkey noises rush out of the *jeroan* to visit each of the households in the village.

The monkeys swarm into the town, singly and in pairs, while the gamelan is picked up and moved to the central street. There, the musicians continue to add to the general din. The clamour is intense; children rush to and fro, and the monkeys invade every household, sometimes 'robbing' the kitchens. Once inside the compound, they visit the *sanggah* and climb any coconut or fruit trees that grow on the property. These are shaken to drive off any harmful spirits.

Twalen and Wredah carry holy water from house to house. They also act as traffic wardens for the monkeys, directing them where to go. The older dancers who have begun the ceremony pass on their masks to younger men who take turns in the game. Everywhere, people give them small presents of food and money.

The special affinity of the monkey for the productive trees of the village is a central aspect of the performance. Alarmed by the tree climbers, the squirrel population of the village also flees, squawking in protest. The demons are also driven out by the din of the private homes in the village into the public streets, where they can be bribed with offerings and then sent on their way out of town.

At about six o'clock in the evening, the dancers gather once again in the inner temple. The forty or so who have taken part are exhausted from the running and hopping and shouting they have done. Now, the pig and five chickens are sacrificed and arranged in an elaborate offering to the demons, which is placed on the ground. The demons are then exhorted to go away, thus preparing the way for a successful Odalan, which will begin the next day with a performance of Baris Gedé or Rejang. The old monkey masks are returned to their storage place in the temple until the next Odalan.

Variations on this ritual performance, one of a very large number of ceremonies still practised on the island involving the expulsion of demons, can be found in many villages. Before the Balinese New Year (Hari Nyepi), for example, many communities attempt to drive off the demons with burning torches, which are flung back and forth by groups of young men in a kind of fire battle.

Wayang Wong

According to Madangan legend, the sacred masks belonging to the Barong Kedingkling rite were copied from a collection of masks kept in the palace of the King of Klungkung, where they had been kept (but not used in performance) since time immemorial. The original set of court masks may very well survive today, in the village of Kamasan, Klungkung Province, which long provided servants and artisans to the royal palace. A group of fine old masks is kept in the Pura Penataran Pulasari, which is the principal temple for the Pulasari clan, a family long prominent in court circles, especially during the nineteenth century. According to members of the family, the masks and musical instruments and other cultural treasures were brought to the temple at the time of the destruction of the palace of Klungkung by the Dutch in 1908.

Fifteen masks are still in this collection. Although it is not clear that all are equally old, they are carved and painted in a style which is noticeably different from that employed by the makers of *topeng*. They resemble other old Balinese masks, such as can be seen at the Bali Museum in Denpasar, representing fantastic or mythical animals. The faces are large, with prominent ears decorated with *rumbing*, a particular kind of ear ornament. Behind the masks is an indispensable part of the costume, the *sekar taji*, a kind of gilded leather ornamental collar. These masks are very similar to the mask worn by the Barong Ket, which we shall discuss in a later chapter. Their style shows Chinese influence and would seem to be very old. In many villages the figures into which the gods descend at an Odalan are guarded by small carved companion figures, called 'lions', with faces carved and painted in this same distinctive manner.

Dalem Gedé Kusamba was King between 1772 and 1825. According to the *Babad Dalem*, a legendary history of the Kings of Gelgel and Klungkung, Dalem Gedé Kusamba ordered his chief dancers to create a new form of dramatic dance using the royal collection of sacred masks.[8] He stipulated that the repertoire for the new genre be taken from the *Ramayana*, and he directed that the dancers create a Wayang Wong, that is, a dance based on the *wayang* (shadow puppet) theatre using men in place of puppets. The resulting form acquired the name of Wayang Wong, by which it is known today. The genre is distinct from the dramatic dance of the same name which exists in Central Java, although some of the ideas behind the two genres are similar.

The *Ramayana* epic, which was to provide the basis for Wayang Wong, has been known and revered on Bali for many centuries. To this day, it is esteemed as a pinnacle of the island's traditional literature. Imagery from the long poem is omnipresent on the island, and the story is widely known by people of all levels and occupations.[9] Even the illiterate are familiar with the most important episodes and characters.

The means by which the *Ramayana* has been kept alive in Balinese life belong to various interconnecting literary, artistic, and theatrical traditions. It has been suggested that much of the Balinese imagery representing scenes from the *Ramayana* was originally based on medieval East Javanese prototypes.[10] Similarly, the basic literary text by which the *Ramayana* is known in Bali, the Old Javanese *Ramayana Kakawin*, was also imported from Java many years ago. Although the Balinese have had access to other literary works based on the Indian *Ramayana*, such as *Uttara Kanda* and *Kapi Parwa*, the Old Javanese *Ramayana Kakawin* has been the principal written source for Balinese knowledge of the *Ramayana* over the centuries. Only since the Second World War has the internationally better known version ascribed to Walmiki been available on the island.

The Old Javanese *Ramayana Kakawin* is a free translation and adaptation of a sixth-century AD Sanskrit poem from India, the *Rawana Vadha* by Bhatti. Manuscript copies of the work have been made on Bali in the form of *lontar* (palm-leaf) manuscripts for hundreds of years. Sections of the epic poem are often recited, with translation and commentary, at Balinese religious festivals and on other important occasions by special groups devoted to the purpose.[11] It thus maintains existence as a specific literary text, as well as providing a source for artists in other media. The old poem is considered to be full of good instruction and *wayah* (ripe, venerable); to recite it is a beneficial and pious act. Unlike certain other works, however, the *Ramayana* is not considered to be magically powerful or dangerous, and except for the recitations just referred to, it does not play an important part in the ritual practice of Balinese Hinduism.

Performances of Wayang Wong have been another way of preserving and reinvigorating the old epic for successive generations of Balinese. Until this century, in fact, Wayang Wong was the only form of dance-drama in which episodes from the *Ramayana* were presented.

The direction to the choreographers that the *Ramadéwa* be used as subject-matter was especially apt, for the *Ramayana* story lends itself very well to ceremonies for frightening or otherwise driving away demons. The epic tells of the defeat of Rawana, King of the Demons, along with his entire army of ogres and imps. The 'good' party in the story, furthermore, is made up largely of monkeys, who are followers of the hero, Ramadewa. These monkeys are no mere simians. Many are hybrids—of a monkey with a tiger, for example, or with a bird or a cow. The monkeys in the Wayang Wong are thus mythological beings. In them, ancient Balinese protectors, in the form of benevolent mythical animals, survive in altered form (Colour Plates 12 and 13).

Dalem Gedé Kusamba's artists created a vocabulary of movement for the monkey characters drawing on those used in the various Sang Hyang and Baris genres. The repertoire employed by Sugriwa is the basis of the monkey moves. But, unlike the simple realistic mimicry of monkey movements seen in the Barong Kedingkling group in Madangan, in Wayang Wong, the hopping, jumping, scratching, and looking around are stylized and formalized. They have been transformed from pantomime into dance.

As the monkeys dance, they shout and squawk in a deafening chorus. Each monkey has a distinctive way of performing the same pattern. The goat-monkey, Arimenda, for example, gallops and butts with his horns; Sempati, the tiger-monkey, creeps and pounces; Satabali, the bird-monkey, hops and pecks much like the *kiuh–keker* 'characters' of the Berutuk rite.

Another important source for the Wayang Wong was Gambuh. The refined human characters—Rama, Sita, Laksmana, and Wibisana—are drawn directly from prototypes in the older Gambuh form. The ogres or demonic characters—Rawana, Kumbakarna, Meganada, Prahasta, and Sukasrana—wear dark red masks similar in style to those of the monkeys. All have prominent fangs. Their movements very much reflect those of the strong characters of Gambuh. The costumes worn by the human characters (Figures 6 and 7) and by the ogres are identical to those worn in Gambuh, while the monkeys wear costumes similar to those of Baris, except that each is fitted with a long and prominent tail.

Another source drawn on by the composers of Wayang Wong, and the one which gives the genre its name, was Wayang Kulit, the shadow puppet theatre.[12] Wayang, like Gambuh, came to Bali from Java, possibly as early as the ninth century AD and was associated with the Hindu culture of the Javanese courts and palaces. This form of theatre became very popular in Bali and remains so today where it is practised by dozens of *dalang*, or puppeteers. From the shadow puppet theatre, the makers of Wayang Wong received a prototype for the dramatization of material from the *Mahabharata* and *Ramayana*.

The *Ramayana* itself was a subject for representation in the shadow theatre. Relief carvings dating from the fourteenth century exist at the Candi Panataran near Blitar in East Java in which episodes from the *Ramayana* are depicted.[13] The servant characters of the shadow theatre are included in the panels, although they do not appear in the old *Ramayana* poem itself, indicating that the story was very likely performed in the Wayang theatre of that time and that the sculptor drew inspiration from it in presenting the *Ramayana* tale in low relief. Some of the characters in the modern set of Balinese Wayang puppets are nearly identical to the figures depicted in the Panataran reliefs. The resemblance extends to the appearance of the monkey and servant characters in Wayang Wong, whose masks and head-dresses definitely show the influence of the old East Javanese style. Other characters of the Panataran group, especially the ogres, like Kumbakarna, bear no particular likeness to modern Balinese shadow puppets or to the masks of the demonic characters in Wayang Wong.

The shadow theatre provided a number of elements to the Wayang Wong. Certain aspects of the dancing, particularly the hand gestures, specifically imitate the movements of the shadow puppets on the lighted screen. The music for Wayang Wong also came from the puppet theatre; accompaniment is provided by the *gamelan batel*.

The percussion element in the *batel* ensemble brought to Wayang Wong the possibility for sophisticated co-ordination of dancers

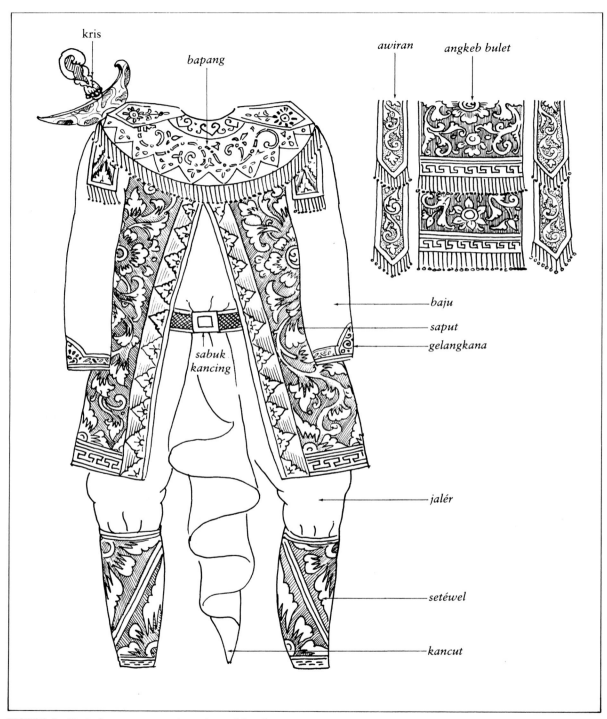

FIGURE 6   Typical costumes worn by males and females in Wayang Wong. (I Nyoman Mandra)

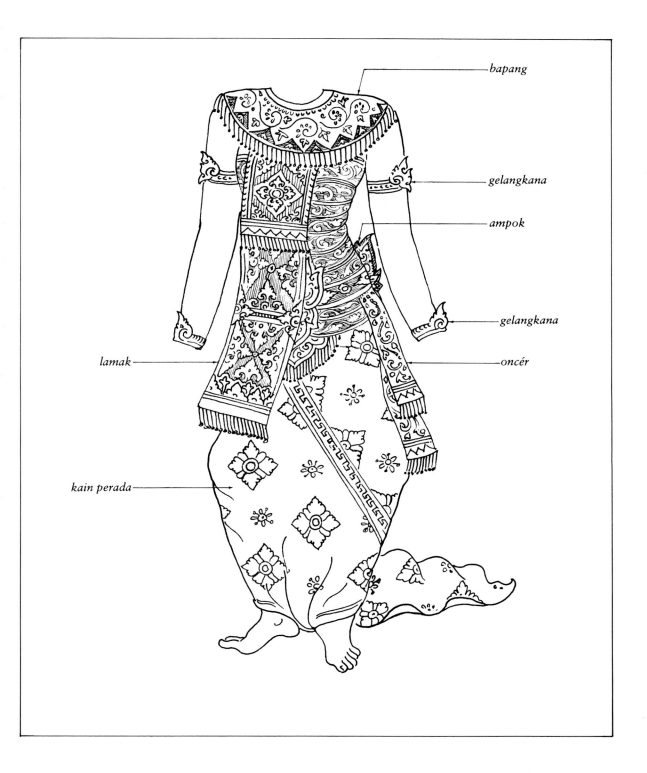

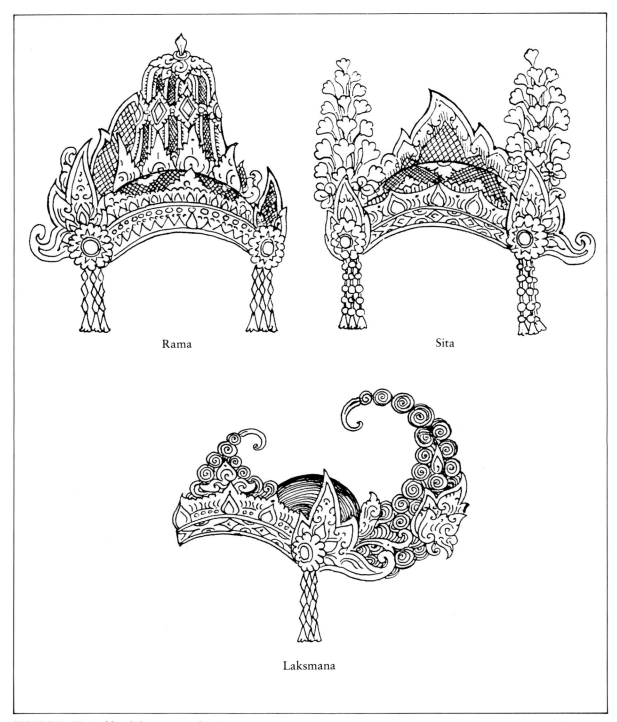

Rama

Sita

Laksmana

FIGURE 7   Typical head-dresses worn by the human characters in Wayang Wong and other genres. (I Nyoman Mandra)

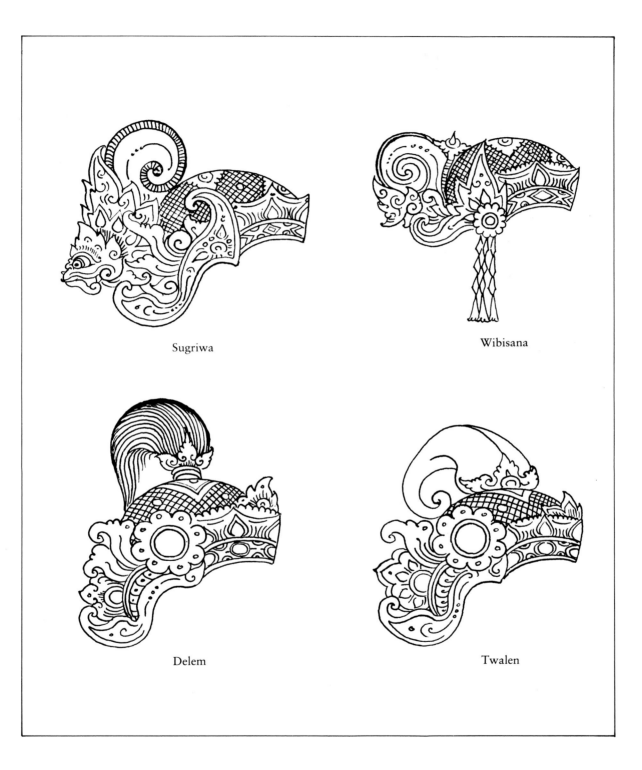

Sugriwa

Wibisana

Delem

Twalen

and orchestra under the guidance of the lead drummer and the cymbal player. At the same time, the *gender wayang* ensemble made available the repertoire of theatrical music from the Wayang Kulit. However, the vocal music, which is sung exclusively by the *dalang* in the shadow theatre, is apportioned among the dancers in Wayang Wong; as in most Balinese ensembles, a lead singer in the *gamelan batel* provides a continuing vocal line.

The makers of Wayang Wong found a ready repertoire in the plays of the *dalang* who performed in the Wayang Kulit *Ramayana*, although the stories had to be simplified and adapted to suit the needs of the dramatic-dance medium. Dialogue in Wayang Wong is much simpler than that in Wayang Kulit, and there is less of it. Correspondingly, the proportion of the performance given over to dance has been enlarged through the incorporation of *igel ngugal*, or abstract introductory dances, adapted from those used in Gambuh.

The typical Wayang Wong performance is devoted to a single episode from the *Ramayana*. Only in Pujungan Kaler, Gianyar Province, has an abridged version of the entire long epic been attempted. In most villages, the choice of story depends on the masks available. The story element is secondary to the dance; the narrative thus serves mainly as a convenient framework for a succession of dances.

In Tejakula, Buleleng Province, the most complete set of Wayang Wong masks in Bali has been preserved. The collection includes masks for each of the four human characters, five principal ogres, four *penasar*, twelve principal monkeys, and twenty-four unnamed monkeys and ogres. These masks belong to the Pasek Dangka clan. According to the four oldest dancers, who were interviewed in 1975, the masks were a gift to the clan in the eighteenth century from the Raja of Bangli.

In Tejakula, two particular tales from the *Ramayana* are still presented with as much fidelity to tradition as the four oldest dancers were able to ensure. The two stories are performed every 210 days on consecutive days: 'The Death of Prahasta' on the first day, and 'The Death of Kumbakarna' on the second. The occasion for the performance is an Odalan at the principal temple of the clan, coinciding with the most important Balinese holiday, Galungun. Participation is limited to members of the 150 families who make up the clan.

The Tejakula performances take place in the *jaba tengah*, or the temple's second courtyard, as in Gambuh. A very large *kalangan* is set up, and over it a temporary ceiling made of fresh greenery, flowers, and fruit is suspended. As in Gambuh, the principal entrance is from the *jeroan* through a low archway. The gamelan and resting mats for waiting dancers are placed at the *kelod* end of the entrance.

In the morning of the first performance day, the dancers gather at the temple to receive their masks and *gelung*. More than fifty men participate, mostly dancers with very little training, except for the older 'masters' who are in charge.[14] Nor has there been a great deal of rehearsal. Participation in the performance is considered a form of devotional service to the temple. The older performers are trained *dalang* and dancers, and they take the most difficult roles: Rama, Kumbakarna, Rawana, and Sugriwa. These roles also entail wearing the magically powerful masks, and therefore are reserved for men of great spiritual strength and learning. The rest of the roles are danced by ordinary farmers and simple craftsmen.

The dancers receive their masks and head-dresses at the temple after a traditional rite for opening the niche in which these are stored between use. Offerings are presented, and the masks sprinkled with holy water before they are distributed. The dancers then retire to make ready for the performance. Some go home to change. Others, especially those who have come from great distances to take part in the ceremony, make their simple preparations near by, outside the temple.

During this time, it is customary for the dancers to hang their masks and *gelung* from the limbs of convenient tangerine and orange trees. Tejakula, located on one of North Bali's mountain slopes, is well-known for its citrus fruit, which provides the village with an important source of income. Throughout the village, the masks and *gelung* hang in the trees like artificial fruit. Just as in Barong Kedingkling, the Tejakula masks have a special association with productive trees and perhaps a special protective role to play on their behalf. The dancers decorate their head-dresses with fresh leaves and flowers for the event.

On both days, the performance begins in the early afternoon. A common pattern is followed. The play starts with a sequence of meeting scenes. On the first day, Rama and his companions meet with the monkey leaders and their army in the first section; then Rawana meets with his ministers and the army of ogres. On the second day, the sequence is reversed. These scenes have very little literary content, and the dialogue consists almost entirely of formal courtesies. Progress in the action is constantly interrupted by extended *igel ngugal*, as character after character are presented, each with their characteristic movements. The audience already knows the general story-line, and the characters on stage therefore do not need to present a detailed exposition.

The four *penasar* characters are very prominent and active in Wayang Wong, and are proportionately much more important than their equivalents in Gambuh.[15] Twalen and Wredah, the attendants of the good party, have their counterparts in Delem and Sangut, who attend the ogres. They serve similar functions as Togog and Semar from Gambuh: they translate from Kawi to Balinese; they elaborate on the words of their masters, interpreting the meaning of the story for the populace; and they take many opportunities to joke and clown. They also serve as on-stage directors during the performance, making sure that the play moves toward its conclusion.

In the Wayang Wong performance, the *penasar* precede their masters on stage. They explain the general situation in the course of their dialogue. However, the comic element is not as extensively developed in the typical Wayang Wong performance as it is in Topeng. The opportunities for verbal humour like puns, sayings, and jokes are impeded by the large masks worn by the *penasar*, which cover the dancers' faces and interfere with speech. The dancers struggle to project as well as they can, but in the realm of comic relief, simple physical comedy is the principal resource. Balinese audiences are very appreciative of this slapstick humour.

The final section of the play is invariably devoted to fighting. First, the ogres and monkeys struggle against one another in groups, and then the principals fight. Between the serious battles are comic interludes among the *penasar*. At the end, Rawana's representative is always overcome, bringing the performance to a quick conclusion. The principal evil character, Rawana himself, is never killed.

In Tejakula, the two performances are treated quite differently by the public, although the production is almost identical on each day. The first performance is always given on the day before the Odalan, and is thus regarded as a means of purifying the temple space and summoning the deities. Human spectators are irrelevant, for as a purely *bebali* performance, it is addressed to the gods. Few people actually watch the performance, for most of the members of the clan are busily engaged with the completion of the preparations for the festival: chopping meat, making offerings, cooking, or perhaps joining the expedition up into the mountains for the purpose of fetching holy water at a sacred spring. Only children and those temporarily free from other responsibilities watch the dancers.

The second day's performance is received very differently, and all the members of the clan, as well as invited guests and other visitors, form the audience. The main difference from the previous day's performance is that the first meeting scene is extended by perhaps half an hour to include an edifying discourse on the nature of patriotism and good government, in Kawi, quoted directly from the *Ramayana*. Delem and Sangut translate and explain for the benefit of those spectators close enough to hear them. On this day, the crowd is very attentive and grave, in keeping with the dignity of the occasion. All are on their best behaviour to honour the distinguished guests, both human and divine.[16]

1. Goris (1954 : I, 55; II, 121).

2. Even these account's give very little descriptive information.

3. Rather more has been written about Topeng than most other forms of Balinese dance. The reader is referred to de Zoete and Spies (1938: 178–95), Emigh (1979, 1984, 1985), Kakul (1979), Young (1980, 1982), Dunn (1983), H. Geertz (1991), and Slattum (1992).

4. Noosten (1941).

5. A copy of this manuscript is on deposit at the Listibya Library, Denpasar.

6. Although the dancer formerly made no use of a curtain at all in Topeng Pajegan, in the performance called Topeng Panca (Five-man Topeng; see Chapter 4, an actual curtain is employed, which is shaken vigorously before a new character enters for the first time. This is similar to the 'curtain look' seen in the Kathakali dance-drama of South India, and may have descended from an ancient Indian source. In recent years, the use of the curtain has also become quite common in Topeng Pajegan.

7. Noosten (1936).

8. A copy of the manuscript is also on deposit at the Listibya Library, Denpasar.

9. See Gralapp (1967) and Forge (1978).

10. See Huyser (1919).

11. See Robson (1972).

12. See deBoer and Bandem (1992) for a Balinese Wayang Ramayana play in translation, with an introduction. DeBoer (1987b) discusses the functions of the *penasar* characters with reference to this play. Another example of a Wayang play, from the *Mahabharata* repertoire, is given in deBoer (1987a).

13. Bernet Kempers (1959).

14. DeBoer (1979) gives a brief account of a typical rehearsal of this type, conducted by another Balinese director, I Nyoman Rajeg, of Tùnjuk village, Tabanan Province.

15. McPhee (1936: 154–5) describes these characters in detail.

16. Bandem (1980) is a comprehensive work on Wayang Wong. It contains the script of a performance given in Tunjuk, Tabanan.

4 Secular Dances in the Outer Temple

THE dance forms considered in this chapter are assigned to the *bali-balihan* group—genres that are essentially secular in nature and presented purely for entertainment. Often they are given on a professional basis to raise money, through the sale of tickets, for the sponsoring group. Performances can, however, acquire a religious significance when they are given as part of a temple festival. Then, they are considered as contributing to the spiritual uplifting of the congregation, with the dancers performing a kind of devotional service. But the same dances may also be performed for purely secular purposes, on purely secular occasions, and in purely secular spaces (although the performance space is invariably purified by the presentation of appropriate offerings.)

The major genres in this category all descend directly from the three *bebali* forms: Gambuh, Topeng Pajegan, and Wayang Wong. In them, emphasis is primarily on aesthetics and entertainment rather than on ritual and ceremony. Natural talent and lengthy training are required of the performers, while audience participation is unimportant. All of these dances can, undoubtedly, be assigned to the highest ranks of classical Balinese artistic achievement. All were created by sophisticated professional artists.

When secular dances are presented at an Odalan, a temporary stage is set up in the temple's outer courtyard, called the *jaba* (literally, 'outside'), which is at once the least sacred and physically the lowest part of the temple (see Figure 2). Although several necessary lesser rituals are performed in this space, it functions primarily as an area for entertainment and relaxation for members of the temple congregation. The *jaba* is thus often crowded with people who are not engaged in formal activities or responsibilities.

As the festival may occasionally continue for as long as ten days, in many temples a dormitory is built in the *jaba* to accommodate participants from distant places. Commerce is permitted in the *jaba*, and during the festival, snacks, drinks, and cigarettes are sold by women at small stands. Gamblers play cards and other games of chance. Often several gamelan groups set up in the area and may play at the same time. The mood is noisy, relaxed, good-natured, and active. Dance performances further contribute to the festive atmosphere.

Legong

Of all the classical Balinese dances, Legong is perhaps most familiar to Western audiences because of exposure to touring dance troupes and film.[1] Delicate, refined, and intricate, the dance is performed by three preadolescent girls, who look as much alike as possible, since in Legong there is no differentiation of the characters according to type. The little dancers wear distinctive head-dresses and costumes, and their highly abstract dance-drama, performed to the accompaniment of an old and sweet-sounding musical ensemble, the *gamelan pelegongan*, is executed in identical style.

Legong is the oldest of the *bali-balihan* dances. An account of its origin, around the turn of the nineteenth century, is given in the *Babad Dalem Sukawati*, a genealogical chronicle of the princes of Sukawati, a village in Gianyar Province long famed for its excellence in the performing arts. According to the story, Legong was created as the result of a vision that came to the ruling prince, I Déwa Agung Madé Karna, renowned for his spiritual powers. When meditating at the Pura Payogan Agung (Temple of the Great Meditation) in Ketewel village near Sukawati, I Déwa Agung Madé Karna dreamed that he saw celestial maidens performing a dance while in a trance, as in the Sang Hyang Dedari, but they were dressed in colourful costumes instead of white and wore golden head-dresses instead of simple head-cloths. When he awoke, the King called for the headman of Ketewel village and asked him to make some masks and create a dance resembling what he had seen in his dream.

Nine sacred masks, representing the nine celestial maidens of Hindu mythology, were carved and painted by an artisan of the village. These masks are still kept at the Pura Payogan Agung, where the dance is performed every six months. Two young Sang Hyang dancers were enlisted to perform with the masks and were taught a new dance—Sang Hyang Legong—composed for the occasion. The choreography of Sang Hyang Legong, also known as Legong Ratu Dari, is quite simple but contains all the basic movements found in present-day classical Legong dancing. Sang Hyang Legong is, however, considered a *wali* dance, and is thus performed in the *jeroan*, or inner courtyard. Although the original masks are now considered too sacred to display or use in performances outside the temple, Sang Hyang Legong was demonstrated to the public at the Walter Spies Performing Arts Festival, held at the Arts Centre in Denpasar in 1988, using modern facsimiles of the original masks.

In the mid-nineteenth century, a group directed by I Gusti Ngurah Jelantik (of the Jelantik family of Blahbatuh) created a new dance, Nandir, in a style similar to Sang Hyang Legong. In this new form, the dancers were three young boys and masks were not used. Nandir was seen by I Déwa Mangis, King of Gianyar, who was so impressed by it that he commissioned a pair of artists from Sukawati to create a similar dance for the young girls of his court. The result of their efforts was the direct source for Legong as it exists today. Unfortunately, Nandir is now extinct, although a similar genre continues to be presented in Tabanan Province. Simpler and slower than contemporary Legong, and by all accounts very beautiful, the old form was lost with the death of I Wayan Rindhi of Denpasar, in 1976. Pak Rindhi had been trained as a young Nandir dancer in Blahbatuh and was well-known as a Legong teacher.

The creators of Legong worked with both *wali* and *bebali* elements in developing the new form. The basic musical and choreographic structures were taken from Gambuh, while the movements were derived from the Sang Hyang Dedari tradition. However, the pure dance passages serving to introduce important characters in the *bebali* genres (*igel ngugal)* were expanded and developed, while the narrative element, although still present in skeletal form, was de-emphasized. The result was more toward a pure dance composition.

The choreography of the Legong performance follows the structure of the music, which, as noted, was adapted from the accompaniment to Gambuh. The lengthy first part of the presentation, which never varies regardless of the story presented, is accompanied by a dance composition in three parts: *pengawit*, or head, *pengawak*, or body, and *pengecet*, or tail. In the *pengawit*, three little dancers are introduced. The first to appear, dressed slightly differently from the other two, is the *condong*, or maidservant (Colour Plate 14). She dances for about ten minutes with two fans which she will present to her mistresses when they enter. Hers is a complicated and difficult solo, which covers the entire stage and demonstrates the full vocabulary of the beautiful Legong style. When her diminutive mistresses enter, she greets them courteously, bending low, and presents them with their fans before departing.

Now, the *pengawak* begins. This section is very elegant and is somewhat slower than the *pengawit*. In the complete classical performance, it perhaps takes twenty minutes. The two dancers move in unison through a symmetrical choreographed pattern, in close co-ordination with the drumming and cymbals.

The final section, the *pengecet*, begins as the gamelan doubles the tempo. The two dancers face each other and dance vigorously, yet precisely. They mirror each other, flicking quick glances of the eyes and jerking their heads from side to side. Their fans are in active motion, almost drawing a design in the air. The tempo accelerates and then comes to an abrupt halt. The dancers pause, but do not leave the *kalangan*.

This signals the beginning of the dramatic section of the performance. The lead singer has sung texts from the old Kawi poem, *Malat*, during the first part of the performance. Now, he serves as narrator, reciting the background to the play in high Balinese from his place in the orchestra, against a background of soft, melancholy music. In the most commonly presented story, 'Lasem', the situation concerns a meeting between the King of Lasem and Princess Rangke Sari, whom he has kidnapped. She does not love him and prefers her betrothed, Prince Panji Inu Kertapati.

The two little dancers begin to dance again, and the scene becomes a *pengipuk*, or courtship dance. The two characters are identical in appearance and style of movement. One of the dancers takes the role of Lasem, the other Rangke Sari (Colour Plate 15). After rejecting Lasem's advances, the Princess tells him that she will only marry him if he can defeat Prince Panji in battle. Dialogue and description are provided by the singer, for although the dancers are not masked, they never speak or sing.

The *pangkat*, or departure, similar to the departure of Panji's group in Gambuh, occurs next. This section is sometimes extended to include mimed riding on horseback as the unlucky King makes his way toward the battlefield. He either dances alone or is accompanied by the second dancer as he travels. Suddenly, the *condong* reappears wearing stylized wings of carved and gilded leather clasped to her forearms to represent a bird of ill-omen, Guwak, the crow. This is a form of *pesiat*, or fight scene. Lasem successfully drives off the crow before he exits to face what everyone knows will be certain death at the hands of Prince Panji. The two dancers return to the stage to dance a short abstract epilogue (*pekaad*) which brings the performance to an end.

Other stories can be told in Legong, with appropriate adaptation of the stock scenes. In Benoh village, Badung Province, for example, a story from the *Ramayana* involving the fight of the two rival monkeys, Subali and Sugriwa, is a favourite. It is called Legong Jobog. Again, no masks are worn, and the characters are difficult to distinguish. Members of the audience who do not understand Balinese may find it difficult to keep track of the details of the story. Although as many as fifteen different stories were adapted to the Legong in the nineteenth century, most of them have fallen out of use. Today, more than ever, Legong owes its popularity to excellence in dancing rather than to the narrative element.

Like other court arts of pre-colonial Bali, Legong served in the traditional palace as an assertion and display of the wealth, power, and glory of the ruling prince. The realm was searched for its most beautiful and talented little girls, many of whom became royal wives and concubines. In contrast to the court dancers of Java, the Legong dancers of Bali were not often themselves of high-caste origin. The dancers were outfitted with expensive costumes decorated with gold leaf and costly jewels. They received a lengthy professional training. When they travelled in public, they were accompanied by a squad of spear-carrying bodyguards.

Like the Sang Hyang Dedari dancers who were their prototypes, Legong dancers were required to cease performing at the onset of menstruation. Thus, in the mid-nineteenth century, there was a movement of trained Legong dancers from the palaces back to the villages, as girls who had studied at court returned to their birth-places or went to other villages. Some of them had served as teachers at court. With the encouragement of lesser gentry in towns, at some distance from the great palaces, clubs were established to perform the popular dance at the local level. These village groups might receive subsidies and encouragement from their sponsors but were free to perform at an Odalan in the village temples, and even outside their villages, for a fee. This was exactly the case at the village of Saba, Gianyar Province, which has been the centre for training teachers and performers of Legong since the early nineteenth century.

Other villages in Gianyar, such as Sukawati, Bedulu, and Peliatan also became known for Legong, and many students from all over Bali were sent to learn the dance from teachers in these cultural centres. By the time of the Dutch take-over of Bali, Legong had spread to many of the larger villages and towns and had become, in many places, a truly popular art form, maintained by and for the village communities. It was and still is performed as entertainment in connection with temple festivals in many villages. Communities that do not themselves have a Legong group might hire a club from one of the famous villages, or might work out an exchange arrangement, performing their Wayang Wong, for example, in return for the borrowed services.

Kebyar

After the Dutch completed their take-over of Bali in 1908, Buleleng Province in North Bali grew in importance, for the capital city, Singaraja, became the seat of the colonial administration. The culture of North Bali had previously been somewhat cut off from the south, for passage was difficult across the great central mountain range, and the border states were often at war. A great cultural renaissance thus began in North Bali in the early years of the twentieth century. Many new gamelan and dance clubs were founded, and creative activity flourished. Among the forms resuscitated or newly created was one which was to take all of Bali by storm, Kebyar. Its source was Legong, but its inspiration was competitive pride.

As noted earlier, it is common at an Odalan for two or even more gamelan to set up and play simultaneously in the *jaba* area of the temple. At times, this can turn into a kind of 'battle of the bands' in which two instrumental groups compete to see who can attract the greatest number of spectators and the loudest support.

In the early years of this century, two villages in North Bali, Bungkulan and Jagaraga, shared an especially intense rivalry and competed on a regular basis in creating new music and dance compositions. Bungkulan contributed a new musical idea—

Palawakia—in which a virtuosic performer alternately sang, gave textual interpretations, and played the *trompong*, a musical instrument consisting of a row of knobbed gongs in a carved wooden case, accompanied by a full gamelan. Texts were taken from the *Bharatayuda*, an Old Javanese poem that deals with the final war at the end of the *Mahabharata*. This form still exists today as a type of dance.[2] In 1914, Jagaraga contributed the Kebyar Legong, a dance performed by two young women dressed in men's clothing, who interpreted the music of the accompanying orchestra in a pure dance medium. There was no plot, but the dancers presented a kind of character study of a young man.

Modern Kebyar grew out of a combination of the forms originated by the two groups, although Jagaraga has received most of the credit for the new development. The new musical ideas, in particular, swept quickly over the entire island of Bali. Kebyar ('lightning') style is florid, complex, dynamic, and highly embellished. Played at blinding speed, with sudden violent shifts of tempo and volume, it sounds much more energetic than the older forms of gamelan music.

The style was well-established when, in 1919, the King of Tabanan, who served also as the regent for his province under the Dutch, sent for a Kebyar orchestra from North Bali to play at an important cremation. In the audience was a young and very talented dancer, I Nyoman Mario, who was much impressed by what he heard, and who undertook to develop possibilities for dance in the new style. His great contribution to Balinese culture—Kebyar Duduk—was presented in 1925 for the first time.

From Palawakia, Mario took the idea of playing the *trompong* during a performance. This instrument had fallen out of favour with Balinese musicians, but Mario restored it to a star role in the ensemble. He developed a flashy style of playing the instrument, with whirling sticks and flamboyant gestures (Colour Plate 16). However, he had to squat behind the instrument to play it, and this led to the idea that the entire composition might be performed in a sitting (*duduk*) position. From Kebyar Legong, Mario adapted the costume, but to facilitate movement in a squatting position, he had to hold up the train with one hand. This became a hallmark of the new genre.

The mood of Kebyar Duduk is determined by the music, and the dancer works in close co-ordination with the gamelan to interpret its shifting colours. Whereas the Legong dancer works in close relationship with the patterns set by the drummers in the gamelan, in Kebyar, the entire ensemble of twenty-five to thirty musicians starts and stops in sudden cadences when the dancer comes to an abrupt, accented pause. Many of the basic poses, gestures, and longer phrases of movement have been adapted from Legong, but they have been made more intricate, more elaborate, and more artificial. In Kebyar Duduk, there is no element of pantomime, and the narrative is absent.

No solo in Balinese dance is more demanding in terms of technique and sheer physical strength than Kebyar Duduk, and for this reason it is a form for the young dancer, as the demands on the performer's legs are very exacting. The dance is set to a single musical composition which lasts for about twenty minutes. The piece progresses through a sequence of moods of an idealized Balinese youth who is on the verge of reaching full maturity. He expresses a gamut of emotions, ranging from sweet flirtatiousness to bashfulness, melancholy, and angry bravado. In a sense, the entire study is a refined distillation of the manifold qualities demonstrated by the young men of Trunyan in the Berutuk rite.

The Kebyar style of music and the new dance by Mario swept with such swiftness over the entire island of Bali that many believed it would be a short-lived fad. Other genres of dance and drama had become—and continue to become—very popular in Bali for a brief time before fading quickly. But the enthusiasm for Kebyar has prevailed since 1925 and shows no signs of abating. Kebyar has become the established modern classical Balinese style of dance and music, and its influence can be felt in every facet of the Balinese performing arts.

A great deal of new dance composition has been evident in Bali since Mario first created Kebyar Duduk, but with a few exceptions, Kebyar has exercised the greatest influence. Between 1925 and the early 1950s, Balinese choreographers created a number of new dances for women in the Kebyar style. The still popular Panji Semirang, for example, was composed in 1933 by the great Legong teacher, I Nyoman Kaler, of Kelandis village, Badung Province, in response to the need for a composition suitable for a female dancer. It had been determined that women could do most of the movements required in Kebyar Duduk, but had trouble capturing the appropriate male moods. In Panji Semirang, the dancer thus portrays Princess Candra Kirana, well-known from the *Malat* poem as well as from Gambuh. Although the dance itself is similar to Kebyar Duduk in form and style, it does not involve squatting.

The Princess, in disguise as a young man, is shown searching the world for her lover, Panji. She visits the court of a foreign kingdom and there performs a dance for the assembled courtiers. As she dances, she searches the crowd with her eyes to see if her lover is present. She reveals a shifting sequence of moods as she searches in vain, and then exults in seeing Panji in the audience. The short piece concludes on a joyful note.

This composition also met with popular success all over Bali, and thereafter Kebyar dance came to be popularly known as Kebyar Bebancihan (Neutered Kebyar), or even plain Bebancihan, because it was no longer restricted to male performers (Plate 14).

Two of the many other new compositions for women were Margapati (King of the Lions), composed by I Nyoman Kaler in about 1942, and Wiranata (Brave King), also by Kaler in about 1943. In these, female soloists presented character studies of

14 Kebyar Bebancihan; Legong Peliatan Group, Ubud. (Stuart Rome)

young men in the manner of Kebyar Duduk, revealing the penchant for travesty common in much of Balinese dance. These androgynous forms survive today. However, in none of them is the difficult squat-walk (*seregseg*) of Kebyar Duduk to be found, although they are otherwise pure Kebyar.

In 1931, the first full group of Balinese dancers and musicians performed in Europe, presenting a series of concerts at the Colonial Exhibition in Paris. The group, from Ubud, Gianyar Province, led by Cokorda Gedé Sukawati, danced before wildly enthusiastic audiences, which included the great French director and dramatic theorist, Antonin Artaud.[3] Legong and Kebyar Duduk were both on the programme. Another important tour to Europe and America was organized in 1952, soon after Indonesia became independent. This tour was organized by an American, John Coast, and included Mario and the Anak Agung Gedé Mandra, Prince of Peliatan, who was a master teacher and the artistic leader of the group.[4]

Accessibility for foreign audiences was already a factor in the development of Balinese dance by this time, and thus when the programme was being planned for the 1952 tour, it became apparent to the leaders that there was a shortage of material suitable for presentation to Western audiences. Because of language and cultural barriers, many of the Balinese dramatic dance genres were felt to be unsuitable. Accordingly, Mario was asked to create a new dance, in Kebyar style, for the tour. His creation, called Oleg Tumulilingan ('Bumble-bees'), is a *pengipuk* for two performers, male and female. They represent, in abstract fashion, two bumble-bees 'courting' in a garden (Colour Plate 17). The new form was greeted with enthusiasm, and accepted by Balinese audiences and dancers at the end of the tour. The duet has since established a secure place in the Balinese repertoire. It is now known simply as Oleg and is performed quite often in connection with temple festivals. Like all *bali-balihan* genres, it acquires religious significance in that context.

Parwa

According to a story told in Sukawati village, during most of the nineteenth century, the Kings of Gianyar were in dispute with their nominal superiors, the Kings of Klungkung. However, in 1885, the King of Klungkung was able to capture the King of Gianyar by trickery. As a result, many members of Gianyar's royal household were sent into exile on desolate Nusa Penida, a small and inhospitable island off the Balinese coast across a strait from Klungkung.

Many dancers and musicians were in the group, and to pass the time they decided to present a performance. Although they had no masks or costumes at hand, they were able to devise a new kind of dramatic dance somewhat similar to Wayang Wong. Realizing, however, that it would be impossible to portray the monkeys and ogres of the *Ramayana* repertoire without special equipment, the artists in exile looked instead to the chapters (*parwa*) of the *Mahabharata* for source material.

The *Mahabharata* epic, which like the *Ramayana* had its ultimate origin in India, likewise came to Bali by way of Java. Its most important incidents and characters are very well known among the Balinese. It tells of a long rivalry and increasingly deadly struggle between two sets of cousins, the virtuous five Pandawa brothers and the hundred evil Kurawas. The climax of the epic is reached when the two groups fight an apocalyptic war in which the Pandawas prevail. Along the way there are many subplots and subsidiary scenes which make the *Mahabharata* a rich source of material for dramatization, especially in the Wayang Kulit.

In the Parwa performance, the characters alternate speech with singing; nearly equal weight is given to each mode of expression.

The musical repertoire comes from the Wayang Kulit, and the dialogue is also in the Wayang manner. The style of dance movement in Parwa shows direct influences from Gambuh: Wayang Wong has an insufficient cast of human characters to provide prototypes for the five Pandawa heroes, their matronly mother, and the hundred evil Kurawas, and all their advisors. Therefore, the Demang and the Temenggung, Prabu, Prabangsa, Panji, Putri, and the *condong* all appear with names and in situations from the old *parwa* of the *Mahabharata*. The Putri's ladies-in-waiting, the *kakan-kakan*, also appear in Parwa, in a dance which shows strong influence of Legong style. Their movements are quick and energetic, and they call to one another as they cross the *kalangan*, gesturing in unison. In Parwa, as in Legong, the eye-flicking movements and side-to-side jerks of the head are very prominently featured.

The Parwa tradition was continued after the courtiers were rescued from Nusa Penida and allowed to return home. For years Sukawati was famous for its Parwa, especially a group under the tutelage of the great *dalang*, I Nyoman Granyam, from Banjar Babakan in the village of Sukawati. Under his supervision, Parwa achieved a high level of performance and fidelity to tradition. Unfortunately, the group was disbanded in 1967 when Granyam died. However, Banjar Babakan continues to be the home for an unusually large number (a dozen or more) professional *dalang*. These expert actors and singers are fluent in Kawi and can even improvise freely in the ancient language.

At present, only a few Parwa groups are active in Bali. One, an organization called the Seka Parwa Agung (Great Parwa Group), is led by Ida Bagus Sarga of Bongkasa village, Badung Province. Pak Sarga was for years Bali's best-known *dalang Ramayana*, and is an expert on many aspects of Balinese performing art. He is now a priest. In the performance given by his group, the *penasar* characters wear no masks, but employ modern make-up. The level of their performance is high, and they are called upon fairly often at Odalan in the villages, and in the government Arts Centre on public holidays, such as Indonesia's Independence Day. Another group, in the village of Mas, now presents Parwa at their regular Odalan, which takes place simultaneously with the island-wide Kuningan holiday (Plate 15).

Arja

In 1825, I Déwa Agung Gedé Kusamba of Klungkung, highest in rank of the Balinese princes, died at the end of a fifty-year reign.[5] His cremation ceremony was said to be one of the most magnificent in Balinese history. Lower-ranked monarchs from all the other Balinese kingdoms attended the ceremonies and contributed generously to the rites. Although the King had quarrelled incessantly with his nominally subordinate neighbours, the Kings of Badung

79

15   Parwa; Mas. (Koes)

and Gianyar, they nevertheless dispatched court Gambuh dancers and musicians to participate in the ceremony. The combined group created a special new performance for the cremation.

The innovation was called Dadap after the two *dadap* trees, traditionally associated with funeral rites on the island, which were planted at opposite ends of the *kalangan*. The all-male company of dancers surprised and delighted the public by singing the dialogue of the play, as in Western opera. Dadap was a great success, and thereafter performing groups were established in most of the court centres.

The new form came to be known as Arja and proved to be very popular among the general population. By the early twentieth century, it had spread all over the island, sponsored by villages and kin groups, and until recently, it was Bali's most popular theatrical genre. However, visitors to Bali have found the form somewhat inaccessible because of the language barrier.

In the Gambuh performance, emphasis has been allotted more or less equally among three major elements: music, dance, and literary-theatrical features. In Legong and its derivatives, stress is placed on the purely 'dancerly' features of Gambuh, and narrative de-emphasized or eliminated. Vocal music has been taken from the dancer and assigned to a special vocalist in the gamelan.

In Arja, by contrast, the vocal music became paramount, especially after the 1920s when women replaced male performers in the principal roles. At the same time, the Kawi language was replaced by Balinese, yielding a more accessible and popular medium. The introduction of female singer-dancers also inspired a new enthusiasm for Arja, for to the Balinese ear, women's voices are better suited to singing the *tembang*, or songs. The audience was also impressed by the beauty of the young female performers.

Arja is technically very demanding. Not only must the performer sing beautifully, but she must be able to dance well at the same time. She must also co-ordinate the phrasing of the vocal line with the phrasing of the gesture, and fit both precisely to the accompaniment. Moreover, although the melodic patterns sung are pre-established, much of the content of the play is improvised during the performance. Long training and great inherent talent are therefore required.

The very best Arja performers soon became known outside their own localities and were sought for professional engagements with other groups. Early in this century, a kind of indigenous 'star system' had come into existence. Dissemination of the genre was also helped by the improvement in communications.

Prior to the colonial period, communications among the various regions of Bali were poor, owing to the constant wars among small kingdoms and to difficult terrain. But after the Dutch pacified the country and constructed modern roads and bridges, and, above all, since the Radio Republik Indonesia station was established, it has been possible for some performers, such as Ni Nyoman Candri of Singapadu village, Gianyar Province, to acquire an island-wide reputation (Colour Plate 18). In 1957, a regular Sunday Arja performance was introduced on Radio Republik Indonesia, under the leadership of I Madé Kredek of Singapadu. The programme has been very popular ever since, with many people planning their weekend schedules around the broadcast. Arja is, in fact, better adapted to radio dissemination than other forms, since the singing is almost continuous throughout the performance, and a listener can readily follow the events. Cassette tape recordings and television have also promoted the reputations of the most popular and well-known performers.

A special feature of Arja performances is the humour and clowning. No fewer than eight *penasar* appear among the standard characters. Even the original Dadap production produced for the cremation of I Déwa Agung Gedé Kusamba contained an important satirical dimension. King Kusamba had two wives, one a beautiful princess from Badung, the other a stout matron from Karangasem. The second wife was as strong-willed and powerful as she was unattractive, and she was heartily disliked, especially in Badung. The story chosen for the Dadap performance at the cremation was 'Kasayang Limbur' (Loves of the Ugly Queen); in it, the deceased King and his wife were discreetly satirized. Limbur, who parodied the Queen from Karangasem, became a favourite type-character in Arja, along with her three comic attendants.

The refined figure in Arja, whatever his name may be in a particular story, is attended by two *penasar*, Punta and Kartala; they are the unmasked counterparts to the *penasar kelihan* and *penasar cenikan* of Topeng Pajegan. Punta is the somewhat pompous and self-important straight man and butt for his more clever partner's jokes and pranks. The *condong* is also prominently featured in Arja, as in other modern dance-drama. Her personality is always frank and direct; she resembles the soubrette of Western tradition.

Modern Baris

It is unclear when and where the first modern variations on the old Baris Gedé were introduced, but they seem to be an early twentieth-century development. The dance is performed by a soloist, for some fifteen minutes, accompanied by the *gamelan gong*. He wears a distinctive costume based on that of Baris Gedé, with its shimmering pointed helmet (Colour Plate 19). The basic movements have also been taken from the older dance, but have been refined and embellished to a considerable degree.

As in Kebyar, solo Baris presents a plotless character study of a traditional Balinese warrior. The character, however, is stronger and more mature than the somewhat effeminate youngster depicted in Kebyar Duduk. The dance is said by some to represent, abstractly, the conduct of the warrior on the battlefield as he manoeuvres to avoid attack. Certainly, the character is tense: he trembles with nervous excitement, and his eyes dart from side to side.

The basic solo Baris dance, which is commonly performed as part of a programme consisting of several different kinds of dance, such as Kebyar, Legong, and Oleg Tumulilingan, has become the fundamental dance in the training of the male dance student. Professional dance teachers feel Baris is an ideal training medium because the form is quite straightforward, yet contains all the essential elements of classical Balinese dance. At STSI, Baris is also included in the first-year curriculum of female dancers, although Legong is considered to be the fundamental female dance style.

Some time after the modern Baris appeared as a pure dance solo, it prompted choreographers in Gianyar Province to create a story-telling dance form using the popular new character, following the example of the creators of Legong a century earlier. Thus, the Baris Melampahan (Story Baris) came into being, employing plays based on stories from the *Mahabharata* and *Ramayana*. Such stories have been especially popular subjects for representation by companies which include one or more Baris dancers, complete with their uniform costume, in leading roles. Just as the Legong dancers do not alter their appearance to differentiate characters, the Baris may represent someone refined or coarse (or even animal) without altering his appearance or characteristic movements.

A Baris Melampahan performance is often preceded by a series of introductory solo Baris dances, similar to the introductory mask dances in Topeng Pajegan. Two *penasar*, Punta and Kartala, always appear. They speak for their masters who, although unmasked, never speak or sing. The *baris* communicates by gesture alone. He may speak to Punta in Kawi, for example, by gesturing at him while Kartala provides the sound, just as if he were dubbing a foreign film. Then Punta will explain what has been said to him, in Balinese, so that the audience can understand.

Topeng Panca

At the end of the nineteenth century, the King of Badung had assembled a truly superior group of dancers to perform at court. Some of the artistes were of the *brahmana* caste, while others were commoners. Ida Bagus Boda, who was to later conceive the modern choreography for the *condong* in Legong, was leader of the group. Since there were five dancers who were all expert performers of Topeng, Ida Bagus Boda was inspired to devise a performance in which the entire group could take part. He called it Topeng Panca (Five-man Topeng). Unlike Topeng Pajegan, it was an entirely secular performance, purely for the entertainment of the ruler and his family. The basic structure of Topeng Pajegan was adapted slightly to serve the needs of the group, and the repertoire was taken from the same historical sources (Colour Plate 20).

The additional performers created new possibilities for humour by comparison with the old Topeng Pajegan, for two clowns had more scope than one. Comic scenes were thus protracted in Topeng Panca, and the performance lasted much longer than the solo form, to allow for extended clowning. The action proceeded more smoothly than in ritual Topeng, since no pause was needed while the dancer was off-stage changing mask and head-dress. The Sidha Karya character did not appear.

The innovation proved to be very popular, and after Badung fell to the Dutch, in 1906, the company went 'on the road'. They performed in many of the larger settlements of the island and inspired many imitators. The genre is still very popular among Balinese audiences. Occasionally, a Baris dancer now performs as part of the introductory group of masks. Television has given the form new exposure.

Prembon

As the twentieth century has progressed, more and more new combinations of previously separate dance genres have sprung up, yielding a bewildering variety of hybrid and composite forms (Plate 16). During the troubled 1940s, the King of Gianyar, I Déwa Mangis VIII, called together the dancers attached to his palace and asked them to create a Prembon (Combination). He asked that favourite type-characters be taken from Gambuh, Baris, Arja, Topeng, and Parwa and a single story presented in which they all appeared. The clowns were taken from Topeng, while the protagonist was drawn from Baris. The Princess and the *condong* from Arja took leading female roles, while Prabangsa from Gambuh appeared as the strong Prime Minister. Once again, the Topeng repertoire, dealing with the historical kings and priests

16   Kunti Seraya scene from the Barong dance; Den Jalan. (I Madé Bandem)

of Bali, was the source of subject-matter. Music for the performance was especially composed for *gamelan gong kebyar* (Colour Plate 21).

This new mixture of traditional and modern elements has found favour with Balinese audiences, as well as with performers, especially in villages where there are dancers who are trained in different styles and genres. Prembon makes it possible for all to contribute to the Odalan in a single performance. Television has also played a role in promoting the popularity of Prembon among the general population.

1. See Bandem (1983) and Scouren (1981) for further discussion of Legong.

2. All origin stories have a mythic aspect, and so it is with Kebyar. For a somewhat different account, see Rubenstein (1992 : 92), referring to accounts by I Wayan Simpen. Informants have their own agendas, and claims for credit conflict, while the 'true story', if there ever was one, recedes into the darkness of the irretrievable past. Our information is based on the testimony of elder Balinese dancers, many of whom have now passed away, and is the best available to us.

3. Artaud's (1958) evocative essays, written after seeing one of these performances, first brought the Balinese theatre to the attention of Western artists. 'In a word, the Balinese have realized, with the utmost rigor, the idea of pure theater. . . .' The essays, although misinformed in a number of particulars, are extremely insightful on many points. On Artaud and Balinese theatre, see Rickner (1972).

4. Coast (1953) describes the story of this tour and its formation.

5. See also Bandem and deBoer (1983).

5 Secular Dances in Secular Spaces

IN this chapter, a group of Balinese dance genres customarily presented in secular spaces is described. These dances are primarily performed for recreation and entertainment; they are rarely performed on occasions connected with religious observances. The genres discussed in the previous chapter, such as Legong and Kebyar, may also be presented for public entertainment, pleasure, and profit outside the context of a religious ceremony, as can *bebali* genres like Gambuh and Wayang Wong, provided authentic sacred objects are not employed.

Secular space in Bali is located at an intermediate point on the *kaja–kelod* axis (see Figure 1). Above the axis are the clearly ranked levels of outer, middle, and inner temple courtyards which rise to the *kaja*, or sacred, end of the scale. Below it are the dangerous haunts of demons, which lie at the *kelod* extreme. Secular performances may be presented in a temporary theatre set up in a public square or street, or in a *balé banjar* (ward association hall), a *wantilan* (arena for cock-fighting), or even in a permanent theatre building. Very often nowadays, tickets are sold, and the audience is provided with fixed, even reserved, seats. Electrical lighting is increasingly common, but modern theatrical equipment is still rare.

Joged Forms

The several sub-varieties of this group have roots in the prehistory of Balinese dance, and are therefore of considerable historical importance. Once wildly popular, they have declined considerably in popularity since the Second World War. The Joged (an old Indonesian term, meaning 'female dancer') genre is distinguished by a social dance feature: after the dancer has completed an extended solo in the Legong style, men from the audience are invited, by turns, to come forward to create a flirtatious improvisation with the skilful performer. *Ngibing*, as the improvisational dancing is called, employs a vocabulary of movement which is generally common to modern classical Balinese dance, but which emphasizes the sensual possibilities of the medium: sexy undulating wriggles, flirtatious gestures with the fan, inviting smiles, and suggestive winks are characteristic. Joged is a somewhat denatured survival from pre-colonial Balinese tradition in which dancing and prostitution were closely linked. Similar 'dance party' customs, in which men come from the throng to dance with professional dancing girls, are common in many other parts of Indonesia, as well as in Bali.[1]

The Dutch scholar, Van Eck, who wrote in 1880, described the public dancers of the period:

After the course of every important cockfight there is for great and small the opportunity to test one's luck at cards or dice. And on these occasions the public girls, or *joged tongkohan* are not lacking; they are sent out by their masters—the princes and headmen—for common account, to save the men and adolescents the trouble of carrying their still remaining coins home. The principal fun consists then in that one, in local fashion, may *ngigel* (dance) for a few minutes with such a *joged tongkohan* (they are called *ronggeng* in Java).

Thereupon there follows another freedom. . . . After the dance has run its course, the dancer separates himself and sits among the many spectators; the girl follows him in order to get her payment, which usually consists of five to six Balinese coins, and for that wretched sum she is obliged to sit on the laps of the dancer and his friends and receive their caresses. It is disgusting to see how such a girl during half the night is pulled hither and thither and regularly tormented with the kisses and embraces of great and small, young and old, without her being permitted to resist.[2]

According to older Balinese informants, in former times the liberties permitted often went far beyond kisses and caresses. Very often, too, a young boy dressed in a woman's costume, called a *gandrung* (see below), danced the solo and received partners from the audience; apparently, the substitution did not inhibit the enthusiasm of the male audience for fondling the dancer.[3]

In pre-colonial Bali, a payment of money or goods was invariably required from the *ibing*, as the males who come forward to dance are called. The dancers formerly belonged to the ruling princes, who held a monopoly of the profession, and who received a percentage of the income from it. Although not all of the royal *penyeroan*, or prostitutes, were trained as dancers, those who were able to dance enticingly earned large sums for the princely coffers. The performers were permitted to keep a portion of their earnings, and many were eventually able to purchase their freedom and retire to more respectable lives in the villages, where some set up as teachers of the dance. Retired Joged dancers became an important factor in the transmission of the forms and standards of performance of the court dance into the village communities.

Too much emphasis should not be put on the distinction between the *joged tongkohan* and the other female court dancers of pre-colonial Bali. The services of dancing girls (and sometimes boys) were often required in the great households of the rulers; the *joged tongkohan* held the lowest in status among them. Above them were the 'private' Joged dancers, whose dancing and sexual favours were reserved for the master and his guests.

Jacobs, a Dutch medical doctor who travelled in Bali in 1881 on government assignment, reported that performances by Joged dancers were presented as part of the official hospitality extended to his party. He was fascinated by the dancers and, almost against his will, found himself responding to their art:

In the late evening the Prince of Mengwi sent us five *joged tongkohan* from his private collection, Balinese beauties, but of course of blemished virtue. For someone who sees the entrance of these ronggeng for the first time it is truly a pleasant appearance and makes, I should almost say, a bewitching impression, to which many circumstances contribute. In the first place, the arena in which the dancing takes place is all wrapped in magical darkness; the costume which the dancers wear, viz. is drawn-up high, many-colored, tightly-fitting sarong, which with difficulty covers both sides of the bosom, the long jet-black hair which partially hangs loose, idyllically woven through with crowns of cempaka flowers, the ornamental line-dance which is performed to the soft tones of the gamelan, the naughty much-signifying glances which they (on orders from on high, to be sure), throw to the guests in turn; all this together brings the older in years who see it for the first time into rapture for a moment.[4]

Jacobs also reported that the traveller who was the guest of a Balinese prince for the first time might discover, with surprise, that the Joged dancers had dawdled after the performance to see if other entertainment, of a more intimate nature, were required. These 'private' dancers do not seem to have performed the *ngibing* improvisation with their audiences.[5]

As far as the music, costume, choreography, and movements were concerned, the Joged and Legong had much in common. Even today, before the *ngibing* section of the performance, Joged dancers perform a pure dance solo in the Legong style. The gamelan used for both Legong and Joged in the courts was the *gamelan semar pegulingan*, or *gamelan pelegongan*, a large ensemble which is accounted the sweetest of Balinese orchestral groups. It is named for the God of Love.[6]

Upon reaching adolescence, the retiring Legong dancer might well have gone on to become a royal concubine and perhaps a Joged dancer. No stigma, however, was attached to the art of dance itself, despite the association between dancing and the royal harem. Members of the noble families received dance training and appeared in the performances. Daughters of the prince often studied Legong, and although they had to give up performing when they reached puberty, some later became Legong teachers in the palaces.

After the Dutch took power in Bali, efforts were made to suppress those aspects of Balinese culture repugnant to the colonists' sensibilities. Along with the traffic in opium, the self-sacrifice of widows, slavery, and civil warfare, the prostitution monopolies held by the nobility in the various states were suppressed. Thus, since the colonial period, princes have no longer 'owned' the Joged dancers. Sponsorship of the Joged groups, consisting of dancers, musicians, and their helpers, passed from the palaces to the ward associations and kin groups and independent clubs, or *seka*. In many instances, however, support and encouragement for the groups continued to be offered by the noble families, even after the *seka* had become public rather than private institutions.

Various types of Joged survive today, a number of which are discussed below.

Leko

This type of Joged, which is very closely associated with Legong, is only found in Tabanan Province, in Tunjuk and Bongan Jawa villages. It is performed by young female dancers, twelve to thirteen years of age, who have previously been performers of Legong.

A performance of Leko opens with a 30-minute introduction identical to the opening section of the Legong dance. The story of Lasem, complete with maidservant and bird of ill-omen, is represented. The *gamelan semar pegulingan* ensemble, played in a very old-fashioned style, furnishes the accompaniment.

At the end of the introductory section, the *ngibing* begins, accompanied by a special, very lively composition played in fast tempo. Only two of the young dancers take part, in turn. Each carries a loose scarf in one hand, and a fan in the other. When the soloist begins the section, men shout from all over the audience, urging her to choose from among them. As the performance will often have been commissioned in connection with the 6-month birthday of a young child, the first partner will be the child's father, who dances holding his baby in his arms. Each dancer improvises with several men, in turn, and then retires while her colleague takes her place. When the girl goes out into the audience to select her partner, she designates the lucky man by tapping him with her closed fan. Once the male reaches the stage, the Leko dancer wraps her scarf around his waist, and the two perform together for a few minutes. Some men, better dancers than others, are permitted to dance longer than the rest. It is characteristic for the male partner to take the lead, and a good Joged dancer is esteemed for her skill at following closely and responding deftly to the dance overtures of her partner. The man attempts to get very close to the dancer, perhaps even close enough to kiss her, but she always darts away in time to evade him. In Leko today, no money is paid to the dancer, and the men never dare to take any indecent liberties with her.

Joged Gudegan

Joged Gudegan, although known by this name in Sukawati village, Gianyar Province, is called Joged Pingitan in Singapadu village, Gianyar, Joged Gandangan in Bangli Province, and Joged Tongkohan in Klungkung. All types descend directly from the Joged dances of the Balinese princes of the nineteenth century. The performers are older than the Leko dancers, perhaps seventeen to nineteen years old. Three girls usually perform in turn. Accompaniment is characteristically provided by a special gamelan ensemble made from bamboo, called the *gamelan rindik*, consisting of five pairs of bamboo xylophones, together with normal percussion and gongs. The repertoire is exactly the same as for Legong.

As in Leko, the first part of the Joged Gudegan performance is pure Legong. In Sukawati village, the Lasem story provides the theme, while in Singapadu village, Calonarang is the subject of the highly abstract drama. The *ngibing* section, however, differs from the Leko. Whereas for the introduction, the stage area is brightly illuminated with many pressure lanterns or by electric lighting, when the *ngibing* is about to begin, these lanterns are quickly removed and are replaced by a sputtering torch. This renders the dancing place much darker and creates a flickering, magical quality of light. Each dancer, in turn, taps her chosen partner with her fan and brings him to the stage area. The dancing begins around the torch, where a kind of seduction is mimicked. The dancers circle the flames of the torch with the Joged dancer making enticing eyes at the *ibing*, then darting to the other side of the fire when he advances, to evade him. After three or four such passes around the torch, the couple comes forward to improvise in the manner of Leko and other varieties. Each of the three dancers improvises with two or three partners in succession.

The Joged Pingitan group in Singapadu village was formed and taught for many years by a former 'private' Joged dancer who served in the Kerajaan Timbul Sukawati, a great palace in pre-colonial times. This dancer brought with her from the palace an old-fashioned *gelungan Joged*, the traditional head-dress worn by the Joged dancers before the Legong costume was more or less universally adopted. This head-dress, now considered a sacred heirloom, has been passed down through sixteen generations of dancers, who worked under the old teacher and her successor, the late I Madé Kredek. *Pingit* means 'secret' or 'selected' and originally designated the Joged dancers reserved for royalty. Nowadays, because of the association of the word with the sacred head-dress, it has acquired a connotation of 'holy' or 'sacred'. The head-dress itself is a simple holder for a crown of fresh flowers and burning incense sticks, furnished with an elaborately worked and gilded piece covering the dancer's forehead. It closely resembles the head-dress used in Rejang.

Adar

This form of Joged is no longer performed although it is not entirely extinct, since it may be revived some day. In the 1930s, Adar (enjoyment) groups existed in several villages in Tabanan Province. In Gebug and Kediri villages, the performing groups were sponsored by the ward associations, while the groups in Selingsing and Kerambitan were under the patronage of members of the former royalty.

The Adar was traditionally offered only at harvest time, with performances normally taking place in the street close by the *balé banjar*, or ward association hall. Around the dancing area many small stands and stalls for vendors were set up, similar to the arrangement which prevails at any Balinese festival, but in this case some of the booths were operated by the seven or eight girls who would take part in the dancing.

Before and during the performance, men from the crowd would gather around the tables, bidding for the little items sold by the girls. The men who made the highest offers of rice, coffee, cash, or other valuables for the cigarettes, peanuts, or wine would later be selected to dance as *ibing*. The highest bidder would earn the opportunity to dance first. Remnants, not so vestigial, of the earlier practice of paying for the privilege of dancing may be seen in this custom, which is called *medagang* (selling). The same manner of bargaining is still customary in some villages where regular prostitutes (who are not dancers) practise their trade. They are paid for sexual favours by accepting greatly inflated prices for small objects of little value. At the Adar performance, men in the crowd, feeling rich from the proceeds of the recent harvest, or with winnings from cock-fights, would bid furiously, inflamed at times with an almost reckless sense of competition, for the right to dance.

The performance took place late at night, and was illuminated by small coconut-oil lamps. It would go on until very late, often continuing until dawn. Before the dancing began, the girls would return from their little vending booths to form a chorus and sing a traditional Balinese folk-song:

Beautiful brother, come and make enjoyment now!
Make your feelings happy right now;
And if you are as happy as I am,
I promise to love and die with you.

The Adar performance contained no introductory dance section. One by one, by the dim light of the lamps, the girls would select their partners and dance in the performance area for a time. Then the dancer and the *ibing* might withdraw to the darker shadows, to dance in a more private place. While she was thus away from the stage, her place would be taken by another girl. When a girl had finished dancing (and perhaps making other 'enjoyment') with her partner, she might return to her vendor's booth to secure a new *ibing* for her next turn as a dancer.

The money brought in by the dancers went to the general fund of the sponsoring organization and was used for community projects. Here, village organizations, with or without support from the former royalty, took over what had been previously a monopoly of the princes.

The independent village groups at Gebug and Kediri possessed only bamboo instruments for the accompaniment of the Adar, but the groups from Selingsing and Kerambitan used the *gamelan semar pegulingan* which had formerly belonged to their high-caste sponsors.

Gandrung

Gandrung (meaning 'infatuation') is another very important form of Joged that is now all but extinct in its traditional, established form. In it, a young boy would take the role of the dancer, and, following a pure dance solo in the Nandir style (see pp. 71–2), would dance with an *ibing* from the audience.[7] Such performances were still given in the 1930s, complete with *ngibing*. Covarrubias reported at that time that the audience could become very rowdy at a Joged performance, and especially in the Gandrung, which he considered a more decadent form.[8] The great dancer/choreographer, I Mario, of Tabanan, was in his youth a Gandrung performer, and the influence of his experience in that medium is clearly visible in his Kebyar Duduk creation, where the dancer flirts outrageously with the head drummer.

Two Gandrung groups in the Denpasar area are still functioning, but in both, the dancers are young girls, rather than boys. The preliminary dance is pure Legong and employs the Lasem plot. In the second section of the performance, a rather stylized *ngibing* is performed in which the sexual element is de-emphasized. The only surviving aspect of the performance specific to the old Gandrung is the musical composition which accompanies the *ngibing*, called 'Gending Gandrangan'. Both these groups perform regularly for tourist audiences and the dancers often 'tap' foreigners in the crowd to come up and participate.

Joged Bumbung

Bumbung is a Balinese word meaning 'bamboo tube', and refers to the particular musical ensemble which accompanies the dancing. This, like the *gamelan rindik*, is made up of a group of bamboo xylophones, here four in number. Such instruments are often played, without accompanying dances, in hotel lobbies and other tourist haunts. The soft and gentle bamboo sound is quite lovely, yet can easily be ignored; it is perfect Balinese 'background music'.

Among the Balinese, Joged Bumbung is the most popular of the surviving Joged types, although interest in it has declined somewhat from its peak during the Second World War. Groups can still be found in the Sanur area, Badung Province, as well as in Tegal Tamu, Gianyar. Several groups also exist in villages in Jembrana and in North Bali. According to the Balinese musicologist, I Nyoman Rembang, the form originally developed in the coffee-growing area in the western part of North Bali, near the Jembrana Province border.

The group typically includes half a dozen girls who dance in rotation. Their costume consists of a simple Balinese blouse (*kebaya*) and skirt (*kain batik*) and a scarf wrapped around the waist. Their head-dresses are of golden flowers woven into the hair. There is no preliminary pure dance section. Instead, the dancers proceed straight to the *ngibing*, which is considered very bold and flirtatious by Balinese standards. The group receives a fee for the performance, so the dancers are not required to make individual transactions with the *ngibing*.

It is traditional for the Joged Bumbung dancers to possess love charms, purchased from a specialist, to help increase their allure. It is reported that the group from Tegal Cangkring, Jembrana Province, had such powerful appeal in the 1940s that at times they had to bring a wooden ox-cart to the performance to carry home all the coffee they had earned.[9]

After Indonesia achieved Independence in 1945, Joged Bumbung fell victim to a new and somewhat moralistic concern for public propriety. Since embarrassing connotations were attached to the Joged dances in general, the number of groups devoted to the form quickly declined. In recent years, however, a certain pressure has been felt to revive Joged dancing, but in a new role. Unlike such other Indonesian islands as Sulawesi, Sumatra, or Maluku, Bali lacks an indigenous social dance tradition. Thus, at the ASEAN summit conference held at the Pertamina Hotel in Bali in 1976, a highly stylized version of the *ngibing* portion of the Joged was introduced as the basis for a new Balinese form of social dancing. A dozen students from the government dance schools danced simultaneously with men from the audience. In such a context, the flirtatious element of the dancing was de-emphasized and conventionalized. According to witnesses, hardly a trace of the 'naughty' Joged wriggle was to be seen. Nevertheless, the guests seemed to enjoy the experience, which has been repeated often at official functions. The dancers wear the simple national costume of blouse (*kebaya*) and skirt (*kain batik*); they do not wear a head-dress, but the traditional fan of the Joged genre is retained. In this practice we see movement toward the creation of a new, popular, social dance based on traditional, if simplified, Balinese classical dance movements.

In the 1990s, Joged Bumbung has regained its popularity, especially among younger audiences. Performances now take place at the Arts Centre, where a lively young crowd is always in attendance.

Abuang Kalah

Although Bali lacks a strong tradition of participatory social dancing, vestiges remain of some manifestations in the social dance realm, especially in the Bali Aga village of Tenganan, Karangasem Province, where the customs of the people are of considerable interest to scholars, tourists, and government officials.

There, the Abuang Kalah takes place annually, on the full moon of the first month of their calendar. (This falls within the Gregorian month of February.)

The Abuang Kalah was originally partly a game, partly a group social dance, and partly a ceremonial presentation of the eligible young men and women of the village to each other and to the community, but is now more of a performance and less of a social occasion. Nowadays at the Abuang Kalah event, a VIP seating area is set up, with comfortable chairs and refreshments. Many visitors attend, and the participants are on display to a much broader audience than formerly, an audience composed, moreover, of strangers to the community.

The adolescent girls of the village wear the traditional costume of Tenganan, the famous *grinsing* cloth skirt, breast-band, and sash with gold flowers in their hair. They dance side by side, their arms held out at shoulder height, to the stately tones of the sacred *gamelan selonding*. Across from them are the young men of marriageable age, wearing skirt and cape, a dagger (kris) thrust through the belt behind, and a head-dress of Karangasem silk. The young women dance modestly, eyes downcast, while the men opposite them wait somewhat shyly. The elders of the village, behind them, look on and comment vociferously. At last, some of the youths gain sufficient courage to move forward to join the girls in dancing, imitating the movements of the girls in mirror fashion. They must enter correctly, or the adult critics will shout and the boys must then stop and wait for the next opportunity given by the music. The participants have not previously rehearsed. The more experienced girls occupy the centre places in the female line, and the younger ones attempt to stay in unison with their more expert colleagues. Many levels of skill and grace are in evidence. After thirty minutes or so, the dancing comes to an end. The women retreat to the women's compound, while the young men scatter to their homes.

Gebyog

One of the glories of Bali is the extraordinary range and variety of its folk music. Little studied by scholars, especially with respect to the folk-song, Balinese folk music far outweighs the folk-dance in importance. In several instances, however, rhythmic music and secular dance are closely associated.

Threshing rice by hand is a traditional Balinese domestic and social activity, although the task is increasingly being taken over by machinery. In many places, however, rice is still stored in granaries in an unthreshed state, to be taken and prepared for use as needed. When rice is threshed by hand, the grains are detached from the husks in long troughs which serve as mortars where the rice is pounded with tall, wooden pestles. Other workers then separate kernels from chaff by flipping the pounded mixture up

17   A female performer in Oleg Tumulilingan. (Ida Bagus Alit Yudhana)

18 Ni Nyoman Candri as Mantri Manis in Arja; Singapadu. (Prastya)

19   Modern solo Baris; Kelandis, Denpasar. (Koes)

20   Mask of Tua, one of many characters in Topeng Panca. (Stuart Rome)

21 The *gamelan gong kebyar* which accompanies Prembon. (Prastya)

22   Courting scene between male and female dancers in Janger; Kedaton. (Stuart Rome)

23 Barong Ket mask; Singapadu. (STSI documentation; courtesy Nik Wheeler)

24   Onying, the trance kris (dagger) dance; Batubulan. (I Madé Bandem)

25   Wong Sakti I Gusti Gedé Raka and his Rangda mask. (STSI documentation; courtesy Nik Wheeler)

26   Entranced dancers in Calonarang; Kerambitan. (Stuart Rome)

27   Jero Gedé and Jero Luh in Barong Landung; Tegalalang. (Stuart Rome)

28   A *pemangku*, or priest, with a Barong Landung performer, one of Jero Gedé and Jero Luh's children. (Stuart Rome)

29 Sekar Jagat welcoming dance; Wredhi Budaya Arts Centre. (I Madé Bandem)

30   Rawana in Sendratari Ramayana; Wredhi Budaya Arts Centre. (Prastya)

31   Kijang Kencana, or dance of the shining deer, depicting the cheerful life of a herd of deer in the forest; Wredhi Budaya Arts Centre. (Stuart Rome)

32 Belibis, or dance of the wild ducks, choreographed by Ni Luh Swasthi Wijaya; STSI Denpasar. (I Madé Bandem)

into the air from flat, circular baskets. The chaff blows off to the side while the heavier grains drop back into the basket.

Formerly, in preparation for a large festival, enormous amounts of rice would have to be threshed in this way, involving the work of many people. Women did the tossing and pounding, while men lent a hand in carrying the heavy baskets of rice. The mood was invariably happy and relaxed, and such a gathering was often the occasion for teasing, gossip, and flirtation. It offered the crowded sense of bustle that Balinese people enjoy so much.

Often, as such a group worked, the women pounding at the long mortar trough would start a kind of improvisation, developing a complex interlocking pattern of polyrhythms from the 'byog-byog-byog' (hence Gebyog) sound created by their falling pestles. The resulting elaborate rhythmic structures are considered by many Balinese musicians to be the source for the patterns used by the Cak chorus accompanying the Sang Hyang Dedari dances.[10] In the cremation or harvest festival context, however, the women would sing a folk-song to the accompaniment of the pounding rhythms, such as 'Crow Steals Eggs', 'Moonlight', or 'Fisherman'. Typical lines from the songs might be: 'Let's go out and catch a big fish; she'll bring us lots of pleasure later on!' All the songs involved a flirtatious element or double *entendre* and an invitation to do something together. They were simple choral melodies in which some sections were sung in unison, while others were in question-and-answer form.

While two dozen or more women pounded the rice and created the 'percussion' accompaniment, another dozen or so would toss the mixture of rice and chaff in their baskets. The tossing motion caused their upper bodies to undulate with a wriggling movement reminiscent of the movements employed—more suggestively—in the *ngibing* improvisation of Joged. As the men carried the heavy baskets from the mortars to the women doing the tossing, they might begin to move in time to the music and then begin to dance as they approached with their loads, or as they walked, they would strut and wriggle in a flirtatious manner as comic as it was sexy. And the girls would call as the men danced: 'Come, on brother, bring your pestle!' Wisecracking and teasing were general. The girls would come out to dance also, one or two at a time, still holding their threshing baskets. They would dance with the boys in *ngibing* style, with each couple 'performing' for a few minutes. There was no overt caressing or embracing, and the work went on without interruption, although whispered arrangements for a rendezvous could easily be made as the dance went on.

Gebyog singing and dancing were common in many parts of Bali until well into this century, especially in connection with cremation ceremonies. They were especially prominent in what is now Jembrana Province in West Bali, in such villages as Batu Agung. Gebyog was also traditionally popular in Karangasem Province. The last occasion known to the authors at which this kind of 'folk' Joged took place was in Sibang, Badung Province, in 1964, although it is entirely possible that unpublicized revivals have taken place since that time.

Cakapung

Cakapung is a male social dance, done strictly for recreation and amusement, and is found today only in Karangasem Province and on Lombok, its former vassal state. Like Gebyog, this folk-dance genre derives its name onomatopoeically from the sound of its accompaniment, a rhythmic vocal sound similar to that produced by the *cak* chorus. In the accompaniment, two dozen vocalists chant 'pung-cakapung' in unison.

A performance of Cakapung might take place any evening during leisure time. The dancers gather at about seven o'clock at the *balé banjar*, wearing the traditional Balinese everyday dress of white shirt and simple head-dress (*udeng*). Some of the participants bring bottles of *tuak* (Balinese palm wine), *brem* (rice wine), or *arak* (rice brandy). Others bring their fighting cocks in bamboo baskets.

The men sit informally in a circle on the floor of the *balé banjar*, with their bottles and other paraphernalia in front of them. One of the participants picks up a palm-leaf manuscript, containing texts of Macapat songs, classical love songs or laments, written in Balinese, which are the staple of Arja, the Balinese opera (see pp. 79–82). The reader sings a sentence from the manuscript to the accompaniment of a *suling*, or small flute, and *rebab*, or spiked fiddle. After each line of the song, another member of the group speaks for a minute or so, elaborating on the sentence from the song and clarifying it for the audience, who may have trouble understanding the highly embellished nature of the melodic setting. The function of the *pengarti*, or explainer, is exactly the same as that of the servant-buffoon characters in Arja, minus the costume and characterization.

As the evening passes, different members of the group take over the reading and explanatory functions. Everyone drinks freely while the singing goes on. Some of the men stroke and groom their roosters, while others prepare *sirih*, or betel-nut, for chewing. As the men feel the effects of the *tuak*, *arak*, and *brem*, the occasion becomes very boisterous. Shouts and arguments may develop over the interpretation of the song.

At last someone abruptly stands up. 'Pung!' shouts the leader, 'Pung-cakapung-cakapung!' The other men join in the chant and several more stand up to dance, some still holding their roosters. One or more of the men may have a *genggong*, a small, lyre-shaped musical instrument made from bamboo or palm-leaf, which he holds between his teeth and strikes as he dances. The movement is improvisational, comic in style, and resembles *ngibing* without the flirtatious element. Some of the men are trained dancers in established classical dance forms, and thus elements of Baris, Topeng, and Gambuh can be seen in their cavorting. A cheering, laughing crowd surrounds the performers. As one dancer gets tired, he sits down and is replaced by another. The fun goes on until late in the evening.

Godogan

The *genggong* mentioned above is a Balinese folk musical instrument whose sound is similar to the Jew's harp, and is often heard at Balinese tourist hotels, where it provides pleasant background music.

In Batuan, Gianyar Province, a group devoted to the performance of a particular folk-tale, using *genggong* accompaniment, was established in 1967 by a well-known Topeng dancer, I Madé Jimat. The tale, 'Godogan', is a Balinese version of the familiar fairy tale about the princess who marries a frog.

I Madé Jimat's group use Topeng masks to present the story. Topeng and Baris provide the vocabulary of movement, supplemented with realistic pantomime in the portrayal of the frog. The frog costume, worn by a small child, is a modern creation, based on a green jumpsuit. The Jimat group performs often, especially at the Sanur hotels.[11] In recent years, other groups have been established, and they also perform regularly in the tourist areas.

Janger

Janger is a genre of Balinese performing art which has its roots in some extinct social dance customs. The genre was created in the early twentieth century, probably in North Bali, although it is not known precisely when.[12] The name Janger can be translated as 'infatuation', with a connotation of someone who is *madly* in love.[13] Unlike Abuang Kalah (see pp. 93–4), which it in some ways closely resembles, Janger is a choreographed, rehearsed presentation, in which variety of elements from many sources—some Balinese, some pan-Indonesian, and some Western—are brought together (Colour Plate 22).

The distinctively Western features in Janger include certain design elements, especially the painted backdrop, or *tenda*. This scenic element provides the setting for the prologue to the performance, and bears a close resemblance to the painted perspective scenery common in theatres in the West in the nineteenth century. The same type of realistically painted scenery is commonly found in professional theatres in Java where the dramatic dance form called Wayang Orang is presented. The Javanese learned to paint scenery in this fashion from the Dutch.

The male costume in Janger also shows Western influence. It consists of a beret, Balinese *bapang*, or fancy collar, short trousers,

97

knee socks, and tennis shoes. Large epaulettes are attached to the jacket, and some groups sport sun-glasses. These Western elements—exotic in Bali—were taken into Janger from an earlier form of dramatic entertainment, created in Java, known as Stambul, which was seen in Bali early in the twentieth century. Stambul was also the ancestral form that gave rise to the Balinese Drama Gong, a theatrical genre which lacks dance features and is therefore not considered in this volume.[14]

The typical Janger performance begins with a tableau vivant, presented in front of the *tenda* and behind a decoratively painted front curtain (*langsé*), which is drawn to the sides to reveal the composition. In a decorative pose, the group sings a song in unison, welcoming the audience and requesting their goodwill. In earlier times, a master of ceremonies, called the *daag*, served to introduce and present the group, but this convention has gone out of use. When the opening song has been concluded, the curtain is closed.

The entrance of twelve men, called *kecak*, begins the main part of the performance. They march in to the accompaniment of a gamelan composed of *gender wayang quartet* (as in Wayang Wong), plus rhythmic instruments. Dressed in their short pants, berets, and sun-glasses, the *kecak* execute an elaborate, highly gymnastic, close-order routine involving marching and counter-marching, acrobatics, saluting, and other movements quite alien to classical Balinese dancing. But for all its exoticism, the drill quite clearly belongs to the ancient Baris Gedé tradition: the movements are new, but the format is traditional.

After the male dancers have completed their manoeuvres, they face one another in two rows of six and sit down, forming two sides of a square formation approximately 4.5 metres wide. Now, the women, who are themselves called *janger*, enter, dressed in the traditional Legong costume but wearing head-dresses resembling those of Joged Pingitan (Plate 17). The entrance of the *janger* is based on the old Rejang processional dance, but the movement is more complicated and reveals a distinct influence of Legong. As the women dance, they sing a folk-song in ordinary Balinese to the accompaniment of chanting and rhythmic sounds made by the *kecak*. The first stanza of the song describes the beauty of the *janger*:

Someone is coming from the East,
Her costume shines, ornamented with flowers,
Her waist is slender, her forehead beautiful.
Whoever sees her falls in love and is filled with joy.

Between the lines of the song, nonsense syllables are inserted as part of the musical composition. These are 'si do re si do', based on the syllables of Western solfeggio, but sung to the pitches of a Balinese tuning system. The syllables are another legacy from Stambul. The women's dance is slow and elegant, with much emphasis on fluid, undulating, arm movements; it has nothing of

17   One of the Janger dancers from Singapadu. (Prastya)

the martial staccato quality of the *kecak* routine. When the women's entrance is complete, the *janger* separate into two lines and also sit facing one another, adjacent to the lines of *kecak*, thus forming a square which will define the performance space.

Before the drama starts, however, two musical interludes are presented. The first, called *tetamburan* (drumming), takes its name from a special single-headed drum, the *tambur* (sometimes called a *rebana*), which is of Arabic origin. The piece is a composition in pure Kebyar style performed by the gamelan and the male dancers, who clap in rhythm and vocalize mnemonic syllables employed in teaching Balinese drumming. 'Byung Pyak Be Byung Pyak' the men chant as they clap, while the *janger*, still seated, move in unison to the rhythm. Their movements are drawn from Kebyar Duduk, and the side-to-side jerk of the head is prominent.

The second musical interlude is more lyrical. The male and female semi-choruses sing back and forth to each other in question-and-answer style. The songs, sung to simple melodies in straightforward rhythm, resemble those in Adar. After several choruses sung in a flirtatious mood, the men and women rise and change places and sing again. Finally, after perhaps twenty minutes, a more serious tone is adopted, to prepare the audience for the start of the drama to follow. This invariably commences with the entrance of the *penasar* characters, who begin a performance in typical Prembon or Baris Melampahan style.

Since its creation, Janger has known periods of intense popularity and periods of total neglect. Powerful waves of interest in Janger have several times swept over the island, only to suddenly die out until the next revival. Such waves occurred in the 1930s as well as in 1965 and 1974. In the latter instances, the resurgence in interest occurred just prior to periods of political turmoil in Indonesia, and thus the genre has come to be associated in popular thinking with a season of madness.

In 1965, during the months leading up to the attempted Communist coup in Jakarta, Janger groups sponsored by rival political parties sprang up all over Bali. Almost all disbanded soon after the failed attempt. The revival of 1974 was given momentum when the government sponsored a competition among Janger groups composed of schoolchildren drawn from villages in every part of the island. This occurred shortly before disturbances broke out among university students in Jakarta which had troubling repercussions all over Indonesia. The 1974 fad was as shortlived as the earlier ones had been.

Today, two permanent groups are devoted to the performance of Janger. One, from Peliatan village, Gianyar Province, presents the *Arjuna Wiwaha* story in Baris Melampahan style. The other, based in Kedaton, Badung Province, presents the story of Cupak and Grantang, an important Balinese folk-story. The principal character is Cupak, a notorious glutton, who eats everything he can get his hands on. In the 1930s, this story was itself the subject of a separate dance-drama, notable for the fact that the actor who played the glutton would go into trance during the eating scene and in that condition devour a staggering amount of food. In that performance, as so often in Balinese dance, one could see an old *wali* element recontextualized, in the same manner as the Sang Hyang Dedari is reframed in Legong. In the Cupak dance-drama, it was Sang Hyang Celéng, the trance pig, who reappeared in the frame of the Cupak and Grantang story.[15]

1. Holt (1967: 111–15). See also Raffles (1817: I, 340–4).

2. Van Eck (1880: 9 (2): 14).

3. Jacobs (1883: 14) reported: 'But you know already that they are boys and it disgusts one to see how, at the end, men from all ranks and conditions of Balinese society offer their coins to perform dances in the oddest attitudes with these children, and it disgusts you still more when you realize that these children, worn out and dead-tired after hours of *perpendicular* exercises, are required yet to perform *horizontal* manoeuvre, first stroked by one, then kissed by another.'

4. Ibid., pp. 186–7.

5. Ibid., pp. 13–14, 56, 101, 112–13, 160.

6. Ibid., pp. 69–70 for a description of Legong in the late nineteenth-century palace setting. McPhee (1966: 140–200) treats the *gamelan semar pegulingan* and related ensembles in detail.

7. Jasper (1902) describes a Gandrung performance he attended at about the turn of the twentieth century; he gives a detailed description of the costume and dancing.

8. Covarrubias (1937: 228–9).

9. Private communication to the authors from I Nyoman Rembang, faculty member at SMKI-Bali, Denpasar.

10. Ibid.

11. De Zoete and Spies (1938: 249–51) describe an interesting performance given to *genggong* accompaniment in Jimat's village of Batuan, Gianyar Province, in the 1930s and earlier. A frog or toad was also an important character in that play.

12. According to the late I Madé Kredek, Janger originated in the village of Menyali, North Bali, and the songs featured in it were those of the horse drivers of that area.

13. De Zoete and Spies (1938: 211) are in error when they define the word as 'humming'.

14. Stambul was the creation of a Eurasian Indonesian, A. Mahieu, toward the end of the nineteenth century. As a high school student, Mahieu had read the classics of Western literature in Dutch, and under their inspiration he sought to create a new form of Malay language theatre, accessible to people all over the Malay Archipelago, which was to be a force for their cultural unification. His Komedie Stambul, as it was called, made extensive use of Javanese popular music in presenting romantic and fantastic tales from such sources as the *Arabian Nights*. The costumes included the Turkish fez (hence 'Stambul') and other exotic Oriental elements, as well as Western features. Mahieu was rather successful and his new genre became popular for several decades. His students established touring companies that travelled widely during the 1920s. Stambul was also performed in Bali, where it influenced Janger, Arja, and Drama Gong. See also Van der Veur (1968: 51–2).

15. De Zoete and Spies (1938: 143–9) describe the Cupak dance-drama. They also describe the Cupak and Grantang story as performed in the Janger context, p. 215.

6 'Magic' Dances of the Street and Graveyard

THE middle world, where humans dwell between the mountains and the sea, is constantly visited by gods from above and demons from below. The gods attend their Odalan and are invariably greeted with respect, while the demonic spirits are bribed with offerings and driven back with the use of exorcistic measures. In Balinese thought, evil can never be entirely defeated, only propitiated and, to a limited extent, controlled. It is necessary, therefore, to attend very frequently to bringing the divine and the demonic into balance.

One way of doing so is through dance performances. We have seen this already in the Sang Hyang dances (pp. 10–15) and in the Barong Kedingkling rite (pp. 56–8). In this chapter, we shall consider a number of dance forms—and their component elements—in which ritually dangerous places, like crossroads and graveyards, are visited and the demonic forces confronted on their own ground. All of them belong to the most sacred group of dances (*wali*), and all are exorcistic.

Barong Ket

When the moon is full, the *taruna* of Banjar Sengguan, Singapadu village, often gather at the *balé banjar* at midnight to take a special mask, known as the Barong Ket, for a walk. Word passes round in the evening, as the young men return from bathing in the river: 'Come on! We're going out tonight!' The *banjar* owns a magnificent Barong mask and costume, highly charged with magical power (Colour Plate 23). Twice a month, the Club for Unmarried Men is responsible for animating the great mythological figure and taking him around the village to drive off evil spirits.

Many other villages near by also have Barong masks (Plate 18). Some are of the same shape as the stylized lion face of Banjar Sengguan's Barong Ket, or Keket, while others possess the features of a wild boar, a tiger, a cow, or even a dog. These types are called Barong Bangkal (Plate 19), Barong Machan, Barong Lembu, and Barong Asu respectively.

Fifteen or twenty young men follow the Barong, which is animated by a pair of dancers at the front and rear. The front dancer holds the mask in his hands and peeps out over it through

18   Barong Ket; Batubulan. (I Madé Bandem)

19   Barong Bangkal; Wredhi Budaya Arts Centre. (Swasthi Wijaya)

103

the great beast's hair. The 2.5-metre frame of his body is shaggy with white palm fibres, and a little bell and a mirror hang from the animal's tail. No music accompanies the magnificent figure as he trots about the ward, stopping now and again to loudly rattle his wooden jaw. His magical beard, made of human hair, waggles as his jaw clacks at crossroads and village corners, chasing the demons back into the outer darkness. His followers shout their approval.

Sometimes the Barong is in such high spirits from his promenading that he refuses to go home. He and his enthusiastic followers pause in front of the *balé banjar*, uncertain for a moment, and then someone calls, 'He wants to see his girlfriend!' The group takes off at high speed down the road to another *banjar* a kilometre or so away, heading for the storage place of the Barong's 'friend'. The *taruna* of the neighbouring ward are pressed to bring out their Barong and allow the two mythical beasts, with bells jingling and mirrors flashing, to dance a simple *pengipuk* at the crossroad, by the light of pressure lanterns. The followers of the Barong might also take the opportunity to engage in a little flirtation with the maidens of the other *banjar*. The entire group makes its way home in time to avoid the sun's first rays.

Every year at the time of the Galungun holiday, the same young men's club of Banjar Sengguan takes the Barong Ket and goes 'on the road' with it, travelling for a week or so into distant areas. This old custom is called *ngelawang*. The young men carry all their food with them, as well as a small gamelan, and camp along the way.

When the club reaches a new village, the gamelan is set up and commences to play, and the dancers in the Barong go through a simple 15-minute routine. The steps are not complicated, but the two performers animating the mask must work in harmony. The long-haired beast shuffles and stomps about, and chases the small children in the crowd who dare to approach too closely. When the dance is finished, the club is happy to accept a small contribution from their hosts in return for the good luck they have brought to the village.

Some villagers bring offerings to present to the visiting 'god', while others beg for lucky fibres from the animal's shaggy coat, or for holy water into which the creature's beard has been dipped. The group then goes on its own way to the next village. The expedition is fun for the members and takes them out of their accustomed territory. Following the Barong is regarded as a pious exercise that happens also to be an excellent way for young bachelors to meet girls.[1]

The origin of the Barong was undoubtedly the mask used in the Chinese Lion Dance, which appeared during the T'ang Dynasty (seventh to tenth centuries AD) in China and spread to many parts of Eastern Asia.[2] Originally, the Lion Dance seems to have been a showman's substitute for a real 'lion act', performed by itinerant professional entertainers who followed seasonal fairs and festivals. Associated with the Buddha, the Chinese Lion Dance acquired exorcist connotations which it still possesses. It is not known when the Indonesian Barong appeared, but it existed in many places in Java, as well as in Bali, until the Second World War.[3]

In the literature on Bali, much has been made of the Hindu influences which reached the island from India, but little attention has been paid to Chinese influences on traditional Balinese culture. It is likely, however, that relations existed between 'Po-li' and China as early as the fifth century AD. An eighth-century Balinese king is thought to have had a Chinese wife.[4] A substantial community of overseas Chinese has lived on Bali for hundreds of years and remains important today, especially in the world of commerce.[5] Chinese coins (*uang kepeng*) were the customary medium of exchange on the island in pre-colonial times, and remain important in the making of offerings.

The different kinds of Barong in Bali all have exorcist qualities and are thought to be the protectors of the villages. Almost every *banjar* in South Bali owns at least one of these fabulous creatures, which are regarded as indispensable in the unrelenting war against demons. In addition to the regular bi-monthly patrol just described, the Barong is called out when an epidemic or other disaster strikes. His territory is the dangerous places of the community: the graveyard, the crossroads, and the special paths favoured by the demons as they go about their troublesome business.

At the time of the Balinese New Year, just before Hari Nyepi, the roads of Bali are crowded with processions of Barong on their way toward the *kelod* extreme of the ritual axis—the ocean (see Figure 1). The Barong are attempting to drive the demons back into the ocean where they come from and where human beings wish they would stay. The Galungan holiday, an island-wide event, is also special to the Barong. People come to the *balé banjar* to present him with offerings and to thank him for his services during the year.

None of the many varieties of Barong is accorded as much prestige and respect as the Barong Ket, honoured though the others may be. The mask of the Barong Ket is readily identified as its appearance is identical wherever it is found. It is similar in style to the masks of Wayang Wong, and it also features the *sekar taji*, or wing-like leather collar. It is thought that the Barong Ket masks of Bali all descend from a prototype carved and consecrated about a century ago by Cokorda Gedé Api of Singapadu village. Cokorda Api's great-grandson, Cokorda Raka Tisnu, is still an active maker of Barong masks, as was his father before him. Indeed, Cokorda Raka Tisnu is the only practising maker of ritually powerful Barong masks in the whole of Bali.

According to Cokorda Raka Tisnu, the *punggawa*, or chief, of Serongga village, Gianyar Province, asked his great-grandfather to make a Barong mask in the form of Banaspati Raja (King of the

Woods). 'I don't know what that is,' said the mask-maker. 'Come to the *pura dalem* tonight,' was the *punggawa*'s reply. The craftsman appeared at the temple at midnight, and waited in the graveyard near by to see what would happen. How would the *punggawa* test his power? If the artisan did not prove to be strong enough, the consequences might be terrible. All at once, an unearthly glow appeared in the south-west, at the *kelod* corner of the temple. An eerie face appeared in the centre of it and the air was charged with power. Cokorda Api made a drawing of the face by scratching the ground with a stick. Subsequently, he used the sketch as the prototype for the likeness of Banaspati Raja. Hundreds of examples of the mask have been produced over the years by the members of the same family. Unconsecrated copies of the same mask have been made by the thousands by craftsmen in such villages as Mas, Gianyar Province.

By the end of the nineteenth century, the Barong had been introduced into a simple form of dance-drama. The Dutch physician, Jacobs, who visited in Bali in 1880, also saw a performance in which the Barong appeared. In the simple story, which resembled the action depicted in the afternoon section of the Berutuk rite, four masked male figures attempted to carry off four masked females. When the Barong appeared to defend the women, the males fought it and killed it before carrying the women off-stage. The approach was comic, according to Jacobs, with the masked males striking ludicrous poses and clowning until the fighting section began.[6]

In general, no special qualifications are required to wear the Barong mask, provided one is a member of the *banjar* group which owns it. The physical requirements are, however, very demanding, especially for the dancer at the front, who must hold the heavy mask and clack the jaws while dancing. If the 34-kilogram frame is carried for a long period, as it often is during Galungan, the members of the Seka Taruna take turns in shouldering the heavy burden. When Barong Ket dances to the accompaniment of his gamelan, he follows an established choreographic pattern, shaking from side to side, walking quickly, turning back to admire his tail, flicking his eyes to the left and right, and rattling his jaws in different rhythms. The choreography is rather complicated, and at least a basic training in the modern Baris style is required.[7]

Jauk and Telek

The masked figures reported by Jacobs are still often seen in Bali. The masks they wear are grouped by Balinese authorities into two types: the coarse and the 'sweet' or refined. The males, called *jauk*, wear a similar bright head-dress in the shape of a Buddhist stupa (Front cover). The style of carving and painting resembles the mask of Rawana in Wayang Wong. The face is fierce, with large eyes, shiny teeth, moustache, and beard. The dancers wear long artificial fingernails. The corresponding female characters are called *telek* or *teledek* (or *sandaran* in the Sanur area). Their 'refined' masks are white. Although the teeth are visible, the expression is pleasant and smiling. The masks are identical to the Sang Hyang Legong ones preserved in Ketewel. The female dancers also wear the identifying pagoda-shaped head-dress and carry fans. The *jauk* and *telek* are vestigial descendants of the characters in the type of folk play described by Jacobs; they are historically associated with the Barong.

At present, *jauk* and *telek* dancers are rarely seen in dance-dramas, although the *telek* were the subject of a special study conducted at Bali's college of performing arts (STSI) in 1982. Two styles of solo dance for a male dancer clad as a *jauk*, however, are commonly included in concerts presenting a sampling of different kinds of Balinese dance. Here, the format, like that of the Baris solo from which it was obviously adapted, is a ten to twenty minute solo accompanied by *gamelan gong*. In one of them, the character is portrayed as 'sweet' and refined, despite his fierce aspect, while in the other, the character resembles a puzzled, fierce demon who, it would seem, has been suddenly wrenched into an alien and dangerous reality. No story is connected with the performance. The solo is similar to the *pengelembar* pure dance section of Topeng (see p. 49). In recent times, the Jauk solo has also been frequently used as one of the introductory masks in Topeng Panca or Prembon.

The Masks of Rangda

In South Balinese villages, it is common for two masks of a truly remarkable type to be kept. These are the masks of the fierce, long-tongued Rangda, the witch, widely shown in films and books about Bali. One of the two Rangda masks, known as Ratu Désa (monarch of the village), is customarily kept in the *pura desa*, where it serves to protect the village from harm, just as the Barong of various kinds are kept to protect the smaller *banjar*. The second mask, Ratu Dalem (monarch of the temple), which, like its counterpart, is cut from the living wood of the *rangdu* (kapok) tree and consecrated in a special ceremony, is kept in the *pura dalem*. There, it protects the village against the demons who congregate in low, dirty, and dangerous places, such as the nearby graveyard. While two is the most typical number, some villages possess and venerate as many as five examples of the mask. In common with every magically powerful thing, the Rangda masks are regarded with respect and considered potentially dangerous, but despite their fierce and grotesque appearance, they are regarded as benevolent forces in the life of the community. It is erroneous to think of Rangda as a devil, or even, in the drama, as a villain.

When either temple has its usual Odalan, the village Rangda masks are displayed in a special shrine in the temple and offerings are presented to them, along with prayers of thanks and requests for future protection. Often the Barong paraphernalia from the three *banjar* that make up the *desa adat*, or traditional village organization, are also displayed and honoured at the same time.

Onying

A singular and very striking form of Balinese religious expression is perpetuated at many Odalan, in which devotees, usually young men and elderly women, but sometimes a few male priests, are 'visited' by the gods and dance in an ecstatic 'trance' state, while carrying heirloom daggers and spears (Colour Plate 24). Like the Sang Hyang dancers, the devotees often inhale quantities of pungent incense before becoming possessed.

The dancing is orderly enough at the beginning with the steps and gestures somewhat resembling ceremonial Baris. But suddenly, first one, then several, and then all the dancers start crying and shouting, their bodies taut and shaking with tension. First, their krises are extended high in their right hand and brandished, and then the dancers press them to their chests, straining to stab themselves. Some dancers hurl themselves to the ground as they try, uselessly, to pierce their bodies with their krises. They report feeling a rush of 'hot' emotion, and an itching of the skin during the rite.

Priests and older female attendants move calmly among the dancers with bottles of holy water, sprinkling those who need restraint or relief. Groups of men help to control particularly violent participants. Then, slowly, one by one, the devotees slump limply as the 'god' leaves them. They are carried into a small pavilion to be brought out of trance with additional holy water.[8]

This ritual dance belongs strictly to the *wali* category; it has no dramatic content. The self-stabbing is believed to both test and demonstrate the strength of the god who possesses the dancer. Once possessed, the dancer is invulnerable to harm and proves it. The same principle applies to the Sang Hyang dancers who run through fire or eat excrement while in the trance state. (As a mode of religious expression, it is similar to snake-handling and other such 'charismatic' Western practices). The dancer experiences supernatural power and glory, and—for a time—feels himself to be as if divine. The self-stabbing is not associated with any particular deity, has no particular story, and is not necessarily connected to any other performance.

Nowadays, the participants in *onying* rarely number more than a dozen, but in the nineteenth century, reliable observers told of seeing entire villages of 500 people—men, women, and even young children—participate simultaneously in the rite.[9]

Wong Sakti

Thrill-seekers in every culture enjoy watching others take great risks and live to tell the tale. Balinese audiences are no exception, although the island has no tradition of wire-walking, high-diving, or other such dangerous athletic pursuits. But in the realm of magic, both black and white, there are specialists, called Wong Sakti (men of power), who will perform feats before your very eyes (Colour Plate 25). The performance involves a contest, either with the ambient spirits in a dangerous location, or with another magician.

Rangda dancers, for example, must be men of power, and so also certain *dalang*, who specialize in a particular kind of shadow play, the Wayang Calonarang and have acquired a reputation for being able to counteract the power of black magicians and other people who can turn themselves into *leyak*, or terrifying creatures. When such a *dalang* performs, the story he presents exists merely to provide a context for him to challenge local sorcerers to fight him with their magic. 'LEEEEEAAAAAK!' he cries, forcing them to come forth, whether they want to or not. Small blue lights then flicker in the dark street and in the graveyard where the brave *dalang* gives his performance.[10] In the past, the Wayang Calonarang might well have been intended as a special rite of exorcism for a household compound or other place troubled by spirits, but it is now a contest, and if local sorcerers are in short supply, an outside expert can be commissioned to ensure an exciting match.

Another professional showman belonging to the Wong Sakti category is the *dusang*, or living corpse. This man's specialty is 'playing dead' in dramatic performances. He lies inert and is stripped, washed, and wrapped while songs for the dead are sung. The ceremony for someone newly deceased is then carried out before the 'body' is carried to the cemetery and left by itself. To submit to this procedure is considered extremely dangerous, for by doing it, the person invites any nasty spirit which may be in the vicinity to come and devour him. The *dusang*, like the kris dancer, feels the exaltation of being invulnerable in dangerous circumstances. Coming out of the experience unharmed proves the power of his magic.

Pengrebongan Ceremony

In Kesiman village, Badung Province, about 3 kilometres from central Denpasar, is the Pura Pengrebongan, a place of worship sacred to the masks of Barong and Rangda. Its Odalan is famous for the cock-fights held in connection with the festivities. All the big gamblers and lovers of fighting cocks from all over Bali attend it, and much chicken blood is shed. The occasion is also host to a great gathering of the Barong and Rangda—thirty or thirty-five of the powerful masks—from the villages near by. The gathering takes place in the *jeroan*, the only time, in fact, the Barong ever enter this sacred place. With their followers gathered around them, the mighty masks and costumes are set down on the ground, while prayers are offered to the goddess of the temple. Tension mounts and the concentration of energy increases as the prayers continue.

The *pemangku* offers a prayer: 'Mother, all of your children have already arrived in your presence. Now please behold them, your loyal children, and give them a sign of your favour!' Suddenly, the entire courtyard is seething with struggling men in a state of trance, as the masks are lifted on to their bearers and are brought to life. All of the Barong and Rangda rush out of the temple, pursued by their followers, many of them deep in trance. Barong and Rangda circle the fighting cock-pit, which is directly adjacent to the temple, in a counter-clockwise direction for up to an hour, while many of their followers practise *onying*, the ritual of self-stabbing. None of the group interacts formally with the other masks or their bearers, and there is no story or even dramatic situation.

The concentration of power in the courtyard and the descent of the goddess into her 'children' brings on the same *onying* possession experienced by the old women and young men described earlier. The young men who follow the Barong are stronger than the old women, and their gyrations with the kris are more acrobatic. Older men also take part, and may be inspired to the most extraordinary feats of *onying*, bending the kris double in an attempt to pierce their stomachs. Each dancer has a personal style of doing the stabbing: some lean back, almost in half, while others throw themselves to the ground with the points of two krises pressed to their eyeballs. The participants are rarely injured. The demons, presumably gorged with blood shed for their benefit at the cock-fight, are driven forth by the horrendous din.

Another purpose of the event is the reconsecration of the powerful masks by the descending goddess. At the end of the ceremony, the masks and their bearers can return home, ready once more to protect the villages which own them.

Rangda in Performance

Few of the men who dare to wear the great head and padded Rangda costume have had any formal dance instruction, for Rangda does not need to keep time to the music. When she appears, she advances into the playing area with a high pouncing step and stops, cackling. Then she arches over backwards, shrieking with high, piercing laughter. Her hands flutter and her long fingernails rattle together. She waves in one hand a magical white cloth with secret 'power' symbols drawn on it. When the mask is not in use, it is wrapped in this dangerous kerchief.

Far more important than technical ability for the man who dances Rangda is spiritual power; he must be a Wong Sakti or a priest. Whenever the Rangda mask appears in public, great forces are unleashed among the people and the other dancers, and many in the crowd may become almost automatically entranced. The association between Rangda and falling into trance is so close, in fact, that in some villages if someone goes into trance for any reason, Rangda will be sent for, if she is not already present. Certain dancers, all men of great inner strength, have made a specialty of playing Rangda, and are called when a village wishes to sponsor a performance in which the mask will be worn by the visiting specialist. It is common for someone to be both a *dusang* and a Rangda dancer, for both require the same kind of power.

In Balinese classical literature, there are a number of epic poems in the Kawi language in which principal characters, when enraged, change suddenly into *pemurtian*, gigantic, terrifying, supernatural manifestations with thousands of heads and arms brandishing weapons. In a number of favourite *wayang* stories, magically powerful characters and their opponents change into *pemurtian* forms to fight. *Pemurtian* puppets were designed for the *wayang* theatre, where quick transformations of appearance can be made easily. The many-armed *pemurtian* are admired by *wayang* audiences because their struggles have a majestic dimension that even on the small screen adumbrates the mightiest forces.[11]

Transformations of appearance are also convenient in Balinese masked theatre, for the performer can make an almost instantaneous change. In Wayang Wong, for example, Rawana takes on the appearance of a *brahmana* in order to trick Sita, and in the same story, Marica is transformed into a supernatural deer. A conventional way to indicate a magical transformation of appearance has evolved: the dancer stops whatever he or she is doing, assumes a special 'meditation' pose, and then withdraws. A substitute dancer takes the first one's place, assumes the same pose, and thus establishes that the original character has been transformed by magic into a new one.

In Balinese dance-drama, the special ten-headed, many-armed representation of *pemurtian* figures found in the Wayang Kulit does not exist. Whenever a powerful manifestation of a god or supernatural being is called for, the Rangda mask is customarily employed. Rangda functions as the *pemurtian* of Balinese dance-drama, and represents the awful face of divinity, without respect to gender or to character. Thus, in the *Arjuna Wiwaha* presentation of the Peliatan Baris Melampahan group, the Rangda is incorporated to represent the highest god, Siva. Even in this highly professional and experienced company, which has performed worldwide, a priest is retained to look after the mask and to dance in it. In the dance-drama based on the old Balinese story *Basur*, the male sorcerer also assumes the Rangda aspect when he is working his charms.

The sacredness of the Rangda mask, the Barong outfit, and the likewise holy Sidha Karya mask (p. 49) is not a matter of appearance, for these faces, regarded as visual motifs, are commonly used in many secular applications in Bali. Indeed, the mask-makers feel

111

no reservation about making perfect copies of the sacred masks to sell to tourists or others. What gives the mask its power is the consecration it receives from the maker, the sacred letters inscribed within it, the holy wood it is made from, and the 'charge' of *taksu* or *pasupati* it receives in the temple or the graveyard. A holy mask literally manifests the divinity, and whenever one is introduced into a performance, the unpredictable can always happen.

Dance of the Sisya

The highest rank of magical power is achieved, not by those who merely purchase a protective amulet, or who get it through some stroke of luck, but by those who study under experts able to interpret ancient magical books written in the old Balinese characters. Traditional Balinese medicine has been conducted by *balian*, doctors knowledgeable about herbal remedies and magical spells, as well as Chinese apothecary principles. Today, certain mountain and coastal villages, such as Sanur in Badung Province, are famous for their sorcerers and witches, who practise both white and black magic, and who sell charms and amulets retail. The most famous of them take students, who are clients desiring to increase their powers. These are *sisya*, the sorcerer's apprentices.

After she had taken the book, she arrived at the graveyard, accompanied by her *sisya* [apprentices], at a place in the shadow of a kapok tree.... There, the Widow of Girah sat down, encircled by her students.... 'Come! Strike up your musical instruments and let us dance, one by one. I will attend to your every movement, and soon when the time for action comes you must all dance, together.' Immediately, Guyang began to dance. She danced with outstretched arms, clapped her hands, and lowered herself to the ground, twirling her skirt around her. Her eyes bulged and she shook her head to left and right. Then Larung began to dance. Her movements were like the tiger when he prepares to attack. Her eyes were red and she was naked. Her hair hung loose in front of her.... (*Calonarang* manuscript)[12]

Black magic may have come to Bali in the tenth century AD, when Tantric rites from Java were introduced on the island.[13] At that time, a Javanese princess named Mahendradatta married the Balinese king, Udayana, who, according to tradition, later cast her off for practising black magic. To the modern Balinese, Mahendradatta has become an archetype: she is the domineering wife who controls her pitifully weak husband through black magic. Her legend has become inseparably entwined with the old Tantric Hindu-Javanese story, *Calonarang*, which tells of such a matron, the Widow of Girah, who is a terrible witch and the owner of two very powerful magical books. She tries to destroy the entire country by means of an epidemic spread by magic, for no man dares to marry her daughter. When Calonarang is angered, she becomes a *pemurtian*: fire shoots from her eyes and nostrils, and she takes on the appearance of a monster. Calonarang's favourite technique is to go with her students at midnight to the crossroads, a magically dangerous place, and there to dance naked until the goddess Durga gives them the power to change into *leyak*, hideous familiar spirits who fly about the country working mischief and spreading disease. *Leyak* are still greatly feared in Bali, and many people report some personal experience with one. The apprentice black magician receives a charm from his or her teacher, enabling the adept to take the form of a monkey, goat, or other animal. More advanced *sisya* learn to become smoke or a little point of blue light, or even—at a very advanced level—a huge cremation tower. The peak of achievement, said to be reached by very few, is to attain the power to become Rangda herself, without need for mask or costume.

Black magicians in Bali are business people, and their wares must be publicized. The enterprising have kept up with the times. In 1975, a *leyak* in the form of a riderless motor-cycle was the talk of night-time Denpasar, and at the finish of a famous battle of magicians at Sanur, in 1976, the crowd reported seeing a magical aeroplane, absolutely silent, flying just above the crest of the surf.

Naked witches no longer dance at the crossroads at midnight in Bali, if indeed they ever did, but the vocabulary of movement described in the *Calonarang* manuscript is referred to in the Dance of the Sisya, a product of a little known esoteric dance tradition. Claire Holt has commented that the dancing described in the *Calonarang* is an inversion of classical Balinese dance. The extended arms, loose hair, immodest and uncontrolled gestures, and nakedness are all antithetical to the deepest essential sensibility of classical Balinese dancing.[14] The dance at the crossroads is an equivalent in choreographic terms to reading the scriptures backwards, as black magicians around the world do to work an evil spell.

Calonarang

The period around the turn of the twentieth century was a difficult one in Bali, but it was also a time of great artistic energy. The Kebyar 'explosion' of the 1920s represented the crest of a wave of innovation and creation that had begun thirty years or so earlier and included Parwa and Topeng Panca. During this time, many new subjects, never before represented in the Balinese dance-theatre, were dramatized. Elements from various genres were combined and recombined in the staging of new stories and made into new dance-dramas. None of the new forms, however, was to make such an impression in Bali, and indeed all over the world, as the Calonarang dance-drama, which is thought to have originated about 1890 in the Batubulan area of Gianyar Province.

Like other Balinese creators, the makers of Calonarang drew from a general cultural pool of pre-established materials, some belonging specifically to 'the dance', others from far and wide in the heritage. Composition was a process of assembly and arrangement of inherited or given motifs and motifemes (atomic units of action). At the heart of the new creation was (as is so often the case in Balinese dance), an attempt to rework a *wali* element in terms of classical Hindu-Balinese style and conventions.

In the Legong, the Sang Hyang Dedari dancer has been caught, set, and embellished. In modern solo Baris, Baris Gedé has been captured. In the Calonarang dance-drama, attempts were made to provide a frame in performance for the Rangda. A crucial difference is that the godhead manifesting in the mask can not be contained by any human agency, for Rangda can not be fully tamed.

The places of performance of the Calonarang dance-drama are the graveyard and the crossroad, two areas at the *kelod* extreme of the sacred geographical orientation that are home to demons (Figure 8). These are also the sites favoured by the witch and her pupils in the old Kawi story. A *kalangan* is made at the centre of the intersection, where paths used by demons and *leyak* meet and cross. The stage area itself is similar to the *kalangan* set up in temples; it is perhaps 5.5 metres wide by 9.0 metres deep. The five-toned *gamelan semar pegulingan* is placed to one side.

The special features of the Calonarang stage include a small temporary *sanggah* made of bamboo, which is placed in one corner. This is identical to the shrines erected outside every Balinese household compound on the day of Kajeng Kliwon, which occurs every fifteen days on the Balinese calendar. At this time, small meat offerings are placed in the *sanggah* to placate the demons. It is said that people who like to become *leyak* pray at such shrines before going out to make the transformation. The *kalangan* is also furnished with a small papaya tree, symbol of the sacred *kepuh* tree which grows in nearly every Balinese graveyard. The crossroad itself is usually shaded by a great Banyan tree, symbolic of shelter.

At one end of the stage, screened by a brightly coloured curtain, is the *rangki*, or dressing area, where the dancers put on their make-up and masks. Entrances are made through the curtain. This is the opposite end to a small shack on stilts which towers high over the space and is reached by a precarious ladder. From here, Calonarang makes her entrance, as do her *sisya*. Later, as Rangda, she comes down the same ladder. The spectators watch from three sides of the enclosure. As always, the *kalangan* is consecrated before the performance by a *pemangku*, with libations and small offerings. The performance then begins with a series of *pengelembar*. Very often, the Barong Ket from the local *banjar* will dance, operated by invited dancers from distant villages and cities. Perhaps three different pairs will animate the great beast, demonstrating their virtuosity. Here, the Barong's followers play no role, and the skill of the dancers is an important concern. Then a Baris dancer may perform, if one is available, followed perhaps by a *jauk* and *telek*, each dancing a 15-minute solo in modern style. The *jauk* and *telek*

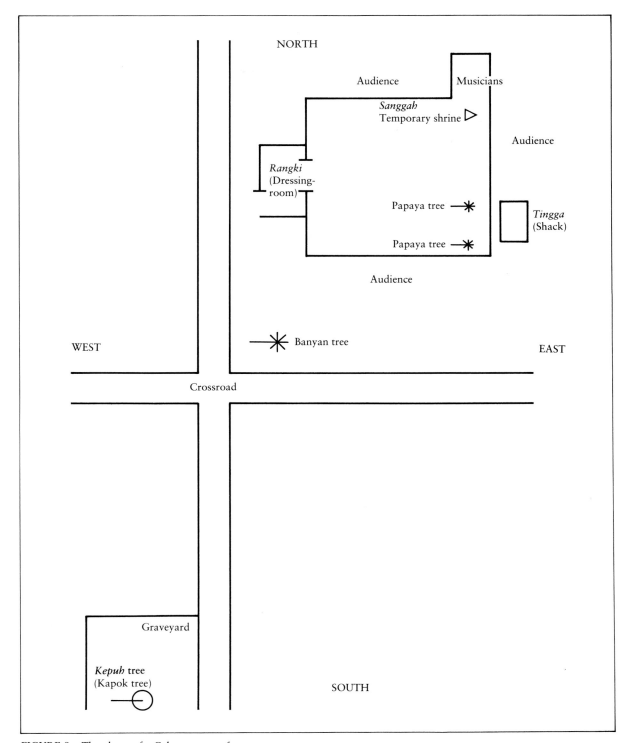

FIGURE 8   The places of a Calonarang performance.

enter from Rangda's elevated shack to show their skill at dancing down a swaying ladder in mask and heavy costume.

After the introductory dances, the play proper begins with the appearance of the *condong*, or attendant, who, in this drama, is usually portrayed by a man. Her entrance and solo are identical to the *condong*'s dance in Gambuh, although minor influences from Arja are clearly audible in her vocal part. The *condong* soliloquizes, explaining the background of the story: no one will marry Calonarang's daughter, Ratna Manggali. The young woman then appears, and as might be expected, is of the same type as the Putri from Gambuh. Ratna Manggali dances and sings before engaging the *condong* in dialogue. 'Why doesn't she have any suitors?' The *condong* suggests that Calonarang may know the reason. But again, following the established Gambuh structure, the subordinates must prepare for the principal's entrance. The *condong* thus calls the *sisya*.

Four to six female dancers usually dance in these roles. Their costume, unique in Balinese dance-drama, consists of calf-length white skirts and yellow tops made by winding a long sash around the upper body, leaving the shoulders and arms bare. Their long hair hangs loose. Here, in their first appearance, the *sisya* do not perform a special choreography but dance a simple variant of the *kakan-kakan* routine from Gambuh. As they dance, they call to one another, in the Kawi language, to make ready. Finally, all take their places, kneeling in a ring on the ground.

Matah Gedé now appears. This name, which is applied to the Widow of Girah, literally means 'the great uncooked one', referring to the fact that fire has not yet issued from her eyes and nostrils. The role is played by a male priest wearing a white head-cloth and skirt. Often a lucky cloak of *kain poleng*, or chequered cloth, is wrapped around her shoulders, and she carries a staff on which to lean as she walks.

Calonarang clambers down the ladder and enters the circle of respectful *sisya*. The vocabulary of movement is pantomimic rather than choreographic, and resembles the movement of the Tua from Topeng. Ratna Manggali greets her mother respectfully, but then begins to weep:

Condong (translating for Matah Gedé)
Don't be full of sorrow, my daughter, even though no man has come to ask for your hand. The goddess Durga has looked with favour on our requests, and has given us permission to punish the people here in the kingdom of Daha. As you can see, all of my *sisya* are spreading disease wherever they can. Now all of you, listen as I explain what we will do.

Now the Matah Gedé explains in Kawi how the magical ceremony is to be conducted and what each of the *sisya* must do and become. The *condong* translates and elaborates in Balinese. The role of the *condong* is considered to be a dangerous one, because her explanation tells both how to work magic and how to combat it. From each kind of *leyak* the proper formulae and antidotes are explained, which requires a knowledge of the magician's art contained in certain sacred manuscripts. Local sorcerers are said to hate the *condong*'s explanation, for it tells the public how to ward off their tricks. The dancer is therefore thought to be in danger of attack by *leyak* at this time—the first challenge to the performance. When the scene ends, Matah Gedé and her followers retire up the ladder into the hut.

Now, the second meeting of the performance takes place. The *penasar* serving the King of Erlangga, Punta and Kartala, enter. They may improvise a comic routine lasting as long as an hour before they come to the root of the exposition: the King is concerned about the epidemic in his country and plans to send the Patih to solve the problem by killing Calonarang with a special kris. The format of the scene is a replica of that of Topeng. The King enters, dancing his introductory solo which duplicates the *igel ngugal* of the evil Prabu in Gambuh. His Patih, called the Pandung, appears without an introductory solo. By this odd bit of type-assignment, it is made clear that the King and his ministers are the villains of the performance.

In the Calonarang dance-drama, the Pandung is one of the performers who must have special protection against the danger of *leyak*. Because he will later attack Rangda with a kris, he is vulnerable to destruction for his temerity. The dancer who plays this role must undergo a special ceremony in which he is consecrated to the part. Very often he wears a protective amulet, purchased from a magician. His characterization is exactly that of the Prabangsa from Gambuh, while his costume is taken from the *arya-arya* in its older form.

The brief scene between King Erlangga and his Patih is interpreted by the *penasar*. The King instructs the Minister to go and kill Calonarang, accompanied by the two servants. Now begins the *pangkat*, or formal departure. The three emissaries travel back and forth across the stage a few times, describing the scenery they pass. They stop several times to search for the correct path. After a while, they 'arrive' at Girah, where they comment on how terribly smelly it is. 'Let's wait over here!' They exit to the dressing area.

The pressure lanterns are now dimmed, and some are removed by members of the gamelan, who do double duty as stage-hands. The central scene is about to take place. This is the transformation, in which the *sisya* dance at the small shrine and before the papaya tree. Their singular choreography has undoubtedly descended from Tantric rites such as those described in the old *Calonarang* manuscript.

Although traces of the Legong are found in the *sisya* choreography, especially during the entrance, the basic vocabulary of movement is unusual in Balinese dance. The girls cover their faces with pieces of white cloth, letting their hair hang loose in front. Some of them immediately begin to mime picking up dead babies—dolls wrapped in white cloth—from the ground, while they all howl with laughter. The *sisya* mime eating the little bundles,

117

and then dance again, shaking their torsos and wiggling their buttocks in a suggestive way, and jumping from side to side in a squatting position. At the end of their 10-minute routine, they sit down on the ground to await Rangda's entrance down the ladder. This is the Widow as *pemurtian*.

Her dancing during the *igel ngugal* at first centres around the little papaya tree in the *kalangan*. She searches for it and stops to shriek with glee when she finds it. She rubs her back against the little plant, symbol of her own *pohon kepuh* (graveyard tree). Then, satisfied, laughing in an unusual snorting high falsetto and waving her cloth, she inspects her students. 'Now daughters, go and kill all the people in Daha. Let not one remain alive! Go to each of the nine directions!' The *sisya* scatter and disappear. Rangda, shrieking with delight, clambers back up the ladder to her house, accompanied by the *condong*.

At this time, the chief comic scene of the performance takes place, much to the delight of the audience, although the joking is in a distinctly macabre, almost ghoulish, vein. It is performed by *bondres* (both comic villagers and comic *leyak*). The rustics, five in number, enter with a dead baby—a doll—wrapped for burial. All wear simple, bold, comic make-up and carry torches to light their way to the graveyard. Some carry digging implements. The woman in the little cortege is crying, while the men sing a mournful dirge.

The procession pauses for a moment. Suddenly, Rangda's chief assistant, Pangpang, appears with two lesser comic demons, and the scene turns slapstick (Plate 20). A favourite section depicts one of the stupid *bondres*, who fancies himself as a black magician. He intones imitation mantras, sits in imitation meditation, and then imitates entering trance. Unbeknown to him, Pangpang creeps up behind and causes the rustic to vomit. After perhaps an hour or more of clowning, and after chasing and beating each other in the confusion, the *bondres* drive off the comic demons, signalling the entrance of the *dusang*.

At this moment in the performance, the mood of the audience changes sharply. People become sombre and tense. Mothers and fathers clasp their children to them, as the professional corpse walks in, and lies down on his pallet of bamboo. He makes no attempt to enact a character or to feign illness. The *bondres* strip off his clothes, except for his loincloth, wash him, place Chinese coins on his eyes, and cross his arms. Then, offerings for the dead, authentic in every way, are presented. An older actor prays while the others chant the liturgy for the dead. They then pick up the pallet and proceed down the road by torchlight, singing a dirge, to the (real) cemetery about a kilometre away. Some members of the audience accompany the procession, while others wait for the climactic and most dangerous moment of the performance, the attack of the Pandung on Rangda.

The Pandung enters the stage area with his attendants. One of the clowns creeps silently up the ladder, peeks into the Widow's

20   Pangpang, Rangda's assistant in
Calonarang; Batubulan. (I Madé Bandem)

shack, and then returns. The Pandung resists the idea of attacking
a sleeping enemy, which his servants urge him to do. Yielding at
last to pressure, he mounts the ladder and steps inside. He drags
out Rangda and hauls her, kicking, down the ladder, stabbing
furiously with his magic kris. The dancer literally tries to kill
Rangda, but is prevented by the magical power of the mask and
that of the man inside it. Rangda laughs exultantly, and quickly
chases the Pandung off the stage. (In the old story, Calonarang
burns him to death with fire that comes from her eyes, nostrils,
and mouth, but this is not represented in the play.)

The dancer performing Rangda is now at the peak of excitement,
and is possibly in a state of trance. He now begins to challenge the
leyak to attack him. In the context of the story, Calonarang as

119

Rangda, in a transcendental state of anger, is here calling her *sisya* to join her for further depredations on the countryside. But more literally, the dancer at this moment invites and dares all local practitioners of the dark arts to test his power. At Kerambitan, at this point in the performance, members of the Barong's entourage attack Rangda with their daggers, but her magical power enables her to proceed unscathed (Back cover, Colour Plate 26, and Plate 21a–c). The performance moves at a double level of being, in which almost contradictory messages are expressed. Rangda dances in character all the way to the graveyard, shouting her challenges, while the remaining spectators follow at a respectful distance. Sometimes the Rangda dancer feels so exultantly invulnerable that he strips off the mask and invites the *leyak* to attack him: 'All you *leyak*, come on! Attack me all together! ME! Attack ME!'

The audience has been steadily dwindling since the *dusang* appeared, as its more timid members decide to go home. The crowd continues to thin out as the group approaches the real graveyard, with its massive *rangdu* tree. Only the braver members of the community follow the dancer into the cemetery, where he repeats the summons and challenge.

The members of the gamelan have followed, however, but are anxious for the performance to come to an end, and to reach the safety of their homes. They struggle to bring the exalted dancer under control, with the assistance of the *pemangku*. Rangda is wrestled to the ground and doused with holy water. He is dragged off to the nearby temple to be restored to his normal condition. The beard of the Barong Ket is dipped into the holy water to give it special strength. The dancer gulps down this restorative and wipes it over his face and upper body to purify himself from the recent experience. Then all go their respective ways. All, that is, except for the *dusang*, who lies motionless and alone in the graveyard. There he will remain until shortly before the sun rises, invulnerable to all the *leyak* of the area. No one usually dares to stay to watch with him. He will return to the *banjar* around dawn: 'Hey, where's my shirt? What kind of cowards are you?' The *dusang* is entitled to brag a little, for he has run a hideous risk and survived. His power has been proven. The performance is over.

The Calonarang dance-drama is still frequently performed in South Bali, especially in Gianyar and Badung Provinces. The villages of Pagutan, Den Jalan, Tegal Tamu, Singapadu, Guang, Sukawati, and Celuk—all in Gianyar Province—maintain groups able to perform, complete with sacred Rangda and the *dusang*. However, the Calonarang production at STSI-Bali in Denpasar, seen by many tourists, employs no consecrated sacralia. This group has even toured abroad. So strong are the conditioned responses to trance-inducing stimuli, however, that some members of the company that performed in the USA in 1983 fell into trance during the performances, despite the unusual context and circumstances of the event.

21a–c   Entranced dancers in Calonarang; Kerambitan. (STSI documentation)

b

122

c

123

In Calonarang, as in Topeng Pajegan, ritual elements are embedded among secular features. No fewer than five members of the company must have special spiritual powers or defence. The Pandung may be protected by an amulet purchased from a *balian*, whereas the *condong* and the Matah Gedé must be literate and have specific magical knowledge. The *dusang* is given his power directly by the gods, but it may not last for more than a few years. In several villages he is the *pemangku* at the *pura dalem*. And Rangda is a professional specialist. Two very active Rangda dancers of the present time are Cokorda Alit, a powerful man of the *ksatrya* caste from Blahbatuh, and I Madé Kengguh of Singapadu, a musician, dancer, and expert teacher of the Rangda dance. These men are often invited to perform with groups from villages in which a man strong enough to 'carry' the deity is lacking.

The Calonarang play was created to counteract and neutralize the supernatural power of black magicians who are *specific* individuals in the community, and the play, like the Wayang Calonarang, can still be applied to this purpose. For this reason, the Calonarang repertoire is quite distinct from ceremonies designed to chase or propitiate evil spirits who are 'natural' demons rather than malevolent humans in transformed shape. It would be absurd to attempt to cleanse a graveyard of demons, for such beings can never be destroyed, but only displaced, and if they were driven from the graveyard, they would enter the village and rice-fields. The Balinese do not hold cock-fights, make offerings, or pour libations, which are all measures to control the demons, in a graveyard. A demon in a graveyard is where it belongs, if it is not in the ocean.

Well-known headquarters for magic, both black and white, are located in a small number of coastal villages, such as Sanur, Ketewel, Matolan, Lebih, and Jempai, situated at the *kelod* extreme of Bali across from Nusa Penida, the traditional haunt of devils. As befits black magic, the principal ingredients in sorcerers' concoctions consist of products associated with the sea, such as fish oil and bones, and seaweed. Inland practitioners of the evil arts must get their medicines from the coastal *balian*, and hence their identities and preferred potions can be discovered through astute detective work.

In the performance of the dance-drama, the *condong* plays a key role. It is she who explains to the public who is practising what kind of magic, and how their spells can be counteracted. Then Rangda and the *dusang* challenge the magicians to throw their worst at them. When the Rangda dancer and *dusang* emerge unscathed, at least a temporary respite from sorcery has been won. In the Wayang Calonarang, the roles of namer and challenger, each requiring special powers, are concentrated in one performer. But in the Calonarang dance-drama, the functions are shared among the five specialists.

In the light of this very specific function, certain perplexities become clear. One source of misunderstanding arises from the fact that the performance concludes with the triumph of Rangda. In Balinese theatre, it is highly unusual for any drama to conclude with the victory of the evil party. In fact, the narrative in Balinese drama, in general, is regarded as a means by which the struggle between the good and evil parties and the final victory of the good can be contextualized. All the stories exist only to provide circumstances for the ritual battle. In Calonarang, Rangda is the heroine of the performance and represents the protection of the village against sorcerers. Although the play concludes very early in the old Javanese story, which is its source, it has reached the perfectly appropriate conclusion. Since Rangda is the village protector, it is no wonder that the Balinese find it difficult—if not impossible—to represent her defeat in the theatre.

Barong Landung

A final type of magically protective effigy is the Barong Landung, which is found in many villages of the Denpasar area in preference to Barong Ket and other types of animal Barong. *Landung* means 'tall', and indeed the 3-metre figures, with their human faces and features, tower over their bearers and attendants (Colour Plate 27). There are five to a set: Jero Gedé (the Big Man), Jero Luh (his wife), and their three children. Jero Luh has Chinese features and yellow skin, while her husband has a black complexion, long hair, and fangs; he is said to represent a Dravidian from ancient India. The children are somewhat shorter and wear masks similar to those used in *telek* (Colour Plate 28).

Barong Landung, like the other Barong types, belongs to the village. The dancers are drawn from among the strongest young men, who alone can handle the size and weight of the giant figures, each of which is carried and operated by a single performer. During most of the year, Jero Luh and Jero Gedé and their children remain in the home *banjar*, but at Galungan time they appear, in the evenings, on the highways of the Denpasar area. At this time, groups with a set of Barong Landung figures walk from village to village, dancing and singing Balinese songs, to the accompaniment of the *gamelan batel*.

When the procession reaches the *balé banjar* of the village to be visited, a small circle of spectators gathers around the figures. There, a simple domestic drama, drawn from daily life, is enacted in song and speech in the Balinese language. The play contains jokes and comic sketches, along with bits of homely good advice from parents to children. The husband and wife quarrel and argue for a short time, but there is no fighting sequence. The little play concludes with songs by the principal characters, and then the procession moves on to the next village.

New Year Processions

Once every fourteen months, the Balinese celebrate their New Year holiday, called Hari Nyepi. This is a time of cleansing and renewal, a time to settle old debts and be reunited with members of one's family. On Hari Nyepi, it is the rule to stay home quietly. Older people fast and meditate, and no one is permitted to make any loud noise. New Year's eve, however, is a very lively occasion. In many villages, noisy purification rites, designed to frighten away the evil spirits, are held, and every family sets out large offerings for the *buta* outside their houseyard. In a sense, the entire island is to be swept clean of demons on this day.

To help accomplish the purpose, the gods in their small *pratima* figures, and the Barong of various kinds, are carried in procession by all the active temple congregations on the island. On this day, it seems that everyone in Bali is on the march with umbrellas and banners and gamelan, going in procession down the highways and byways to the sea or to a river that leads to the sea. Every *banjar*, village, kin group, and irrigation society takes to the road, dressed in traditional temple costume. By evening, hundreds of thousands of people have gathered on the normally deserted shore near Sanur.

As many as a thousand Barong are present here, at the *kelod* extreme of the island. The marchers and their protective figures form a mighty barrier at the edge of the sea, shutting out the demons, if only temporarily. And here, at the edge of the ocean, our account of the traditional dance of Bali is complete; from the inner court of the Berutuk temple in Trunyan to the beach at Sanur, we have come from *kaja* to *kelod*.

1. Mead (1939).
2. Laufer (1923: 29–30).
3. They are discussed in Pigeaud (1938: *passim*).
4. Suleiman (1974: 41).
5. C. Geertz (1963: 135–6).
6. Jacobs (1883: 109).
7. Belo (1949). See also Bandem (1976).
8. Compare Belo (1960).
9. Liefrinck (1886: 1235–7).
10. McPhee (1946: 138–52) describes circumstances that called for Wayang Calonarang and other exorcist measures, as well as the performance of the shadow play. See also Sumandhi (1979).
11. Hooykaas (1971).
12. Poerbatjaraka (1926: 152).
13. Stutterheim (1935: 14).
14. Holt (1967: 288).

7 Balinese Dance in Transition

DURING the nineteenth century, Bali had seen the emergence of professional companies of dancers, often with members drawn from the same *banjar*, who travelled to other villages to perform for hire at Odalan and other festivals. It was, therefore, no surprise when troupes of dancers and musicians were engaged during the 1920s to perform for tourists at the Bali Hotel in Denpasar and at the hotel built by the Dutch in Kintamani village above Lake Batur.

In the second and third decades of the twentieth century, the well-known expatriate painter, Walter Spies, and other Europeans who came to live for long periods in the newly discovered 'island paradise', also commissioned performances in those villages where they had personal contacts.[1] The companies they hired gained much-needed revenue from these engagements. At the same time, the European and American visitors enjoyed reliable access to Balinese dance and music, without the inconvenience caused by the complicated Balinese calendar of festivals and ceremonies.

In the 1930s, the trickle of visitors became a steady flow. Halted for a time by the Second World War, the stream resumed and gained momentum in the post-war era, becoming a flood in the late 1960s when the modern Bali Beach Hotel was opened. In 1994, nearly 3 million visitors came to Bali. More than a dozen separate resort locations have been opened, generously equipped with accommodation, restaurants, shops, and other tourist services. In keeping with Balinese government policy, great stress has been laid on 'cultural tourism', meaning that, in addition to the island's natural beauty, fine beaches, and other attractions, emphasis is placed on the arts and ceremonial life of the Balinese. Attendance at performances is considered to be an indispensable part of a vacation in Bali. The dance could not remain unaffected by the inundation.[2]

In the 1930s, new creations and adaptations of traditional art forms of all kinds were devised in response to the tastes of the tourist market. The art shop came into being at this time, and objects previously made to order by craftsmen began to be mass-produced for sale to foreigners. Copies of sacred objects were particularly sought after. A similar process occurred in the dance. Various *wali* forms, as well as some of the secular genres, came to be performed in some villages on an almost daily basis, without regard for the calendar of religious festivals. Under the circumstances, such performances could not remain truly sacred for very long. Too much is required in the way of offerings and special preparations for an authentic ceremony to be given so frequently and without relation to the religious calendar of the people. Furthermore, many of the traditional forms contain a great deal which is unintelligible to the foreigner and hence fails to please.

New composite genres were developed in response to the need for intelligible, fast-moving, hour-long performances which did not require the use of actual sacralia. These 'imitation' traditional forms have assumed a life and place of their own in the spectrum of Balinese performance, and have been, to some extent, authenticated through constant repetition. Although the Balinese themselves seldom attend these mass-produced performances, they have taken on a very important economic role in the life of many villages and hence have become vital to Balinese life. After all, a tourist performance may be given a hundred times more often than its 'authentic' prototype.[3]

Cak

One such new form is Cak, or Kecak, sometimes called the 'Monkey Dance'. This composite genre was first created by dancers in Bedulu village, Gianyar Province, at the request of Walter Spies.[4] The group was commissioned to devise a new kind of *Ramayana* performance, accompanied solely by a Cak chorus like that found in Sang Hyang Dedari. In that old exorcist rite, the choral group consists of perhaps a dozen men, each making a distinctive 'chek, chek, chek' sound that blends into a complex rhythmic pattern to assist the dancers in sustaining their trance condition (Plate 22).

This *wali* nucleus, much developed, is the basis for Cak, a purely secular performance given almost exclusively for tourists. It is not usually presented in the context of village life. The first simple version created in Bedulu achieved instant success and rapidly became very popular with tourists and other visitors to Bali. Today, several dozen professional groups perform regularly at the larger hotels and on special stages built for the purpose in their *banjar*. Every day, tourists come by the busload to see the show.

In Cak, a chorus of chanting men, whose number has been increased to a hundred or more, sit in concentric rings around a small oil-lamp (Plate 23). One of the chanter-dancers serves as the leader. Instead of the simple repetitive continuous chanting of the original version, the chorus now performs a highly structured piece of vocal music, exactly an hour long. Melodies and musical ideas from the modern Balinese concert repertoire are heard, and the influence of the Kebyar musical style is apparent.

The creators of Cak included a dramatic episode in the performance, executed by a small number of skilled dancers wearing

22 Sugriwa, the King Monkey from the *Ramayana* epic; Cak; Teges, Peliatan. (Stuart Rome)

simple costumes. Drawing on the *Ramayana*, the first episode was a very simple representation of the abduction of Sita. Later, a battle sequence was added, in which Sugriwa was pitted against Rawana's son, Meganada. This and subsequent innovations were quickly copied by the various villages as more and more Cak groups came into being. Because Balinese choreographers and musicians are very alert to the efforts of their colleagues and rivals, a successful local novelty can become standard practice all over the island in a matter of months. The process has been facilitated by the many improvements in transportation and communications, especially over the past twenty-five years.

23   Cak, male chorus performing the *Ramayana* story; Wredhi Budaya Arts Centre. (Koes)

In 1969, a number of important changes were made in the Cak performance. The single *Ramayana* episode was lengthened to represent the whole epic tale, from the banishment of Rama to the death of Rawana. New costumes were brought into use, and the music was made more elaborate. These innovations were adopted almost everywhere within a few months, under pressure from travel agents, who threatened to stop taking tourist buses to villages refusing to adapt their play to the newer style.[5]

Barong and Rangda

Of all the forms of Balinese dance, the Barong, the Rangda, and the genres involving trance possession were the most fascinating to early Western residents and visitors. Followers of the Barong frequently practised self-stabbing during a performance, to the great interest of scholars and curiosity seekers alike. In the early 1930s, Walter Spies directed many visitors to the villages of Pagutan and Tegal Tamu in the Batubulan area of Gianyar Province, where variants of the Calonarang dance-drama were performed. Many special performances were commissioned by Walter Spies and his guests, and in Pagutan, especially, Calonarang performances became something of a local industry; three or more might be requested in a single week.

With the resumption of tourism in 1948, the Bali Hotel in Denpasar requested that a Barong performance be specially created to suit the needs of the tourist trade. In response, a group of traditional artists led by I Madé Kredek and I Wayan Geria established the form as it is seen by the tourist today. Carefully tailored to a 1-hour performance, the show is performed with unconsecrated masks and with minimal offerings to protect the dancers (Plate 24). Sacred objects are not employed. It is rare that a performer actually enters trance in the performance. The company is made up of members of the *banjar*, who divide the profits monthly, after setting aside a percentage for the general fund.

Although the performance is based on a *Mahabharata* story called 'Sudamala', or 'Kunti Sraya', the masks and general format are taken from the Calonarang performance described in Chapter 6. In this plot, which has been standardized so that a synopsis can be distributed to the audience, two Rangda masks are employed, worn by the goddess Durga and by her servant-priestess, Kalika. When the Barong appears at the end of the play, his followers practise simulated self-stabbing and other trance-like behaviour according to a precise timetable. After the tourists depart, the everyday life of the village resumes.

131

24   Barong play for tourists; Den Jalan.
(I Madé Bandem)

Prembon

The term *prembon* was originally applied to a dance-drama made up of elements from a number of separate genres, but has now come to refer to a revue-style presentation, first given at the Bali Beach Hotel. The permanent performing space at this modern international facility is located as close to the Sanur beach as possible. The dancers have their backs to the sea when they step on to the permanent stage, placed by the swimming-pool under waving coconut palms. Imitation shrines conceal the spotlights. The stage is not consecrated.

The concert consists of half a dozen items, all much like the introductory dances of Topeng. No dialogue or story features are included. A welcoming dance derived from Gabor, such as Pan-yembrama, is invariably presented first, usually followed by Kebyar Duduk, Legong (much abbreviated), solo Baris, Jauk, Panji Semirang, and a single Topeng mask. Perhaps influenced by the example, many Balinese village performances now take the Prembon form; it is especially favoured for presentations featuring the village children.

The tourist performances have obviously yielded both advantages and disadvantages to the artists of Bali. Among the benefits is the contribution that income from tourist performances has made to the organizations of dancers and musicians. The clubs (and the individual *banjar* from which their members are drawn) have been able to buy new gamelan, new costumes, and so on, and these expensive items are regularly used for traditional performances given in the village context for Balinese audiences. Thus, tourism serves the Balinese religion, which is the basis for the entire performing arts tradition.

On the negative side, the endless repetition of performances for audiences composed entirely of people who are experiencing Balinese dance and theatre for the first time has undoubtedly led, in many cases, to a deterioration in standards. The regular tourist dances have been given in identical form for more than a decade, leading to some performances that seem quite stale. On the other hand, the best groups reach a high level of accomplishment, achieved through lengthy practice.

The tourist is by definition a curiosity seeker in search of new sensations. Since the more exotic and (to the Westerner) sensational forms of Balinese dance are in the *wali* category, there has been increasing pressure to exhibit sacred dances for commercial purposes. This trend has been resisted by Balinese religious, cultural, and political leaders, especially since 1971 when a seminar on the subject, 'Sacred and Secular Art', was held. At this, I Gusti Bagus Sugriwa, the well-known expert on traditional Balinese religion and culture, proposed the basic three-part set of categories of sacred performance which has been followed in this volume. It was the consensus of the seminar participants that the *wali* and *bebali* genres should not be exploited for commercial gain.[6]

Nevertheless, pressure to mount sacred dances has been intense. In the Sang Hyang Dedari performance given twice a week at Bona, the little girls are put into trance strictly for the tourist audience. In that village, too, Legong has been added to make a more interesting show. And in 1977, amid great controversy, a Baris Gedé troupe from Sebatu village performed a number of *wali* dances for audiences in Europe and America. Since no sacred objects were employed, no great harm was done in the eyes of many Balinese dancers, although some regretted that the quality of the Sebatu performance was not up to standard.

Modern 'Classical' Forms

The creation of new pieces in Kebyar style continued into the post-war period, under the example of I Mario's Oleg Tumulilingan (1952). These efforts resulted in the creation of a number of new genres in Bali based on pantomime and patriotic thematic material. The pantomimic gestures were developed from observed activities of everyday life among the common people.

Tari Tenun

Tari Tenun (Weaving Dance), composed by I Nyoman Ridet and I Wayan Likes in 1957, is an example of a dance based on everyday activities. In it, a soloist or small group of female dancers execute a choreography showing characteristic movements from

133

the action of weaving cloth using traditional Balinese equipment. No props are employed, and the movement is synchronized with the orchestral accompaniment. The simple costume is based on traditional Balinese attire, and includes a head-dress called *lelunakan*, commonly worn by women attending a cremation ceremony.

Tari Tani

In the early years of Indonesian independence, the new national government and a number of emerging political parties actively supported the development of new forms of dance as a vehicle for political gain. Tari Tani (Peasant Dance) is a work of this type which was sponsored by the Nationalist Party (PNI), and choreographed by a group of artists in Kerambitan, Tabanan Province, In this piece, seven dancers, six women and a man, mime the sequence of tasks involved in planting, cultivating, and harvesting rice. Other dances sponsored by such groups portrayed the daily tasks of fishermen and of coffee plantation workers. In his seventieth year, Pak Kaler of Kelandis even attempted to create a dance based on the movements of a badminton player. None of these dances makes use of speech, although some end with choral singing in Balinese on the benefits of mutual aid and co-operation.

The vocabulary of movement employed in these programmatic dances is entirely new and, growing out of the direct observation of nature, is quite realistic. For the first time in hundreds of years, Balinese choreographers were prompted to look for sources beyond their traditional heritage. The dances, however, are firmly set to the musical accompaniment provided by the *gamelan gong kebyar*, the newest and most brilliant (and possibly the loudest) of the orchestral ensembles of Bali. In good Kebyar style, the compositions feature complicated patterns of rhythmic accents and quick cadences in which the gamelan and the dancers come to sudden, simultaneous, halts.

Kebyar style here is overlaid on movement quite foreign to the traditional Balinese dance vocabulary, and it can therefore be seen for what it is: a mode of embellishment growing out of a set of rhythmic ideas. The basic pattern might be spoken as 'Tut cheng cheng, tut cheng!' Like flamboyant art all over the world, Kebyar's highly ornamented surfaces are best supported by relatively simple structures.

Panyembrama

This purely secular composition, meaning 'Greeting', was created in 1967 by I Gusti Gedé Raka, a well-known Legong teacher from Saba village, Gianyar Province. Based on the sacred Rejang dance, it took its present form after some reworking by I Wayan Beratha in 1970. The piece, which is always performed first in a dance programme, is a group work, in modern Kebyar style, for five female dancers. The dancers, who wear an elaborate new creation based on the simpler Rejang costume, carry bowls of flower petals and burning sticks of incense. Developed from rites to honour the visiting gods, the piece has been adapted to show honour to the guests at a performance. At the conclusion of the dance, the young women throw flower petals toward the audience.

Recently, Panyembrama has come to be regularly performed at Ngurah Rai Airport when distinguished guests from Jakarta or foreign dignitaries arrive. As many as thirty dancers may take part. Certain villages near the airport have organized groups for hire by travel agents, hotels, or the government.

Other new variants of the 'Welcoming Dance' have also been developed. One of them, Puspawresti (Rain Flowers), employs a group of young men and young women whose movements are derived from Rejang and Baris Gedé. It is performed, like Panyembrama, to welcome distinguished guests, and often serves as the opening number in a Prembon revue. It was composed in 1981 by I Wayan Dibia, with music by I Nyoman Windha, on the occasion of a visit by the Governor of Bali to Singapadu village. Like Panyembrama, Puspawresti concludes with the dancers strewing flower petals toward the audience as a gesture of respect.

Another welcoming dance, called Sekar Jagat (Flower of the World), was composed in 1993 by Ni Luh Swasthi Wijaya, based on the sacred Rejang performed in the Bali Aga village of Tenganan (Colour Plate 29). The costume is exceptionally colourful, being made of the special woven cloth of Tenganan, and the head-dresses, which are based on the traditional golden helmets, are prominent. The seven female dancers carry elaborate bowls of offerings and dance slowly and elegantly as they proceed through the routine, conveying a more solemn atmosphere than that created by the other dances of this type. The music was again composed by Windha, based on the sacred ritual music of Tenganan.

In recent years, it has become common for women who have received dance training to perform Panyembrama in the context of a village Odalan, where once Mendet or Gabor might have been done. This indicates a movement from the secular toward the sacred, as a *bali-balihan* genre becomes a *wali* one. The same process can be seen with the other welcoming dances.

Sendratari

In 1962, a team of Balinese artists connected with the government high school for the performing arts, Sekolah Menengah Kesenian Indonesia, or SMKI, led by I Wayan Beratha, one of Bali's foremost choreographers and composers, created a new dance composition in which the Kebyar style was employed for the presentation of a lengthy dance-drama (Plate 25). The drama was based on a popular Balinese story, *Jayaprana*, which was told in its entirety by a large company of student dancers through gesture and

135

25 Composer and choreographer
I Wayan Beratha. (STSI documentation;
courtesy Nik Wheeler)

pantomime, ornamented with Kebyar embellishments. Although no words were necessary for an understanding of the dance-drama, educated Balinese were treated to a narrative in Kawi and Balinese provided by the *juru tandak* from his place in the gamelan. The new form was called Sendratari (modern dance-drama) Jayaprana (from the name of the story). Audiences were very enthusiastic, both at the school where it was first performed, and later in villages all over Bali.

In 1965, the SMKI group, again led by Beratha, produced another dance-drama of the same type, this time based on the *Ramayana*, which met with even greater success (Colour Plate 30). The creators of the genre were much influenced by the success of the Javanese Ramayana Ballet, first shown at Prambanan in Central Java in 1961. That performance had been initiated, with government support, to provide a cultural entertainment intelligible to foreigners as well as to Indonesians from all over the Republic. Balinese Sendratari was thus devised to meet the same needs, but took on an independent life among the local audience as villages began to establish Sendratari Ramayana groups of their own to perform as *bali-balihan*, either in connection with their own village Odalan, or for hire to other villages, or even for tourist audiences at hotels and elsewhere.

By 1978 seven Balinese classics had been adapted for presentation in the Sendratari mode by faculty members at SMKI working under the artistic leadership of Beratha. These formed the prototypes for village performances of Ramayana, influenced, no

136

doubt, by the fact that all of the teachers who brought the genre into the villages were alumni of the school. Just as the court culture of the Hindu-Balinese rulers of the eighteenth and nineteenth centuries served to standardize Balinese culture, government-sponsored schools, research teams, and creative projects now tend to exert a unifying influence across the island.

The early Sendratari performances were all conceived for an 'end stage', similar to a Western proscenium stage, which is the theatre form on the former SMKI campus. In the villages, alternative arrangements had to be made. Most often performances are given in the *bale banjar* or in a cock-fighting arena in the *jaba* area of the temple. This disposition of the stage space has led to the use of many Western principles of stage composition at the expense of some of the intimacy generated by the three-sided *kalangan*.

The development of Sendratari was given an impetus by the establishment of the annual Bali Arts Festival, in 1979. Each year, four new productions are mounted in a large thrust-stage arena theatre, two by each of the government schools of the arts—SMKI (which is high school level) and STSI (which is an undergraduate institution). These presentations have been enormously popular with the Balinese public. Not only does every performance play to a packed house, but they have been disseminated by radio and television to every corner of the island.

As in the programmatic dances, in Sendratari the Kebyar style of ornamentation is applied over a simple foundation of panto-mimic story-telling, so that even young children can follow the narrative. At the same time, the difficult accents and flourishes of the Kebyar style provide interest and pleasure for the connoisseur of pure dance. The musical structure brings together compositions from a number of different Balinese dance traditions into a clever anthology, several hours long, unified by its stylistic treatment. In good Balinese tradition, the play includes audience scenes, comedy, fight sequences, love scenes, scenes of weeping and lament, elaborate processional entrances, movement by large groups of dancers, and all the spectacular effects that can be mustered.

Since the inception of the Bali Arts Festival, Sendratari has changed in response to popular demand. Perhaps the most significant innovation is that the *dalang sendratari* has assumed a more important role in the show. Sitting at the side with his assistants and chorus of singers, he provides the complete text for the evening, doing all the voices, guiding the actors with his interjections, and elaborating on the verbal content of the story. The tourist audience has receded in importance as the verbal dimension has expanded, since the tourist cannot understand the dialogue, which makes use of Kawi, Balinese, Indonesian, and even a few words of English and other foreign languages.

Although the largest theatre in the Wredi Budaya Arts Centre is equipped with electric lighting, the technical apparatus available on the big stage is still relatively unsophisticated. Nevertheless, lighting effects are attempted and the voices of the *dalang* and his assistants electrically amplified. Much emphasis has been placed on the costuming, and many new costumes have been created by such artists as Ni Luh Swasthi Wijaya. Giant effigies, carts, chariots, fantastic animals, and other impressive properties have become essential to the performance, although some consider these elements unnecessary and vulgar.

The size of the giant Arts Centre thrust stage has also encouraged the dancers to enlarge and exaggerate their movements, hoping to better communicate with the large crowd. Delicate eye movements and trembling hand gestures do not 'read' well from a distance. Consequently, the dancing in these mega-spectacles is less refined than is the norm in a traditional *kalangan*, where the spectators are very close to the action. In terms of the dance itself, the emphasis in Sendratari has shifted to the choreographic patterns, the co-ordination of group effects, and expressive tableaux.

The musical accompaniment has also changed. The former *gamelan gong kebyar* has been supplemented with a seven-tone *gamelan semar pegulingan*, making possible a greater variety of moods and tonalities during the performance. Other instruments, such as the *kulkul* (slit drum) and *okokan* (cow bells), have been introduced into particular performances. The result is a much larger orchestra. The entire performing group—cast, musicians, and crew—may number 200.

Sendratari-based Dances

An important consequence of the Sendratari creations has been the detachment from them of solo and group numbers that can be performed outside the context of the dance-drama. In the style of the Prembon revue discussed above, these *tari lepas* (free dances) can be presented alongside other, older forms in the context of an Odalan or elsewhere.

Manuk Rawa

The first *tari lepas* to make a great impression was Manuk Rawa (Waterbird), created in 1981 by I Wayan Dibia as part of a Mahabharata Sendratari called Balé Gala-gala, (House of Lacquer). The dance presents a flock of waterbirds who live peacefully and freely in a pond in the mountain forest. In the dance, movements from the traditional Balinese movement lexicon have been combined with movements drawn from a dance depicting peacocks that the choreographer observed in West Java. Music for *gamelan gong kebyar* was composed by I Wayan Beratha, and the costume devised by Dibia.

Kijang Kencana

Kijang Kencana (Shining Deer) was composed in 1983 by I Gusti Agung Nugrah Supartha, former head of SMKI. The dance depicts the cheerful life of a herd of deer in the forest. It was created as part of a revised Sendratari Ramayana, to show that portion of the story when Rama is deceived by Marica, who transforms herself into a deer in order to lead Rama away from Dewi Sita whom Rawana wishes to abduct. The dance as a *tari lepas* has no dramatic content, however. It is highly energetic and features a distinctive innovation—leaping—hitherto rarely seen in Balinese dance. The music was composed by Beratha and the vocal music provided by I Gusti Bagus Arsaja. The costume is distinguished by an antlered head-dress and yellow blouse and trousers (Colour Plate 31).

Belibis

This composition—the Wild Duck Dance—portrays the behaviour of a flock of wild ducks in their natural surroundings, stressing the beauty and grace of their movements (Colour Plate 32). It was composed for the Sendratari Angling Dharma in 1984 by Ni Luh Swasthi Wijaya of the STSI faculty. The story tells of a king who has been changed into a duck, cursed by his three wives for spying on them when they have practised black magic. He is joined by other ducks, and in this dance (which like Kijang Kencana and Manuk Rawa lacks a narrative element) he plays joyfully with the others. Five to seven female dancers take part, each wearing a pink and white costume with white wings. Belibis has become quite popular in Indonesia and is part of the standard repertoire at the Presidential Palace in Jakarta. The music was composed by I Nyoman Windha.

Cendrawasih

The three previous dances, created as part of a Sendratari, have become detached from the original drama and attained a life outside that context. Cendrawasih is an example of a contrary movement. In this case, the dance originally choreographed by Ni Luh Swasthi Wijaya as a duet for presentation at the Walter Spies Festival, held at the Bali Arts Centre in 1988, became the basis for a large-scale, full-length, semi-dramatic work presented at the Nusa Dua Convention Hall to audiences composed mainly of tourists and other foreign visitors.

The duet depicts the courtship of two Birds of Paradise (probably the best-known symbol of Indonesia's state of Irian Jaya, which occupies the western half of New Guinea.) As a subject for Balinese dance, it thus reaches outside Bali for material and reflects the growing international outlook and cosmopolitan sophistication of the Balinese creative teams. The Cendrawasih itself, well-known for its beautiful plumage, is also called 'the dancing bird'. Known to the Balinese as the *manuk déwata* (bird of the gods), a preserved specimen of the species is commonly carried in cremation processions as a symbolic guide to lead the human soul up to heaven. The dance duet reveals the beauty and grace of the birds' movements and may be seen as a modern rendering of the *keker–kiuh* motif found in the Berutuk rite in Trunyan.

The full-length version that grew from this duet is called 'Apoda-poda', which is a legendary story about how the Cendrawasih acquired its beautiful feathers. His name is Logohu, and he feels very jealous of the other birds of the forest because they have beautiful coloured feathers, while he only has black ones like a crow. Accordingly, he requests the gods of the forest for more colourful ones. His request is granted, but he is told to choose the colour he wishes to wear. Therefore, he has to travel around to search for the correct choice. Confused by the profusion of colours available, he returns to the gods and requests that he be made multicoloured. This proves acceptable, but he soon learns that people are eager to catch and kill him to get his feathers. Although his life is more colourful, it is much less secure. Moreover, his wife is distressed by the change in his appearance and weeps. The finale displays a group of eight dancers whose costumes turn from black to a veritable rainbow of bright hues. Hunters come and chase them away. Beneath the story there is a plea for conservation of Indonesia's wildlife species, many of which are under threat of extinction.

When the Cendrawasih was created, the colours were chosen, not by searching in the forest, but by going to the different islands of Indonesia. The performance thus became an expression of unity in diversity—'bhineka tunggal ika, tan hana dharma mangrwa'—as the national motto puts it, of the Indonesian peoples. It was presented for a Convention of Pacific Area Travel Agents and the World Tourism Organization Conference in 1990.

Cendrawasih has subsequently been followed by similar works, such as 'Beautiful Indonesia', in which Dewi Sri, the rice goddess, travels around the whole of Indonesia teaching people how to cultivate rice. Here, too, is an element celebrating national unity. These dance programmes celebrating Indonesian identity are usually given in a large indoor room at the Nusa Dua resort complex with an end stage decorated in keeping with the theme of the convention being held. Stage design blends with interior decoration and the practical requisites of the particular occasion. Dancers adjust their choreography to suit the available electronic and other facilities.

The most important feature of the choreography is that the individual numbers presented have been drawn from the dance traditions of the different areas represented. Thus, Kalimantan was brought into Cendrawasih by way of a dance based on the Topeng Hudoq, a masked dance form of that area. Central Java was represented by more classical Javanese court dance sources, and Sulawesi by the Pakarena dance. In all cases, the Balinese choreographer reworked the 'borrowed' source materials and unified them within a recognizably Balinese dance style. Dance elements from China, Korea, India, Japan, and the West have similarly come into various Balinese modern dance creations, as their makers have increasingly had experience and training outside Bali.

With Cendrawasih, we near the end of our discussion of dances which have emerged thus far in the Kebyar style. We have seen that Kebyar developed from Legong, and that it gave rise to many forms of modern composition. It should be noticed as well that Kebyar's influence also extended backward, affecting its sources. In 1932, Ida Bagus Boda, of Kaliungu, Badung Province, re-choreographed the *pengawit* section of the Legong in a style heavily influenced by Kebyar. Subsequently, the body of the dance was also elaborated. These changes were adopted quickly everywhere.

Legong itself has influenced its own sources. The Sang Hyang Dedari dancers of Bona village, Gianyar Province, now dress in the complete Legong costume complete with golden aprons and head-dresses rather than the traditional simple white cloth costume. At the conclusion of their 'tour' in trance around the village, the little dancers of Bona stay outside the temple and give a complete performance. The pattern of interrelations among the genres becomes ever more complex with time, because new creation in Bali, especially in Balinese music and dance, arises very often from the transposition of the materials from one genre into the medium of another.

New Creations

As the artists of Bali, and especially the faculty members of the government-sponsored arts schools, have travelled abroad, they have become increasingly aware of the great body of contemporary and avant-garde work done by their counterparts in other countries. Just as elements from the traditional acrobatic Chinese Lion Dance have been recontextualized in a Sendratari performance, so too the artists have been exposed to the work of modern dancers, composers, performance artists, and directors while abroad. And with the sponsorship of STSI and of the Walter Spies Foundation, programmes of Balinese contemporary work have been presented, featuring new compositions in several media.

'Kosong', (Empty), a multifaceted work by I Ketut Gedé Asnawa, involves a group of musicians and dancers who perform contemporary music using stones, plates, cymbals, and other unlikely instruments. They also sing *kidung*. The theme is taken from the Balinese New Year celebration, Hari Nyepi. The performers mime such activities as chopping meat, decorating the houseyard, marching in procession with musical instruments,

141

carrying the large effigies, and coming suddenly to the abrupt silence of Nyepi, when the entire island becomes quiet and public areas are deserted.

Another new composition, made by the young choreographer, I Ketut Suteja, in 1993, is 'Ngelawang'. The title refers to the practice alluded to in Chapter 6 in which groups of young men go 'on the road' with the village Barong mask. Here, no Barong is employed, and the travelling is done by people. The vocabulary of movement owes much to modern Western dance, featuring crawling, jumping, leaping, and other elements alien to the Balinese dance tradition. Here, a more cosmopolitan—even global—approach is apparent. The dance is abstract in quality, but suggests a journey into the forest, graveyard, and strange villages. Various moods—anger, love, sadness, etc.—follow upon one another. The work is accompanied by musicians who play such instruments as flutes, drums, gongs, even a violin and guitar, individually rather than as an ensemble. This creation has become a model in Bali for contemporary dance composition. Western modern dance technique has been taught at STSI since 1973 in classes devoted to improvisation, technique, and composition, and the effects of that curriculum are being revealed in works like 'Ngelawang'.

In conclusion, mention must be made of the numerous discotheques that have sprung up in beachside areas like Kuta and Sanur, centres of tourist accommodation. Here, visitors from all over the world—as well as young Western-oriented Balinese—dance the latest international rock and disco crazes. The resemblance of the nightly activities in these locations at the *kelod* extreme of the island to the dancing described in the old *Calonarang* is not too far-fetched:

Gandi danced while jumping up and down, and her hair hung to one side. Her eyes were red as a mangosteen. Lende danced on tiptoe. Her face glowed like fire and her hair hung loose. Woksirsa danced pecking like a chicken while staring blankly. Her hair was loose and she was naked. Mahisawadana danced hopping on one foot. Then she turned upside-down and stuck out her tongue, licking. Her hands clutched as if to capture her prey.

1. Rhodius and Darling (1980).

2. Hanna (1976: xi–xiii, 92–128). See also Picard (1992).

3. Many guidebooks have been published about Bali. Some of them seem more intended for display on a coffee-table than for use by travellers, while others are dense reference works, crowded with sometimes obsolete information. Dalton (n.d.) is frequently updated. We can also recommend Oey (1991), with its many articles by noted experts. Eiseman (1990), though strictly speaking not a guidebook, is a fascinating compendium of lore about the island, with much of interest about Balinese dance.

4. Rhodius and Darling (1980: 37).

5. For an interesting analysis of Kecak, see McKean (1979).

6. 'Proyek Pemeliharan dan Pengambungan Kebudayaan Daerah Bali' (1971) is the report issued at the conclusion of this pivotal seminar.

Glossary

Abbreviations

C = Costume element.

D = Choreographic element. Only a few of the more than 800 named gestures, poses, transitional movements, and locomotive movements are listed.

G = Genre.

L = Literary source or other written work.

M = Musical term.

R = Role or character.

S = Term applying to the stage or properties.

Abuang Kalah (G)	Old social dance ritual performed in Tenganan, a Bali Aga village.
Adar (G)	Joged dance of the Tabanan region, now virtually extinct.
adat	Custom or tradition.
agem (D)	Pose or basic standing position. There are various types.
agung	Great or large.
alus	Refined, soft, or delicate.
ampok (C)	Carved and gilded waistband, part of certain female costumes.
Anggada (R)	High-ranking officer in the monkey army in the *Ramayana*.
angkeb bulet (C)	Decorative cloth panel, worn at the back.
angsel (D & M)	Abrupt rhythmic pattern of syncopated accents executed simultaneously by dancer and orchestra, culminating in a sudden pause which suspends music and dance at a definite point in the musical cycle.
Anoman (R)	The white monkey in the *Ramayana*. Able to fly, he is very popular with Balinese children.
anteng (C)	Type of sash.
arak	Spirits distilled from rice wine.
Arja (G)	'Balinese opera', formerly very popular but now in decline.
Arjuna Wiwaha (L)	Well-known classic of Old Javanese literature, suggested by an episode in the Indian *Mahabharata*. It is a popular subject in the shadow theatre and the dance-drama.
arya-arya (R)	Four dancers who represent the common soldiers in the army of Prince Panji in Gambuh.
awiran (C)	Apron simulating monkey fur, worn in Wayang Wong.
Babad (L)	Balinese historical/genealogical chronicles, ordinarily devoted to a single lineage. These accounts form the basis for the Topeng repertoire.
Babad Blahbatuh (L)	Chronicle of the Jelantik family of Blahbatuh.
Babad Dalem (L)	Chronicle of the family of the Kings of Klungkung, nominally the highest-ranking Balinese principality in the pre-colonial era.
Babad Dalem Sukawati (L)	Chronicle of the Princes of Sukawati.
babi guling	Roast suckling pig, a Balinese delicacy.
baju (C)	Jacket.
balé	Hall or pavilion.

143

balé agung	Great hall or council chamber, seat of civic power in Bali Aga villages.
balé banjar	Ward association hall.
Bali Aga	People considered by the Balinese to be the original inhabitants of the island. Living in certain more or less remote villages, Bali Aga people differ from their more 'Javanized' neighbours with respect to burial practices, composition of the priesthood, calendar, etc.
balian	Traditional healer, ritual expert, sometimes a spirit medium.
bali-balihan	Dance performances presented purely for the entertainment of the audience.
Bali kasar	Low Balinese, the vulgar vernacular.
Banaspati Raja (R)	'King of the Woods', a title given to the Barong Ket.
bancih	Neuter or bisexual. In the dance, the term refers to modern Kebyar compositions which may be performed by either male or female dancers.
bandrangan (S)	Decorative lance which serves as part of the furnishings of the kalangan.
banjar	Ward of a village or larger settlement.
bapang (C & M)	Decorative neckband or collar. Also the title of a composition used to accompany dancing by the comic characters.
Baris (G)	Group of warrior dances for males, based on manoeuvres derived from military drill. In most varieties, a distinctive pointed helmet is an essential part of the costume. Modern solo Baris is a set piece for the young male dancer, often the first dance he will learn.
Baris Dadap (G)	In this variety, the dancers carry boat-shaped shields.
Baris Gedé (G)	'Great Baris'. Generic term for the sacred Baris dances performed in groups.
Baris Melampahan (G)	Secular variety of Baris in which a drama is presented with one or more Baris dancers in the leading roles.
Baris Pendet (G)	In this variety, the dancers carry ritual vessels filled with flower petals.
Baris Tamiang (G)	In this variety, the performers carry shields provided with spikes in the middle.
Baris Tumbak (G)	In this variety, the dancers carry lances.
Barong (G)	General term for a mask representing an animal or supernatural being. Masks of this type have costume elements attached and cover at least the head and shoulders of the bearer. Often they are animated by two dancers, one behind the other.
Barong Asu (G)	Barong in the form of a giant dog.
Barong Bangkal (G)	Barong in the form of a wild boar.
Barong Kedingkling (G)	Old *wali* form associated with Wayang Wong. The masks represent monkeys and are worn by male performers.
Barong Keket (G)	Also known as Barong Ket. The best known of the Balinese Barong types, resembling a dragon-like lion.
Barong Landung (G)	A kind of giant effigy figure 3-metres tall, representing a human character. Each mask is operated by a single performer. A complete group of Barong Landung involves five characters, who on some occasions act out a little play.
Barong Lembu (G)	Barong in the form of a cow.
Barong Machan (G)	Barong in the form of a tiger.
Basur (L)	Old Balinese tale about a sorcerer; it is the source for a dance-drama similar to the Calonarang play. The Rangda mask is used to represent the central character when he is at the height of his magical powers.
batel (M)	Cyclical musical piece, played to accompany battle scenes and other scenes of vigorous action.
batel gender wayang (M)	Musical ensemble used to accompany Wayang Wong and certain other genres of dance and drama. It consists of a quartet of *gender wayang* metallophones, supplemented with percussion and gongs.
bayu	Action.
bebali	Category of semi-sacred or ceremonial dances.
Bebali Sidha Karya (L)	Rules and lore of the Topeng Pajegan dancer.
bebonangan (M)	Ensemble like a marching band, used to accompany processions.

144

belas-belasan	Going in all directions.
Belibis (G)	Dance of the wild ducks, a modern creation.
bendesa (R)	Village headman, a character in Topeng and other dance-drama.
Berutuk (G)	Masked dance ritual performed in Trunyan village.
bondres (R)	Any of a number of comic and eccentric characters, usually belonging to the lowest caste.
brahmana	The highest-ranked or priestly caste.
Bratayuda (L)	Poem in Old Javanese dating from the twelfth century. It recounts the story of the great final war between the Pandawas and the Kurawas from the *Mahabharata* epic. The poem is the source of episodes represented in Parwa dance-drama, the shadow theatre, and Arja.
brem	Rice wine.
buta	Demonic spirit.
Cak (G)	'Monkey dance', a popular type of tourist performance incorporating a much enlarged *cak* group. (M) the male chorus which provides *cak* accompaniment for some of the exorcistic Sang Hyang dances.
Cakapung (G)	All-male improvisatory dancing and poetry reading party popular in Karangasem Province.
Calonarang (L)	Old Javanese prose work, telling the story of the Widow of Girah, a witch, who is defeated by the great sage, Empu Bharadah; a second section tells of a visit by the sage to Bali, which he reached by crossing the ocean while riding on a leaf. The first section provides the basis for Wayang Calonarang and Calonarang dance-drama. (R) the name of the witch in the dance-drama of the same name. See also Matah Gedé and Rangda.
candi bentar (S)	Open archway in the temple wall, used by dancers as a principal entrance or exit. Gateways of this type are also found on other buildings. The design is made to look as if the two sides of the gateway had been split down the middle.
capung mandus (D)	Movement imitative of a dragonfly playing on the water.
caru	Offering placed on the ground to placate demons.
Cendrawasih (G)	Dance of the Bird of Paradise, a modern creation with a national theme.
Cokorda	Feudal title applied to the highest-ranking members of the Ksatrya caste. The Cokorda was the reigning monarch.
condong (R)	The maidservant, a type character resembling the soubrette or pert maid of Western tradition. She interprets the Kawi and High Balinese of her mistress in Gambuh and many other genres.
daag (R)	Formerly the master of ceremonies at the Janger performance. This figure has been used as the basis for a modern dance composition by I Wayan Dibia of STSI.
dadap	Shrub with powerful symbolic and medicinal qualities.
Dadap (G)	Early form of Arja.
dalang	Shadow puppeteer. A literary expert, the *dalang* often serves as dramaturge and choreographer.
dalang sendratari	Narrator at the Sendratari performance. Like the shadow puppeteer, he provides voices for the mute dancers from his place near the orchestra.
dalem	Deep, inner, majestic.
Dalem (R)	The King, a highly refined character, in Topeng.
dedari (R)	From the Sanskrit *vidyadhari*, the heavenly nymphs of Hindu mythology. Synonymous with *widyadari*.
Delem (R)	Chief *penasar* to the antagonist party in Wayang Kulit, Wayang Wong, and Parwa. Pompous and ridiculous, Delem (also called Melem) is very popular with the audience.
Demang (R)	Prince Panji's Prime Minister and Commander of the Armed Forces in Gambuh.
desa	Village.

145

desa adat	Traditional village government.
dewa, dewi	God, goddess.
Déwagung	Title for the highest ranking king.
Dharma Sangging (L)	Manuscript containing the lore, prayers, rituals, and special prescriptions applying to a maker of sacred masks.
Drama Gong (G)	Modern theatrical form, created in 1965 by Anak Agung Gedé Raka Payadnya, with spoken dialogue and very little dancing. It is a descendent of Stambul and depicts stories based on the Arja repertoire.
dukun	Folk doctor, sometimes a magician.
dusang (R)	Person who portrays the corpse of one of the Widow's victims in the Calonarang play.
Gabor (G)	Ritual dance for females in which offerings are presented.
Galuh (R)	The heroine in Arja.
Galungan	Major Balinese holiday held every 210 days and lasting for ten days. It is the occasion for countless ceremonies and performances all over the island.
Gambuh (G)	'Expert', the oldest surviving form of dance-drama. Belonging to the *bebali* group, it is considered to be the source of all subsequent dramatic dance.
gambuh suling (M)	Long end-blown flute which is played with a difficult circular breathing technique. It is the main instrument in the *gamelan gambuh*.
gamelan (M)	Any Balinese orchestral ensemble which includes rhythmic and punctuating instruments. There are many different types.
gamelan batel (M)	See *batel gender wayang*.
gamelan gambuh (M)	Ensemble which accompanies the Gambuh dance-drama. It consists of four *gambuh suling*, plus drums, other percussion instruments, *rebab* and gongs.
gamelan gong (M)	Traditional large orchestral ensemble, used to accompany Topeng and other dance genres. There are a number of different types, distinguished by instrumentation and the tuning system.
gamelan gong gedé (M)	The largest of the pre-twentieth century gamelan ensembles, now very rarely found as most were melted down to make *gamelan gong kebyar* sets.
gamelan gong kebyar (M)	Large modern instrumental ensemble, used to accompany the Kebyar genres and Sendratari, as well as for purely musical compositions.
gamelan legong (M)	See *gamelan semar pegulingan*.
gamelan pelegongan (M)	See *gamelan semar pegulingan*.
gamelan rindik (M)	Bamboo xylophone ensemble, accompanying Joged Gudegan.
gamelan semar pegulingan (M)	This traditional orchestral ensemble, once reserved for the nobility, is associated with amorous dalliance. It accompanies certain Joged and Gandrung dances, as well as Legong. In recent years, it has been brought into the ensemble accompanying Sendratari, where it plays in alternation with a *gamelan gong kebyar*.
Gandrung (G)	Dance of the Joged group, formerly performed by young teenaged boys. Now rare.
Gebyog (G)	Social dance related to Joged, formerly performed improvisationally during the rice harvest.
gedé	Large, great.
gelangkana (C)	Wristband.
gelatik nguwut papah (D)	Movement imitative of a bird jumping sideways on a tree branch.
gelung (C)	Head-dress. There are many types. Often *gelung* have or acquire sacral qualities, especially in unmasked genres like Gambuh.
gelungan Joged (C)	Special head-dress formerly worn by Joged dancers.
gender wayang (M)	Metallophone consisting of ten bronze keys suspended over resonating bamboo tubes. They are played in pairs, with a difficult two-handed technique.
gender wayang quartet (M)	Small instrumental ensemble used to accompany Wayang Kulit. It is comprised of four *gender wayang* played in two pairs. The musical parts interlock in complex syncopation.

146

genggong (M)	Instrument resembling a Jew's harp played singly or in groups.
Godogan (G)	Balinese folk-tale that has been made into a modern dance-drama that is popular with tourists. The story is a variant of the tale of the Princess who marries a frog.
grinsing (C)	Special handwoven fabric made in Tenganan Pagrinsingan.
Hari Nyepi	Balinese New Year holiday.
ibing	Male dancer, most often an amateur, who comes up from the audience to dance with a *joged*.
idep	Thought, belief.
igel	dance
igel ngugal	Section of a scene in a dance-drama in which an important character is introduced. It may be long or short in duration, depending on the character and the place of the scene in the structure of the drama as a whole. After the *igel ngugal*, the dramatic action may begin.
igel pajeng (D)	Section of a dance composition during which the performer dances with an umbrella.
igel sambir (D)	Section of a dance in which movement involving the *sambir* is featured.
jaba	Outside the temple's third or outer courtyard, the lowest caste, to which the great majority of the Balinese people belong.
jaba tengah	The temple's second or middle courtyard, ante-room to the *jeroan*.
jalér (C)	White trousers, part of the male costume.
Janger (G)	Twentieth-century genre in which elements from many sources are combined. Circus stunts, question and answer singing, and military drill are characteristic.
Jauk (G)	Fifteen-minute solo performed by a *jauk* dancer.
jauk (R)	Masked dancer depicting a demonic male character, in which a particular stupa-shaped conical helmet is worn.
Jayaprana (L)	Balinese romantic story, a popular subject for Sendratari.
jeroan	Sacred innermost courtyard of a Balinese temple.
Jero Gedé (R)	'Big Man', the father in Barong Landung.
Jero Luh (R)	The mother in Barong Landung, wife of Jero Gedé.
Joged (G)	Group of dances in which the performers dance sequentially with men from the audience (*ibing*) who improvise flirtatiously.
Joged Bumbung (G)	Joged genre, now again popular after a period of decline, accompanied by an ensemble made up of bamboo (*bumbung*) xylophones.
Joged Gudegan (G)	Old Joged genre, also known as Joged Pingitan, Joged Gandangan, or Joged Tongkohan.
joged tongkohan	A public dancing girl, common in the nineteenth century. The term has passed out of use. Another name for *ronggeng*.
juru tandak (M)	Principal male singer who sits in the gamelan and provides sung narration for the dancers in Legong. Formerly, this was also his role in Sendratari. I Nyoman Sumandhi of SMKI became famous for his singing in this capacity in Sendratari Jayaprana and Sendratari Ramayana. But since the advent of the Bali Arts Festival, much of the role of the *juru tandak* has been superceded by the *dalang sendratari*.
kade-kadehan (R)	Heralds in the court of Prabu in Gambuh.
kain batik (C)	Batik cloth or sarong.
kain perada (C)	Wrap-around skirt made of gilded cloth, part of the basic female costume.
kain poleng (C)	Chequered cloth used for flags, banners, and various costume pieces. Thought to have beneficial magical properties.
kaja	Direction toward the north; high, holy.
Kajeng Kliwon	Day in the Balinese calendar when offerings to demons are set out.
kakan-kakan (R)	Female retainers attending Putri in Gambuh.
kakawin (L)	Poem in the Old Javanese language, composed according to Sanskrit metrical principles. Quotations from the most venerated kakawin, like the *Ramayana*

147

	and *Arjuna Wiwaha*, are used as lyrics by dancers who sing.
kalangan (S)	Traditional Balinese arena stage.
kancut (C)	Folded cloth panel that hangs down in front of the male costume.
Kartala (R)	Name of the younger attendant in Arja and Topeng. Also known as *penasar cenikan*.
kasar	Coarse, vulgar, rough.
Kawi	A living, if restricted, language used on Bali today for ceremonies and in the theatre. It is based on Old Javanese.
kebaya (C)	Traditional Indonesian blouse for women.
Kebyar (G)	'Lightning', the popular modern Balinese style of music and dance.
Kebyar Bebancihan (G)	Neutered Kebyar, or dances in Kebyar style performed by women.
Kebyar Duduk (G)	'Seated Lightning', a highly virtuosic dance of the Kebyar group created by I Mario of Tabanan in the 1920s. The male soloist performs in a squatting position, plays the old-fashioned *trompong* instrument, and flirts with the drummer.
Kebyar Legong (G)	Early twentieth-century dance for two women in Kebyar style.
Kebyar Trompong (G)	A synonym for Kebyar Duduk.
kecak	Male semi-chorus in Janger.
Kecak (G)	Another name for the Cak dance.
kedingkling	Hopping.
keker	Forest cock, a variety of pheasant, complement to the *kiuh*.
kelod	Direction toward the south; low and demonic.
kendang (M)	Drum.
kepeng	Chinese coin with a hole in the centre, once the basic unit of Balinese currency.
keras	Strong, rough, forceful.
kerawuhan	In a state of possession or trance.
kidang rebut muring (D)	Movement imitative of a deer pestered by biting flies.
kidung (L)	Poem or scriptural song in Old Javanese following Indonesian metrical principles. Also (M) a style of singing associated with such texts.
Kijang Kencana (G)	Dance of the shining deer, a modern creation.
kiuh	Forest hen, complement to the *keker*.
kris	Indonesian dagger, often with a carved handle.
ksatrya	Knightly caste, second in rank to the *brahmana*. From this group, Bali's feudal rulers were drawn.
kulkul (M)	Large wooden slit drum, found in every *banjar*, which serves as an alarm, etc.
Kuningan	Major Balinese holiday falling ten days after Galungan.
lamak (C)	Decorative apron, part of the female costume.
langsé (S)	Decoratively painted front curtain.
Legong (G)	Classical female dance form, semi-dramatic in nature, performed by two or three young girls. Formerly only preadolescent girls were permitted to dance, but in recent years the age limit has been lifted.
Leko (G)	Type of Joged dance.
leyak	Sorcerers and their apprentices as transformed terrifying creatures (e.g. goat, pig, monkey or even Rangda) who spread pestilence.
Limbur (R)	Comic matron, a popular stock character in Arja.
lontar	Balinese palm-leaf manuscript.
mabasan	Ceremonial reading aloud (i.e. chanting) and interpretation of the Balinese literary classics.
Mabuang (G)	Dance ceremony in Trunyan.
Mahabharata (L)	Indian epic poem, source for much of the Balinese dramatic repertoire, known in Bali principally through the medium of Old Javanese works such as the prose *parwa*, the *Bratayuda* poem, and adaptations such as *Arjuna Wiwaha*.
Malat (L)	Old Indonesian epic poem, the source of the Panji stories as they are represented in Gambuh, Legong, and Arja.

manis	Sweet, refined, gentle.
manuk déwata	Bird of the gods, the Bird of Paradise.
Manuk Rawa (G)	Dance of the waterbird, a Kebyar dance choreographed by I Wayan Dibia.
Margapati (G)	Dance belonging to the Kebyar group in which a character study of a young man is depicted.
Matah Gedé (R)	'The Great Uncooked One', a name applied to the Widow of Girah in the Calonarang play, as she appears before transforming into Rangda.
medagang	'Selling', the process of bargaining employed in former times by certain Joged, Gandrung, and Penyeroan dancers.
Melem (R)	A synonym for Delem.
Mendet (G)	Ritual dance, counterpart to Gabor, performed by priests and other male members of the temple congregation.
mengigel	To dance.
Merdah (R)	Another name for Wredah.
mudra (D)	Sacred hand poses and gestures employed by priests in their rituals and in certain dances.
mungkah lawang (D)	Movement involved in opening the front curtain (*langsé*) in order for a dancer to make his or her entrance. When no curtain is present, the gesture symbolizes that process.
nadab gelung (D)	Touching the head-dress with a particular gesture.
nadi	To enter a state of trance (from *dadi*, 'to become').
Nandir (G)	Classical dance genre, similar to Legong, formerly performed by young boys.
ngelawang	To go 'on the road' with the Barong, done by groups of young men at the time of the Galungan holiday.
ngelayak (D)	Bending movement, imitative of a tree bowing under the weight of many flowers.
ngibing	To dance as an *ibing*.
ngigel	To dance.
ngurek	To attempt to stab oneself while in a possessed state.
Odalan	Temple festival, occurring every 210 days.
okokan	Cow bell.
Oleg Tumulilingan (G)	'Bumble-bees', a duet in Kebyar style by I Mario.
oncér (C)	Long sash, worn by the female dancer in Tumulilingan.
onying	Another name for *ngurek*.
padmasana	Stone shrine for the highest gods.
pajegan	'The whole thing', refers to the Topeng performance in which the principal dancer performs all the roles.
Pandung (R)	The villainous Prime Minister in Calonarang.
pangkat	Formal exit or departure sequence.
Panji (R)	Refined hero in Gambuh.
Panji Semirang (G)	Kebyar dance portraying Panji's beloved Candra Kirana, the refined heroine of the *Malat*.
pantun	Indonesian song style, in which semi-choruses sing back and forth in question and answer format.
Panyembrama (G)	Modern dance composition, based on temple dances, now used to welcome distinguished guests and to open a concert.
parekan (R)	Servants, retainers.
partapukan	Old Javanese for masked dancer.
Parwa (G)	Dance-drama like Wayang Wong, based on the *Mahabharata* repertoire.
parwa (L)	Old Javanese prose work, a more or less faithful translation of certain sections of the *Mahabharata*.
pasupati	Magical power.
Patih (R)	Prime Minister and Commander of the Armed Forces, a strong character found in many genres. He may belong to either party in the drama.
pedanda	Brahmana or high-caste priest.

pegunem	Audience or meeting scene.
pekaad	Final section of the Legong performance.
pelinggih	Shrine.
pelog (M)	Tuning system in which successive intervals between the pitches vary greatly. In its most complete form, it consists of seven tones within the octave, but in most modern practice five-tone scales are drawn from the seven, with the omitted tones serving only as passing or substitute tones.
pemangku	Lower-caste priest.
pemurtian (R)	Powerful and wrathful form which certain divine and demonic characters have the power to assume.
penasar (R)	Clown or buffoon characters who serve as attendants to the leading male characters. They interpret the Kawi spoken by their masters and add comic relief. They may also point out moral and social issues.
penasar cenikan (R)	Sly, younger *penasar* in Topeng.
penasar kelihan (R)	Pompous, older *penasar* in Topeng.
pengarti	'Explainer', in Cakapung the performer who interprets the chanted poetry.
pengawak	'Body', the main section of the dance composition.
pengawit	'Head', the opening or prologue section of the dance composition.
pengecet	'Tail', the final section of the dance composition.
pengelembar	Introductory series of masks in Topeng, also known as *pengempat*.
pengipuk	Courtship or love scene.
penudusan	Purifying the Sang Hyang or other ritual dancers with smoke to assist them in entering a trance state.
penyeroan	Prostitute.
penyor (S)	Decorative, flag-like banner.
pepaosan	Another word for *mabasan*.
pesiat	Fighting scene.
pinggel (C)	Armband.
pingit	Secret, sacred.
pohon kepuh	Kapok tree, which grows in the graveyard. Also known as *pohon rangdu*.
potet (R)	Comic group of soldiers, led by Prabangsa in Gambuh.
Prabangsa (R)	Patih to Prabu in Gambuh, prototype of the strong character.
Prabu (R)	Antagonist king, the villain in Gambuh.
Praçasti Bebetin	Ninth-century copperplate village charter.
pratima	Wooden effigies into which the visiting deities descend at an Odalan.
Prembon (G)	Dance-drama created by combining stock characters from several genres. Also a revue made up of short dances from various genres.
punggawa	Village headman.
Punta (R)	Name of the *penasar kelihan* in Topeng, Arja, and other genres.
pura	Temple. There are a great many different kinds of them, from the great temple at Besakih (the 'Mother Temple'), other all-island temples, village temples, and others supported by kin groups, irrigation societies, etc.
pura dalem	Inner or death temple, one of the important village temples.
Pura Dalem Madangan	Inner temple in Madangan.
pura desa	Village temple.
Pura Pancering Jagat	'Navel of the World' temple in Trunyan.
Pura Payogan Agung	Temple in Ketewel village, where King Déwa Agung Madé Karna dreamed of the Legong dance.
Pura Penataran Pulasari	Temple in Kamasan village, Klungkung Province.
Pura Penataran Topeng	Temple in Blahbatuh, where some very old Topeng masks are kept.
Pura Pengrebongan	Temple in Kesiman, Badung Province, sacred to the Barong and Rangda masks.
pura puseh	'Origin temple', a village's principal temple.
puri	Palace.

150

Puspawresti (G)	Modern welcoming dance in Kebyar style, for a group of male and female dancers.
Putri (R)	Heroine or principal female character of the Gambuh performance, the Princess. She is the prototype for refined female characters in all the more recent genres.
rajeg (S)	Spear or lance, used to define the stage area.
Ramayana (L)	Indian epic poem, known in Bali by means of an Old Javanese *kakawin*. It is frequently read by *mabasan* groups and forms the basis for the repertoire of Wayang Wong, Wayang Kulit Ramayana, Cak, Sendratari Ramayana, and, to an extent, Barong Kedingkling.
Rangda	'The Widow', a mask of demonic aspect named perhaps for Calonarang. In fact, the Widow is only one of a number of characters which may be represented by this mask. These masks are charged with potent magical power and are considered protectors of the community against bad luck and demonic influences.
rangki (S)	Dressing and retiring room for the dancers.
Ratu Dalem	'Monarch of the Temple', a name given to the Rangda mask.
Ratu Désa	'Monarch of the Village', a name given to the Rangda mask.
Ratu Pancering Jagat	'God Navel of the World', object of devotion in Trunyan, a Bali Aga village.
rebab (M)	Spiked fiddle, played in Gambuh and optionally in more recent forms.
rebana (M)	Single-headed Arab drum, featured in Janger. Also known are *tambur*.
Rejang (G)	Female temple dance.
ronggeng	Public dancing girl, a *joged*. Also known as *joged tongkohan*.
rumbing (C)	Ear ornament.
sabda	The word, language.
sabuk kancing (C)	Belt.
sakti	Supernaturally powerful.
sandaran (R)	Another name for *telek*.
sanggah taksu	Shrine devoted to the artist's power of inspiration.
sang hyang	Protective divinity.
Sang Hyang (G)	Group of exorcistic dances or rites characterized by spirit possession.
Sang Hyang Bojog (G)	In this variety, the performer is possessed by a monkey spirit.
Sang Hyang Celéng (G)	In this variety, the performer is possessed by a pig spirit.
Sang Hyang Dedari (G)	In this genre, the performers are possessed by the spirits of celestial nymphs.
Sang Hyang Deling (G)	In this variant of Sang Hyang Dedari, puppet figures on a string are vibrated as the performers enter trance.
Sang Hyang Jaran (G)	In this variety, the performer is possessed by a horse spirit.
Sang Hyang Legong (G)	Sacred old masked genre, found only in Ketewel village.
sanggah	Family temple, temporary shrine.
Sangut (R)	Younger *penasar* serving the antagonist party in Wayang Kulit, Wayang Wong, and Parwa. A great favourite of the audience, Sangut, also known as 'Ngut or Uludawa, is more prudent and better-natured than his elder brother, Delem.
saput (C)	A belt or sash.
sebel	Ritually polluted, unclean.
seka	Club or voluntary association.
Seka Daha	Club of unmarried young women.
Seka Mabasan	Club devoted to *mabasan*.
Seka Parwa Agung	Group devoted to Parwa, now defunct.
Seka Taruna	Club of unmarried young men.
Sekar Jagat (G)	Modern welcoming dance in Kebyar style.
sekar taji (C)	Wing-like decorative collar.
selonding (M)	Sacred iron gamelan ensembles of great antiquity, preserved mainly in Bali Aga villages.

Semar (R)	*Penasar*, or clown-servant, to Panji in Gambuh.
sembah (D)	Gesture of respect and obedience, involving a bow with clasped hands.
Sendratari (G)	Modern pantomimic dance-drama, often on a very large scale, based on traditional Balinese literature.
seregseg (D)	The very difficult squat-walk of Kebyar Duduk.
setagen (C)	Long sash.
setéwel (C)	Leggings.
Sidha Karya (R)	Character who is part of the ritual in Topeng Pajegan. The mask worn in this portrayal is sacred.
sisya (R)	Students, apprentices, or witches in the Calonarang play.
slendro (M)	Tuning system in which successive intervals between the pitches do not vary greatly. There are five tones to the octave. Ensembles in *slendro* tuning accompany Wayang Kulit, Wayang Wong, Parwa, Janger, and Joged Bumbung.
SMKI	Sekolah Menengah Kesenian Indonesia—Bali, the government high school of traditional performing arts.
soyor (D)	Movement imitative of a tree swaying in the wind.
Stambul (G)	Pan-Malay dramatic genre based in part on imitation of Western drama and operetta.
STSI	Sekolah Tinggi Senian Indonesia—Bali, the government College of the Arts.
Sugriwa (R)	King of the monkeys in the *Ramayana*.
suling (M)	Small flute.
Sutri (G)	Temple dance similar to Rejang performed in Batuan, Gianyar Province.
taksu	Magical power, the artist's inspiration.
tambur (M)	Single-headed Arab drum, a synonym for *rebana*.
tapel	Mask covering the face, usually fastened to the dancers' head with an elastic band.
tari	Dance.
tari lepas (G)	'Free' dances, i.e. dances that stand on their own outside a dramatic performance.
Tari Tani (G)	'Peasant Dance', a modern composition employing stylized movements derived from the activities of rice cultivation.
Tari Tenun (G)	'Weaving Dance', a modern composition employing stylized movements derived from preparing thread and weaving on a traditional Balinese handloom.
taruna	Young unmarried man.
telek (R)	Also known as *teledek*. Female counterpart to the *jauk*. She wears a refined smiling mask with visible teeth and a pagoda-shaped helmet like that of the *jauk*.
tembang (M)	Song.
Temenggung (R)	Partner to the Demang, a member of Panji's entourage in Gambuh.
tenda (S)	Painted backdrop used in Janger.
tenget	Magically dangerous.
tetamburan	Section of the Janger performance in which the *tambur* is featured.
tingga (S)	Rangda's shack in the Calonarang play.
Togog (R)	Attendant buffoon to the Prabu in Gambuh.
Topeng (G)	Masked dance-drama based on historical chronicles of the Balinese ruling families.
Topeng Pajegan (G)	A ritual masked dance-drama, performed by a single actor-dancer-priest, who brings a dozen masks to life during the performance.
Topeng Panca (G)	'Five-man Topeng', a genre in which a historical story is performed by a group of masked dancers.
Topeng Wali (G)	Another name for Topeng Pajegan.
trompong (M)	Old-fashioned instrument consisting of a row of tuned knobbed gongs placed side by side in a wooden case. This is played by the dancer, who spins and flourishes the mallets in Kebyar Duduk.
Trunajaya (G)	Dance of the Kebyar group, similar to Margapati, Wiranata, and Yudapati.

Tua (R)	Dignified old man who frequently is portrayed as part of the group of *pengelembar* masks in Topeng.
tuak	Palm wine.
tumbak	Lance carried by dancers in certain Baris Gedé forms.
Twalen (R)	Leading *penasar* of the protagonist's party in Wayang Kulit, Wayang Wong, and Parwa.
uang kepeng	Chinese coins, tied in strings through the holes in their centres.
udeng (C)	Typical Balinese male head-dress, worn on festive occasions.
Uludawa (R)	Another name for Sangut.
Usaba Nini	Type of Balinese temple festival.
wali	Sacred, the group of most sacred dance genres.
Wangbang Wedeya (L)	Panji stories.
wantilan (S)	Cock-fighting arena, which can serve as an indoor secular theatre for Drama Gong, tourist performances, etc.
wayah	Venerable, ripe.
wayang	Shadow.
Wayang Calonarang (G)	Subcategory of Wayang Kulit, devoted to the *Calonarang* story, usually performed for exorcistic purposes.
Wayang Kulit (G)	Shadow puppet theatre of Bali. It is quite different from its Javanese counterpart in certain respects.
Wayang Lemah (G)	Ritual shadow puppet play, performed in the daytime without lamp or screen. The puppets are pressed against a string which is stretched between two *dadap* stalks. Addressed to the gods, rather than a human audience, it often takes place simultaneously with Topeng Pajegan in the *jeroan* during a ritual. When the priest concludes his prayers, the performer may break off abruptly, without regard for completing the story.
Wayang Orang (G)	See Wayang Wong.
Wayang Ramayana (G)	Subcategory of Wayang Kulit, devoted to stories from the *Ramayana*.
Wayang Wong (G)	Dramatic dance genre in which episodes from the *Ramayana* are presented. To a certain extent, the masked actor-dancers imitate the movements of the puppets of the shadow theatre.
widyadari (R)	Another name for *dedari*, the heavenly nymphs or demigoddesses.
Wijil (R)	Another name for the sly younger attendant-buffoon in Topeng and other genres. See also *penasar cenikan*.
Wiranata (G)	Dance of the Kebyar group in which a brave king is depicted.
wong	Human being.
Wong Sakti	'Man of power', a specialist in dangerous ritual tasks.
Wredah (R)	Also known as Merdah, the younger retainer attending the protagonist in Wayang Kulit, Wayang Wong, and Parwa.
Wredhi Budaya	Bali Arts Centre, in Denpasar, a performance venue with three theatres, small, medium, and very large. Site of the annual Bali Arts Festival which takes place in late June and early July.

Select Bibliography

Artaud, Antonin (1958), 'On the Balinese Theater', and 'Oriental and Occidental Theater', in *The Theater and Its Double*, New York: Grove Press, pp. 53–73. First published in French, 1938.

Bandem, I Madé (1975), 'The Baris Dance', *Ethnomusicology,* 19: 259–66.

———— (1976), 'The Barong Dance', *World of Music*, 18(3): 45–52.

———— (1980), 'Wayang Wong in Contemporary Bali', Ph.D. dissertation, Wesleyan University.

———— (1983), 'The Evolution of Legong from Sacred to Secular Dance of Bali', *Dance Research Annual*, 14: 113–19.

Bandem, I Madé and deBoer, Fredrik Eugene (1978), 'Gambuh: A Classical Balinese Dance Drama', *Asian Music*, 10(1): 115–27.

———— (1983), 'Notes on the Development of Arja Dance Drama', *Indonesia Circle*, 30: 28–33.

Belo, Jane (1949), *Bali: Rangda and Barong*, Seattle: University of Washington Press.

———— (1953), *Bali: Temple Festival*, Locust Valley, NY: J. J. Augustin.

———— (1960), *Trance in Bali*, New York: Columbia University Press.

Belo, Jane (ed.) (1970), *Traditional Balinese Culture*, New York: Columbia University Press.

Bernet Kempers, A. J. (1959), *Ancient Indonesian Art*, Amsterdam: Van der Peet.

———— (1978), *Monumental Bali: Introduction to Balinese Archaeology— Guide to the Monuments*, The Hague: Van Goor Zonen; Revd. edn. Berkeley: Periplus Editions, 1991.

Boon, James (1977), *The Anthropological Romance of Bali 1597–1972*, Cambridge: Cambridge University Press.

Coast, John (1953), *Dancers of Bali*, New York: G. P. Putnam.

Covarrubias, Miguel (1937), *Island of Bali*, New York: Alfred A. Knopf; reprinted Kuala Lumpur: Oxford University Press, 1972.

Dalton, William (n.d.), *Bali Handbook*, Chico, California: Moonbooks.

Danandjaja, James (1985), *Upacara-upacara Lingkaran Hidup di Trunyan; Bali/Life Cycle Ceremonies in Trunyan, Bali*, Jakarta: Penerbit Nasional Balai Pustaka.

deBoer, Fredrik E. (1979), 'Pak Rajeg's Life in Art', *Drama Review*, 23(2) [No. T82]: 57–62.

———— (1987a), 'The *Dimba* and *Dimbi* of I Nyoman Rajeg: A Balinese Shadow Play', *Asian Theater Journal*, 4(1): 76–107.

———— (1987b), 'Functions of the Comic Attendants (*Penasar*) in a Balinese Shadowplay', in Dina and Joel Sherzer (eds.), *Humor and Clowning in Puppetry*, Athens, Ohio: Popular Press, pp. 79–105.

———— (1989), 'Balinese Sendratari: A Modern Dramatic Dance Genre',

Asian Theater Journal, 6(2): 179–93.

deBoer, Fredrik E. and Bandem, I Madé (1992), 'The "Death of Kumbakarna" of I Ketut Madra: A Balinese Wayang Ramayana Play', *Asian Theater Journal*, 9(2): 141–200.

De Kleen, Tyra (1924), *Mudras: The Ritual Handposes of the Buddha Priests and the Shiva Priests of Bali*, London: K. Paul, Trench, Trubner & Co.; reprinted New York: University Books, 1970.

de Zoete, Beryl and Spies, Walter (1938), *Dance and Drama in Bali*, London: Faber and Faber; reprinted Kuala Lumpur: Oxford University Press, 1973.

Djelantik, A. A. M. (1986), *Balinese Paintings*, Singapore: Oxford University Press.

Dunn, Deborah (1983), 'Topeng Pajegan: Mask Dance of Bali', Ph.D. dissertation, Union of Experimenting Colleges, Cincinnati, Ohio.

Eiseman, Fred (1990), *Bali: Sekala and Niskala*, 2 vols., Berkeley: Periplus Editions.

Emigh, John (1979), 'Playing with the Past: Ancestral Visitation in the Masked Theater of Bali', *Drama Review*, 82: 11–36.

———— (1984), 'Dealing with the Demonic: Strategies for Containment in Hindu Iconography and Performance', *Asian Theater Journal*, 1(1): 21–39.

———— (1985), 'The Domains of Topeng', in Robert Van Niel (ed.), *Art and Politics in Southeast Asian History: Six Perspectives*, Southeast Asia Paper Number 32, Center for Southeast Asia Studies, University of Hawaii.

Forge, Anthony (1978), *Balinese Traditional Paintings*, Sydney: Australian Museum.

Geertz, Clifford (1963), *Peddlers and Princes*, Chicago: University of Chicago Press.

———— (1973), *The Interpretation of Cultures*, New York: Basic Books.

———— (1980), *Negara: The Theater State in Nineteenth Century Bali*, Princeton: Princeton University Press.

Geertz, Hildred (1973), 'Indonesian Cultures and Communities', in Ruth McVey (ed.), *Indonesia*, New Haven: Human Relations Area Files, pp. 24–96.

———— (1991), 'A Theater of Cruelty: The Contexts of a Topeng Performance', in H. Geertz (ed.), *State and Society in Bali*, Leiden: KITLV Press, pp. 165–98.

Goris, Roelof (1954), *Praçasti Bali*, 2 vols., Bandung: Masa Baru.

Gralapp, Leland (1967), 'Balinese Painting and the *Wayang* Tradition', *Artibus Asia*, 29: 239–66.

Hanna, Willard (1976), *Bali Profile: People, Events, Circumstances 1001–1976*, New York: American Universities Field Staff.

Hauser-Schäublin, Brigitta et al. (1991), *Textiles in Bali*, Berkeley: Periplus Editions.

Hinzler, H. I. R. (1980), 'The Balinese Baris Dadap: Its Tradition and Texts (A Preliminary Study)', in W. Voigt (ed.), *XX deutscher Orientalistentag vom 3. bis 8. Oktober 1977 in Erlangen: Vorträge*, Wiesbaden: Steiner, pp. 450–3.

Holt, Clarie (1967), *Art in Indonesia: Continuities and Change*, Ithaca: Cornell University Press.

Holt, Claire and Bateson, Gregory (1944), 'Form and Function of the Dance in Bali', in Jane Belo (ed.), *Traditional Balinese Culture*, New York: Columbia University Press, 1970, pp. 322–330.

Hooykaas, C. (1971), 'Pamurtian in Balinese Art', *Indonesia*, 12: 1–21.

Huyser, J. G. (1919), 'Wayang Stil', *Mudiato: Tijdschift tot Bestudeering van de dans- en toneel-kunst van Oost en Westindië*, 1(1): 3–22.

Jacobs, Julius (1883), *Eenigen Tijd onder de Baliérs*, Batavia: G. Kolff.

Jasper, J. E. (1902), 'De "Gandroeng Bali": Fragment van een verslag in de Javabode over de tentoonstelling te Bondowoso', *Tijdschrift voor Binnenlandsche Bestuur*, 23: 414–18.

Kakul, I Nyoman (1979), 'Jelantik Goes to Blambangan: A Topeng Play', translated by John Emigh and I Madé Bandem, *Drama Review*, 82: 37–48.

Laufer, Berthold (1923), *Oriental Theatricals*, Chicago: Field Museum of Natural History.

Liefrinck, F. A. (1886), 'De rijstcultuur op Bali', *De Indische Gids*, 2: 1033–59, 1213–37, 1557–68.

Lingis, Alphonso (1980), 'Rangda and the Nostalgia for Glory', *Philosophy and Literature*, 4(1): 66–79.

McKean, Phillip (1979), 'From Purity to Pollution? The Balinese Ketjak (Monkey Dance) as a Symbolic Form in Transition', in A. L. Becker and A. Yengoyan (eds.), *The Imagination of Reality: Essays in Southeast Asian Coherence Systems*, Norwood, NJ: Ablex, pp. 293–302.

McPhee, Colin (1936), 'The Balinese Wayang Kulit and Its Music', in Jane Belo (ed.), *Traditional Balinese Culture*, New York: Columbia University Press, 1970, pp. 146–97.

———— (1946), *A House in Bali*, New York: John Day; reprinted Kuala Lumpur: Oxford University Press, 1979.

———— (1948), 'Dance in Bali', *Dance Index*, 7: 156–208.

———— (1966), *Music in Bali*, New Haven: Yale University Press.

Mead, Margaret (1939), 'The Strolling Players in the Mountains of Bali', *Natural History*, 43: 137–45.

Noosten, H. H. (1936), 'Maskers en Ziekten op Java en Bali', *Djawa*, 16: 311–17.

———— (1941), 'De heilige maskers van de Poera Penataran Topeng te Blahbatoe (Bali)', *Mededeelingen van de Kirtya Liefrinck Van der Tuuk*, 14: 1–26.

Oey, Eric (1991), *Bali: Island of the Gods*, Berkeley: Periplus Editions.

O'Neill, Roma M. G. Sisley (1978), 'Spirit Possession and Healing Rites in a Balinese Village', MA thesis, University of Melbourne.

Picard, Michel (1992), *Bali: Tourisme culturel et culture touristique*, Paris: Editions L'Harmattan.

Pigeaud, Th. (1938), *Javaanse Volksvertoningen*, 2 vols., The Hague: Martinus Nijhoff.

Poerbatjaraka, R. N. G. (1926), 'De Calon Arang', *Bijdragen tot de Taal-, Land- en Volkenkunde*, 82(2): 110–80.

'Proyek Pemeliharan dan Pengambungan Kebudayaan Daerah Bali' (1971), *Seminar Seni Sakral dan Seni 'Profan' Bidang Tari*, Denpasar, Bali: mimeograph.

Raffles, Thomas Stamford (1817), *The History of Java*, 2 vols., London: Black, Parbury and Allen, and John Murray; reprinted Kuala Lumpur: Oxford University Press, 1965.

Ramseyer, Urs (1977), *The Art and Culture of Bali*, Fribourg: Office du Livre; reprinted Singapore: Oxford Unversity Press, 1986.

Ras, J. J. (1973), 'The Panji Romance and W. H. Rassers' Analysis of Its Theme', *Bijdragen tot de Taal-, Land- en Volkenkunde*, 129(4): 411–56.

Rassers, W. H. (1959), 'On the Meaning of Javanese Drama', in *Panji the Culture Hero*, The Hague: Martinus Nijhoff, pp. 1–62. First published in Dutch, 1925.

Rhodius, Hans and Darling, John (1980), *Walter Spies and Balinese Art*, Zutphen: Terra.

Rickner, Robert (1972), 'Theater as Ritual: Artaud's Theater of Cruelty and the Balinese Barong', Ph.D. dissertation, University of Hawaii.

Robson, S. O. (1971), *Wangbang Wedeya: A Javanese Panji Romance*, The Hague: Martinus Nijhoff.

––––––– (1972), 'The Kawi Classics in Bali', *Bijdragen tot de Taal-, Land-en Volkenkunde*, 128(2–3): 307–29.

Rubenstein, Raechelle (1992), 'Pepasosan: Challenges and Change', in Danker Schaareman (ed.), *Balinese Music in Context: A Sixty-fifth Birthday Tribute to Hans Oesch*, Winterthur: Amadeus Verlag, pp. 85–114.

Sanger, Annette (1985), 'Music, Dance, and Social Organization in Two Balinese Villages', *Indonesia Circle*, 37: 45–62.

Scouren, Leslie (1981), 'Legong Keraton of Bali: An Analysis of Style and Structure in Relation to Social Environment', MA thesis, University of California, Los Angeles.

Slattum, Judy (1992), *Masks of Bali: Spirits of an Ancient Drama*, San Francisco: Chronicle Books.

Soekmono, R. (1973), *Pengantar Sejarah Kebudayaan Indonesia*, Jogjakarta: Penerbit Yayasan Kanisius.

Spies, Walter (1936), 'Bericht über den Zustand von Tanz und Musik in der Negara Gianyar', *Djawa*, 16: 205–27.

Spies, Walter and Goris, Roelof (1937), 'Overzicht van Dans en Tooneel in Bali', *Djawa*, 17: 205–27.

Stutterheim, W. F. (1935), *Indian Influences in Old Javanese Art*, London: India Society.

Suleiman, Satyawati (1974), *Concise Ancient History of Indonesia*, Jakarta: Archaeological Foundation.

Sumandhi, I Nyoman (1979), 'Wayang Calonarang', MA thesis, Wesleyan University.

Suryani, Luh Ketut and Jensen, Gordon D. (1993), *Trance and Possession in Bali: A Window on Western Multiple Personality, Possession Disorder, and Suicide*, Kuala Lumpur: Oxford University Press.

Tenzer, Michael (1991), *Balinese Music*, Berkeley: Periplus Editions.

Van Bloemen Waanders, F. L. (1859), 'Aantekeningen omtrent de zeden en gebruiken der Balineezen, inzonderheid die van Boeleleng', *Tijdschrift van de Bataavische Genootschap van Kunsten en Wetenschap van Nederlandsche-Indië*, 3rd series, 8(2): 105–279.

Van der Veur, Paul (1968), 'Cultural Aspects of the Eurasian Community in Indonesian Colonial Society', *Indonesia*, 6: 51–2.

Van Eck, R. (1880), 'Schetsen van het eiland Bali', *Tijdschrift voor Nederlandsche-Indië*, New Series, 9(2): 14–15.

Vickers, Adrian (1986), 'The Desiring Prince: A Study of the Kidung Malat as Text', Ph.D. dissertation, University of Sydney.

––––––– (1989), *Bali: A Paradise Created*, Berkeley: Periplus Editions.

Worsley, P. J. (1972), *Babad Buleleng*, The Hague: Martinus Nijhoff.

Young, Elizabeth (1980), 'Topeng in Bali: Change and Continuity in a Traditional Drama Genre', Ph.D. dissertation, University of California, San Diego.

———— (1982), 'The Tale of Erlangga: Text Translation of a Village Drama Performance in Bali', *Bijdragen tot de Taal-, Land en Volkenkunde*, 138(4): 470–91.

Zoetmulder, P. J. (1974), *Kalangwan: A Survey of Old Javanese Literature*, The Hague: Martinus Nijhoff.

Index

Numbers in italics refer to Colour Plates

ABUANG KALAH, 93–4, 97
Adar, 90–2, 100
Agung, Gunung, vii, 1, 21
Alit, Cokorda, 124
Ancestor spirits, 1
Anggada, 57
Animal sacrifices, 57–8
Anoman, 57
Api, Cokorda Gedé, 105–6
'Apoda-poda', 140
Arimenda, 60
Arja, 27, 79–82, 96, *18*
Arjuna Wiwaha, 100, 111
Arsaja, I Gusti Bagus, 139
Artaud, Antonin, 77
Arya-arya, 35–6, 41, 117
Asak, 16
Asnawa, I Ketut Gedé, 141

BABAD, 55–6
Babad Blahbatuh, 47
Babad Dalem, 59
Babad Dalem Sukawati, 71
Badung, 23, 44, 83, 120
Balé Gala-gala, 138
Bali Aga villages, 1–2, 8, 16
Bali Arts Festival, 24, 137
Bali Beach Hotel, 127, 132
Bali Hotel, 127
Bali Museum, 59
Balian, 112
Bali-balihan dances, 70, 78, 135, 136
Banaspati Raja, 105–6
Bangli Province, 44, 89
Banjar Babakan, 79
Banjar Sengguan, 102
Baris, 97
Baris (modern), 21, 82–3, 106–7, 114, 132, *19*
Baris Dadap, 20
Baris Gedé, 18–21, 82, 98, 114, 135
Baris Melampahan, 21, 27, 83, 100, 111
Baris Pendet, 23

Baris Poleng, 20, *4*
Baris Tamiang, 20
Baris Tumbak, 19
Barong, 109, 111, 120, 126, 131–2
Barong Asu, 102
Barong Bangkal, 102–3
Barong Belas-belasan, 57
Barong Kedingkling, 56–8, 60
Barong Keket, 102
Barong Ket, *59*, 102–6, 114, 120
Barong Landung, 125, *27–8*
Barong Lembu, 102
Barong Machan, 102
Basur, 111
Batara Surya, 3
Batu Agung, 95
Batu Renggong, Dalem, 47, 49, 56
Batuan village, 18, 38, 42, 97
Batubulan, 113
Batur, 18–20
Batur, Lake, 3, 8
Bayu–sabda–idep trinity, 22–3
Bebali dances, 26, 44–5, 133
Bebali Sidha Karya, 55
Bebancihan, 76
Bebarisan, 18
Bedulu, 74, 128
Belibis, 139, *32*
Bendesa, 54
Benoh village, 73
Beratha, I Wayan, 134–6, 138–9
Berutuk, 3–10, 106, *1*
Bharatayuda, 75
Bhatti, 60
Black magic, 109, 112, 124
Blahbatuh, 46
Boda, Ida Bagus, 83, 141
Bona village, 133, 141
Bondres: Calonarang, 118; Gambuh, 38, 41; Topeng Pajegan, 52, 54, *11*
Bongan Jawa village, 89
Buffoon, *see Penasar*
Buleleng Province, 23, 74
Bumbung, 92

Bungkulen, 74
Buta, 14, 126

CAK, 128–31
Cak chorus, 12, 95, 128
Cakapung, 96–7
Calonarang, 90, 112–25, 131, *26*
Calonarang manuscript, 112–13, 117
Candi bentar, 28
Candi Panataran, 61
Candra Kirana, Princess: Gambuh, 31–2, 40; Panji Semirang, 76
Candri, Ni Nyoman, 81, *18*
Celuk, 120
Cemengawon village, 13
Cendrawasih, 139–41
Chinese influence, 105
Chinese Lion Dance, 104–5, 141
Choral groups, 12–13, 22
Clown, *see Penasar*
Coast, John, 77
Cock-fights, 109
Colonial Exhibition, Paris, 77
Condong: Arja, 82; Calonarang, 116, 118, 124; Gambuh, 32–4, 41; Legong, 72–3, 83, *14*; Parwa, 79; Prembon, 84
Covarrubias, Miguel, 92
Crossroads, 104, 113–14
Cupak and Grantang story, 100

DAAG, 98
Dadap, 80–2
Dadap trees/leaves, 20–1, 35, 80
Dalang, 61, 66–7, 79, 109
Dalang sendratari, 137
Dalem, 52–5, *10*
Danawa, *9*
Dance-dramas, 22–43, 71, 113, 135
Dance of the Sisya, 113
Delem, 67–8
Demang, 35, 79, *6*
Demonic spirits, 1, 10, 29, 58, 102, 105, 107, 124

Den Jalan, 120
Denpasar, 92, 113, 125
Desa Pinggan, 3
Dewi Sri, 140
Dharma Sangging, 45
Dibia, I Wayan, 135, 138
Discotheques, 142
Divine spirits, 10
Dolls, 12
Drama Gong, 98
Dukun, 40
Durga, 113, 131
Dusang, 109, 111, 118, 120, 124
Dutch, 42, 59, 74, 81, 88, 97

EMIGH, JOHN, 49
Epidemics, 11, 14, 56
Erlangga, King of, 117
Exorcistic dances, 102, 105, 109

FIRE WALKING, 14
Flute, *see* Suling
Folk music, 94

GABOR, 1, 22–3, 132, 135
Gajah Mada, 26
Galungan, 66, 104–6, 125
Gambuh, 20, 27–43, 61, 66, 72, 79, 81, 97, 116, 6
Gamelan, 21–2, 70, 74–5, 104, 106, 126, 136
Gamelan batel, 57, 61, 66, 125
Gamelan gambuh, 28–9, 31–2, 38, 57
Gamelan gong, 22, 49, 82, 107
Gamelan gong gedé, 18, 19–20
Gamelan gong kebyar, 85, 134, 138, 21
Gamelan legong, 12
Gamelan pelegongan, 71, 88
Gamelan rindik, 90, 92
Gamelan selonding, 94
Gamelan semar pegulingan, 88–9, 92, 138
Gandrung, 92
Gandrung, 87
Gebug village, 90
Gebyog, 94–6
Gelatik nguwut papah, 33
Gelgel, 44, 46–7
Gelung, see Head-dresses
Gender wayang, 28, 57, 66
Gender wayang quartet, 98
'Gending Batel', 55
'Gending Gandrangan', 92
Genggong, 96–7
Geria, I Wayan, 131
Gianyar, 44, 83–4, 120
Girls, preadolescent, 10, 71, 73–4
Godogan, 97

Gods, vii, 1, 16, 21, 24, 29, 68, 102
Granyam, I Nyoman, 79
Graveyard tree, 45, 107, 114, 118, 120
Graveyards, 107, 114
Guang, 120
Guwak, 73

HARI NYEPI, 58, 105, 126, 141
Head-dresses: Abuang Kalah, 94; Cakapung, 96; Gambuh, 29, 32, 35–6, 38, 45; Janger, 98; Joged Bumbung, 93; Joged Pingitan, 90; Sekar Jagat, 135; Tari Tenun, 134; Topeng Pajegan, 54; Wayang Wong, 64–7
Hindu-Balinese courts, 26–7, 41–2, 44
Hindu-Javanese culture, 1, 26, 61
Hindu mythology, 10
Hindu religion, 22, 26
Holt, Claire, 113
Horse spirits, 10, 14

IBING, 87, 90–2
Igel ngugal: Calonarang, 118; Legong, 72; Wayang Wong, 66–7
Inner temple courtyard: dances 1–24
Irian Jaya, 45

JABA, 70, 74
Jaba tengah, 28, 66
Jacobs, Julius, 88, 106–7
Jagaraga, 74–5
Janger, 97–101, 22
Janger, 98–100
Jauk, 132
Jauk, 106–7, 114, 116
Jayaprana, 135
Jelantik, I Gusti Ngurah, 71
Jelantik family, 46–7, 49, 71
Jembrana, 92, 95
Jempai, 124
Jero Gedé, 125
Jero Luh, 125
Jeroan, 1, 28; dances, 1, 48, 57, 71
Jimat, I Madé, 97
Joged, 33, 86–93
Joged Bumbung, 92–3
Joged Gandangan, 89
Joged Gudegan, 89–90
Joged Pingitan, 89–90, 98
Joged Tongkohan, 89
Joged tongkohan, 87–8
Juru tandak, 136

KADE-KADEHAN, 38–9, 41
Kaja–kelod ritual axis, vii–viii, 21, 29–31, 51, 86, 105, 114, 126
Kajeng Kliwon, 114

Kakan-kakan: Gambuh, 33–4, 116; Parwa, 79
Kalangan: Calonarang, 114; Gambuh, 29–31; Wayang Wong, 66
Kaler, I Nyoman, 76, 134
Kalika, 131
Kalimantan, 45
Kamasan, 58
Kapi Parwa, 60
Kapok tree, 107
Karangasem Province, 95–6
Karna, I Déwa Agung Madé, 71
Kartala: Arja, 82; Baris Melampahan, 83; Calonarang, 117
Kawi: Arja, 81; Baris Melampahan, 83; Calonarang, 116; Gambuh, 32, 34, 37–8; Parwa, 79; Sendratari, 136–7; Topeng Pajegan, 50–3, 56; Wayang Wong, 67–8
Kebyar, 74–8, 82, 128, 134–7, 141
Kebyar Bebancihan, 76–7
Kebyar Duduk, 75–7, 82, 92, 100, 132, 16
Kebyar Legong, 75
Kecak, *see* Cak
Kecak, 98, 100
Kedaton, 100
Kediri village, 90
Kendang, 28
Kengguh, I Madé, 124
Kerajaan Timbul Sukawati, 90
Kerambitan, 92, 120, 134
Kerawuhan, 12, 14
Kesiman village, 109
Ketewel village, 71, 124
Kidung, 12–13, 22, 141
Kidung Sunda, 18, 27
Kijang Kencana, 139, 31
Kintamani, 12
'Klincang Klincung', 23
Klungkung, 44, 46, 56, 58–9, 89
'Kosong', 141
Kredek, I Madé, 81, 90, 131
Ksatrya, 46, 53
Kulkul, 138
Kumbakarna, 61, 67
Kuningan holiday, 79
'Kunti Sraya', 131
Kusamba, Dalem Gedé, *see* Kusamba, I Déwa Agung Gedé
Kusamba, I Déwa Agung Gedé, 59–60, 79, 82

LAKSMANA, 61
Langsé, 98
Lasem: Gandrung, 92; Joged Gudegan, 90; Legong, 73; Leko, 89
Lebih, 124
Legong, 27, 71–5, 77, 79, 81–3, 88–90,

92, 98, 101, 114, 117, 132–3, 141, *14–15*
Legong Jobog, 73
Legong Ratu Dari, 71
Leko, 89–90
Lelunakan, 134
Leyak, 109, 113–14, 116–20
Likes, I Wayan, 133
Limbur, 82
'Lions', *59*
Logohu, 140
Lombok, 96
Lontar manuscripts, 46–7, 56, 60, 96
Luh Géro, *11*

MABUANG DANCE CEREMONY, 9
Madangan, 56
Mahabharata, 57, 61, 75, 78, 83, 131
Mahendradatta, 112
Majapahit Empire, 26–7
Malat, 31, 33, 39, 45, 72
Malayo-Polynesians, 1
Mandra, Anak Agung Gedé, 77
Mangis, I Déwa, 71–2
Mangis VIII, I Déwa, 84
Manuk déwata, 140
Manuk Rawa, 138
Margapati, 76
Marica, 111, 139
Mario, I Nyoman, 75–8, 92, 133
Marriage: Trunyan, 8–9
Mas village, 79, 106
Masked dancing, 44–5
Mask-makers, 45–6
Masks: Barong Kedingkling, 56–7; Barong Ket, 102–7, *23*; Gambuh *5, 7*; Rangda, 107–8, 109–12, *25*; Sang Hyang Legong, 71; Topeng Pajegan, 44–53, *8–13*; Wayang Wong, *59*, 67–8
Matah Gedé, 116–17, 124
Matolan, 124
Medagang, 91
Meganada, 61, 129
Mendet, 23, 135, *5*
Monkey spirits, 10, 14
Monkeys: Barong Kedingkling, 56–8; Wayang Wong, 60–1, 66, 68, *12–13*
Mudra, 21, 23
Mungkah lawang, 49

NADI, 14
Nagara Kretagama, 27
Nandir, 71–2, 92
National unity performances, 140
Nationalist Party (PNI), 134
'Ngelawang', 142
Ngelawang, 104

Ngibing, 86, 88–90, 92–3
Nusa Penida, 78, 124

ODALAN, 3, 9, 18, 20, 22, 26, 28, 42, 58, 66, 68, 70, 79, 85, 102, 107–9
Ogres, 61, 66, 68
Okokan, 138
Oleg Tumulilingan, 78, 82, 133, *17*
Onying, 108–10, *24*
Opium, 88
Overseas tours, 77–8

PAGUTAN, 120, 131
Pakarena dance, 141
Palawakia, 75
Pandanus, 35
Pandung, 117–19, 124
Pangkat: Calonarang, 117; Gambuh, 38; Legong, 73
Pangpang, 118
Panji, Prince: Gambuh, 32, 34–8, 40–1, 7; Panji Semirang, 76; Parwa, 79
Panji Inu Kertapati, Prince, 31, 45, 73
Panji Semirang, 76, 132
Panyembrama, 132, 134–5
Partapukan, 45
Parwa, 78–80
Pasek Dangka clan, 66
Pasupati, 44
Patih: Calonarang, 117; Topeng Pajegan, 49–50, 53–5
Patih Tua, 36
Pedanda, 21–2
Pedungan village, 34
Pegunem, 37
'Pekaad, 73
Peliatan village, 74, 100
Pelinggih, 17–18, 20–3, 57
Pemaksan Gusti Ngurah Jelantik, 46–7, 49
Pemangku, 10–13, 21–4, 29, 57, 110–11, 114, 120, 124
Pemayan, I Dalem Agung, 56
Pemurtian, 111, 112
Penasar: Arja, 82; Baris Melampahan, 83; Barong Kedingkling, 57; Calonarang, 117; Gambuh, 40; Janger, 100; Parwa, 79; Prembon, 84; Topeng Pajegan, 52–5; Topeng Panca, 52, 83; Wayang Wong, 66–8
Pengarti, 96
Pengawak, 72
Pengawit, 72
Pengecet, 72
Pengelembar, 49, 52, 107, 114
Pengipuk: Barong Ket, 104; Gambuh, 40–1; Legong, 73; Oleg Tumulilingan, 78, *17*
Pengrebongan ceremony, 109–10

Penudusan, 12
Pesiat, 73
Pig spirits, 10, 14
Pohon kepuh, *see* Graveyard tree
Possession, 1; Onying, 108; Sang Hyang, 10, 12
Potet, 38–9
Prabangsa: Gambuh, 38–9, 54, 117; Parwa, 79; Prembon, 84
Prabu: Gambuh, 38–9, 41, 117; Parwa, 79
Praçasti Bebetin, 45
Prahasta, 61
Pratima, 44; Baris Gedé, 18, 20; Gabor, 22; Hari Nyepi, 126; Rejang, 16–17; ritual cleansing, 21
Prembon, 84–5, 100, 107, 132–3, 135
Priests, *see Pemangku*
Procession, 21–2
Professional performers, 127; Arja, 81; Rangda, 124; Topeng Pajegan, 55–6
Prostitutes, 86–8, 91
Public dancers, 87
Puja, Ida Bagus, 48
Pujungan Kaler, 66
Pulasari clan, 59
Punta: Arja, 82; Baris Melampahan, 83; Calonarang, 117; Topeng Pajegan, 52
Pura Besakih, vii
Pura Dalem Madangan, 57
Pura Pancering Jagat, 3
Pura Payogan Agung, 71
Pura Penataran Pulasari, 59
Pura Penataran Topeng, 46
Pura Pengrebongan, 109
Puspawresti, 135
Putri: Gambuh, 32–4, 40–1; Panji Semirang, 76; Parwa, 79; Prembon, 84

RADIO REPUBLIK INDONESIA, 81
Raka, I Gusti Gedé, 134, *25*
Rama, 61, 67, 131, 139
Ramadewa, 60
Ramayana, 56–7, 59–61, 66, 68, 73, 78, 83, 128–31
Ramayana Ballet, 136
Ramayana Kakawin, 59–60
Rangda, 107–8, 109–12, 114, 116–20, 124–5, 131, *25*
Rangdu tree, *see* Graveyard tree
Rangke Sari, Princess, 73, *15*
Rangki, 114
Ratna Manggali, 116
Ratu Dalem, 107
Ratu Désa, 107
Ratu Pancering Jagat, 3, 5–6, 8–9

Rawana, 60–1, 67–8, 106, 111, 129, 131, 139, *30*
Rawana Vadha, 60
Rebab, 32, 96
Rebana, 100
Rejang, 15–18, 98, 134–5, *3*
Rembang, I Nyoman, 92
Ridet, I Nyoman, 133
Rindhi, I Wayan, 72
Rumbing, 59

SABA, 74
Sacred dances, 1–24
Samprangan, 44
Sandaran, 107
Sanggah, 114
Sanggah taksu, 29
Sang Hyang Bojog, 10, 14–15
Sang Hyang Celéng, 10, 14–15, 101
Sang Hyang Dedari, 10–15, 71–3, 95, 114, 128, 133, 141
Sang Hyang Deling, 12
Sang Hyang Jaran, 10, 14, *2*
Sang Hyang Legong, 71
Sangut, 67–8
Sanskrit, 51
Sanur, 92, 112–13
Sarga, Ida Bagus, 79
Satabali, 61
Sebatu village, 23, 133
Seka, 89
Seka Parwa Agung, 79
Seka Taruna, 3, 102, 104, 106
Sekar Jagat, 135, *29*
Sekar taji, 59, 105
Sekolah Menengah Kesenian Indonesia, *see* SMKI
Selingsing, 92
Selonding ensemble, 18
Semar, 36–8, 40–1, *7*
Semarapura, 44
Sempati, 61
Sendratari, 135–8
Sendratari Angling Dharma, 139
Sendratari Mahabharata, 138
Sendratari Ramayana, 136, 139, *30*
Seregseg, 77
Serongga village, 105
Sibang, 96
Sidha Karya, 49, 55, 111, *8*
Singapadu village, 22, 89–90, 102, 105, 120, 135

Singaraja, 74
Sisya, 112–14, 116–18, 120
Sita, 61, 111, 129, 139
SMKI, 135–7
Social dancing, 93
Sorcerers, 112
Spies, Walter, 42, 127–8, 131
Stambul, 98, 101
STSI, 43, 83, 107, 120, 137, 141
Stutterheim, W. F., 1
Subali, 73
'Sudawala', 131
Sugriwa: Cak, 129; Legong, 73; Wayang Wong, 57, 67, *12–13*
Sugriwa, I Gusti Bagus, 24, 133
Sukasrana, 61
Sukawati, Cokorda Gedé, 77
Sukawati village, 71–2, 74, 79, 89–90, 120
Sulawesi, 45
Suling, 27–8, 32, 96
Supartha, I Gusti Agung Ngurah, 139
Suteja, I Ketut, 142
Sutri, 18

TABANAN PROVINCE, 72, 89–90
Taksu, 14
Tambur, 100
Tari lepas, 138–9
Tari Tani, 134
Tari Tenun, 133–4
Tegal Cangkring, 93
Tegal Tamu, 92, 120, 131
Tejakula, 23, 66–7
Teledek, see Telek
Telek, 107, 114, 116
Television, 82, 84–5
Tembang, 81
Temenggung, 35, 79, *6*
Temples, 1–3; *jaba*, 70; *jaba tengah*, 28; *jeroan*, 1, 28
Tenda, 97
Tenganan, 16, 18, 93, 135
Tenget, 44
Tetamburan, 100
Tisnu, Cokorda Raka, 105
Togog, 40–1
Topeng, 46
Topeng, 27, 97, 132
Topeng Hudoq, 45, 140

Topeng Pajegan, 22, 44, 46–56, 83, *8–11*
Topeng Panca, 52, 69, 83–4, 107, *20*
Topeng Wali, 48
Tourist performances/products, 97, 112, 127–8, 131–3, 135, 140
Trance, 1, 10, 14, 23, 108, 110–11
Trompong, 75
Trunyan, 3–4, 8–9
Tunjuk village, 89
Twalen, 57–8, 67, *13*

UBUD, 77
Udayana, King, 112
Udeng, 96
Ugrasena of Bedulu, King, 45
Usaba Nini festival, 18
Uttara Kanda, 60

VAN ECK, R., 87

WALI DANCES, 1, 33, 44, 71, 102, 108, 127–8, 133, 135
Walmiki, 60
Walter Spies Foundation, 141
Walter Spies Performing Arts Festival, 71, 139
Wangbang Wedeya, 45
'Wargasari', 22
Wayang, 46
Wayang Calonarang, 109, 124
Wayang Kulit, 61, 66, 78–9, 111
Wayang Lemah, 20, 22
Wayang Orang, 97
Wayang Wong, 27, 44, 58–68, 78–9, 98, 105–6, 111, *12–13*
Wibisana, 61
Widow of Girah, 112, 116, 118
Widyadari, 10
Wijaya, Ni Luh Swasthi, 135, 138–9
Wijil, 52
Windha, I Nyoman, 135, 139
Wiranata, 76
Wisnumurti, 29, 55
Witches, 112
Wong Sakti, 109, 110, *25*
Woodfowl, 6, 9
Wredah, 57–8, 67, *13*
Wredi Budaya Arts Centre, 137–8; *see also* STSI

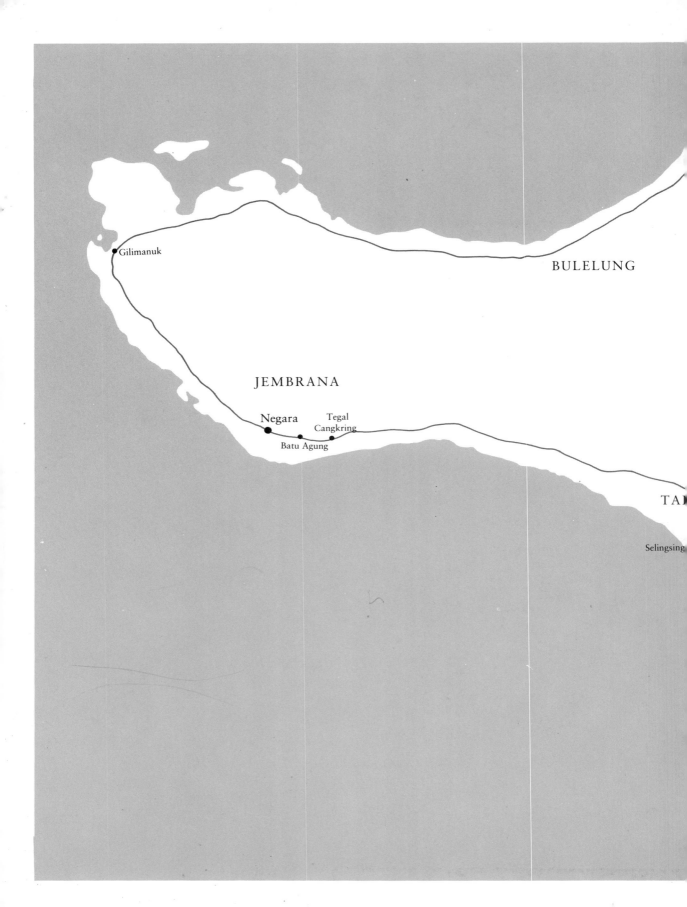

BULELUNG

Gilimanuk

JEMBRANA

Negara   Tegal
                Cangkring
      Batu Agung

TA

Selingsing